G000147316

The Human Difference

Published by
Lion Publishing plc
Sandy Lane West, Littlemore, Oxford, England
ISBN 0 7459 1284 2
Lion Publishing Corporation
1705 Hubbard Avenue, Batavia, Illinois 60510, USA
ISBN 0 7459 1284 2
Albatross Books Pty Ltd
PO Box 320, Sutherland, NSW 2232, Australia
ISBN 0 7324 0147 X

First edition 1989

Library of Congress Cataloging-in-Publication Data
Allan, John, 1950–
The human difference.
Bibliography: p. 157
Includes index.
1. Psychology—Miscellanea. 2. Man—Miscellanea.
I. Title.
BF145.A63 1989 128 89–8242
ISBN 0–7459–1284–2 (U.S)

Printed and bound in Yugoslavia

The Human Difference

John Allan

A LION BOOK
Oxford · Batavia · Sydney

Contents

Part I

Introducing Human Life 7

Part II

The Potential of Human Beings 37

Part III

People Together 87

Special Features

Part I

Introducing Human Life

1

BIRTH, LIFE AND DEATH

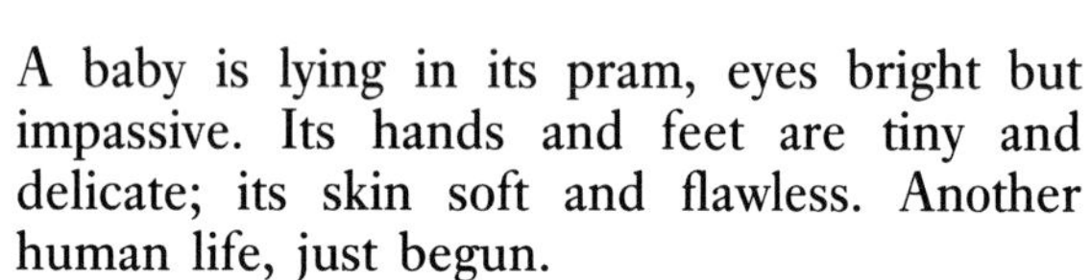

A baby is lying in its pram, eyes bright but impassive. Its hands and feet are tiny and delicate; its skin soft and flawless. Another human life, just begun.

How does it feel to be a baby? And how will it develop?

What does the future hold for this eight-and-a-half-pound packet of human life?

Obviously, no one can tell exactly. There are over five billion of us on this planet, and many new human beings arrive every minute. Human lives take a tremendous variety of courses, dictated by family circumstances, accidental occurrences, culture, health and intelligence. But some things are fairly standard. Let's assume that our baby survives infancy and lives through a generally typical lifetime (typical, that is, for that part of the world's population which isn't facing daily starvation and health risks). Which phases will this human being pass through? What will the landmarks be?

Birth and babyhood

There is no definite answer to the question, 'When does human life begin?' But it is clear that even before the moment of birth, a child already has a well-developed existence inside its mother's body.

In fact, as soon as the egg cell of the mother is penetrated by the sperm cell of the father, the child-to-be already has its distinct identity determined. Sex, intelligence, size and shape, colouring and temperament—all these details are already firmly decided. Four weeks later, still only a quarter of an inch long, its heart will be beating, eyes and mouth will have started to appear, and ears will have begun to form. Before the pregnancy is two-thirds complete, the new human will be able to cry, to use its hands to grasp and hit, and to kick its legs.

What is it like to be inside the womb? Brain activity begins early, at six or seven weeks, but there can only be a very rudimentary kind of

awareness. There can be no real understanding of space or sense of time. The new life is completely insulated from the many different stimuli it will encounter in the world outside. Its needs for nourishment, warmth and shelter are automatically met. Life couldn't be simpler.

And so the moment of birth must come as a tremendous shock! Suddenly we come into contact with all sorts of things we have never encountered before: pain, for example, and cold. The brightness of daylight must seem terrifyingly dazzling. And hunger becomes a reality: our food needs are no longer automatically supplied, and even if our mother hurries to feed us as soon as she realizes we are hungry, there is still a slight delay between the need and the fulfilment. No wonder we cry. This has never happened before!

The change in our mother is bewildering, too. Up until birth, she had been the whole of our world. We lived inside her. Now, after one traumatic upheaval, she shrinks to just one part of that world, outside us and operating independently. She can even leave us and walk away!

(Perhaps we never quite forget the first view we have of our mother. Some psychologists claim that many men are attracted to women with pale faces and dark eyes because that is how a baby first glimpses its mother: a blurred white oval in which only the dark shadow of the eyes is discernible. Perhaps this is true; certainly women in many different civilizations have tried to increase their sex appeal by whitening their faces and darkening their eyebrows.)

As brand new babies, we have difficulty at first in deciding what is 'me' and what is 'something else'. For example, a baby can watch with great curiosity its own hand moving and waving while not really appreciating that the hand is actually connected to its own body, or that baby itself is causing the birth movements. But gradually we begin to settle down in our new world. We start to learn how to use our eyes, to follow objects visually as they move away from us, rather than just registering blankly those sights which happen to drift in front of us. Our hands start to grasp objects firmly. Our ears start to distinguish between sounds.

Now the world is becoming less terrifying. Our mother may have changed her position in relation to us, but she does not appear to be abandoning us, she is still meeting our needs and feeding us; we start to develop a sense of trust in our new environment. (Obviously, if our needs are not met sufficiently at this critical stage, it can cause problems in our development later on. The more stroking and caressing a baby receives, for example, the greater its chances of adjusting naturally to sexual activity when it grows up.)

We begin to develop the first faint stirrings of memory. This gives us a growing sense that there is a continuity in the things which are

CAN LIFE START IN TEST-TUBES?

When Louise Brown was born in Oldham, Lancashire, in July 1978, she was a perfectly normal, very attractive human baby. Yet she made history. For no human being had ever come to life in the same way that she had.

Louise was born through 'in-vitro' fertilization. This means that the egg cell from her mother's body and the sperm cell from her father's had not come together in the normal way—within the body of the mother, after sexual intercourse—but that the egg cell had been removed from the mother, cultured in a laboratory until it reached ripeness and then artificially fertilized with sperm. After a period of growth outside the mother's body it was re-implanted inside the womb, where it grew and developed like any other normal growing foetus.

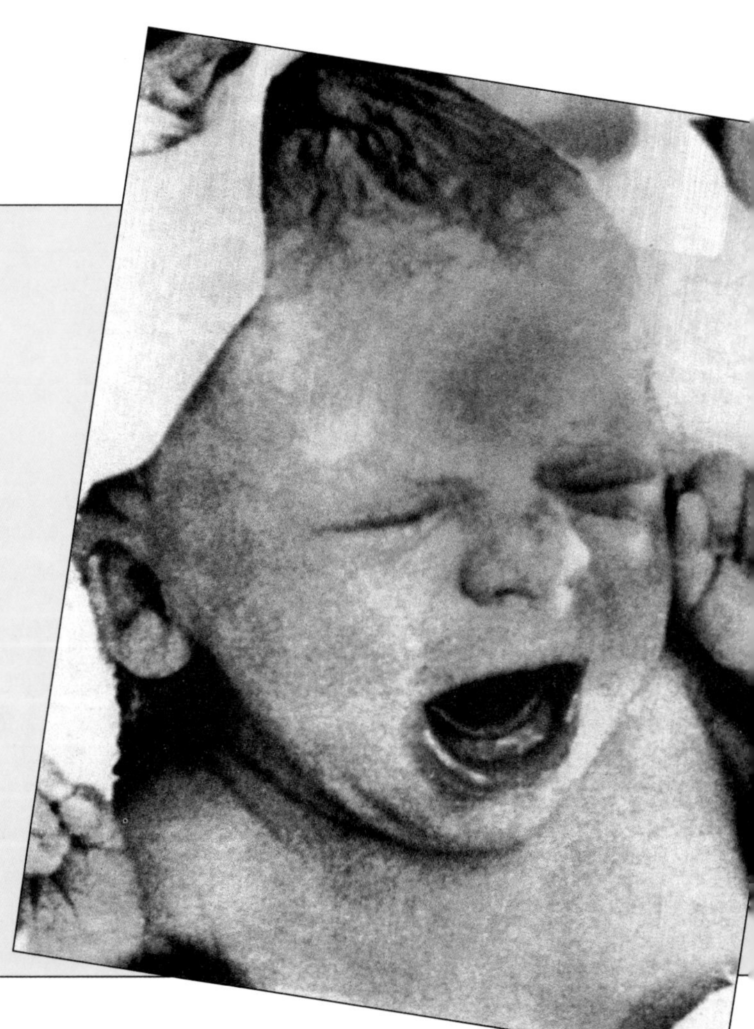

On 25 July 1978, at Oldham General Hospital, England, Louise Joy Brown was born by caesarian section. Louise was the world's first test-tube fertilization baby. She is a perfectly normal child, and lives with her mother Lesley and father John.

happening to us; life is not all just a parade of inexplicable events. Around now we start to become aware for the first time that we have an individual identity. 'Myself' has started to arrive.

Being a toddler

We start to leave the baby stage when we gain some control over our bodies. We discover that we can stand upright and learn to walk. And our excretions—until now quite involuntary, leaving an endless procession of nappies on the line—we suddenly find to be susceptible to our own control. This gives us a lot of satisfaction. Psychologist Sigmund Freud wrote that we gain two different kinds of pleasure from this new achievement: first from co-operating with our parents and doing it when they want us to; but then also from refusing to do it, so as to defy their authority and enjoy the power this gives us. Independence is beginning to develop. . .

It is often when children are two years old that their parents suddenly find, to their horror, that what was once a sweet, compliant baby has all at once developed a determined mind of its own! Screaming matches, stubborn disobedience and deliberately naughty behaviour start to develop. The child is beginning to realize its own independent identity, and test out how much it can afford to defy the wishes of others.

This was a tremendous breakthrough, which had been forecast for over a decade—ever since in 1966 Dr Robert Edwards had shown that it was possible to extract oocytes (undeveloped cells) and develop them artificially. It doesn't exactly happen in test-tubes, but certainly in a laboratory, under the direction of scientists.

Since then, many other 'test-tube babies' have been born, and extravagant claims are being made for the future. It is said that some time soon scientists will be able to manufacture eggs—rather than taking them from the mother—and so create a living baby from scratch, without using already existing human material. A geneticist in San Marcos, California, has founded a 'Repository for Germinal Choice', a sperm bank where the donors are distinguished scientists, Nobel Prize-winners, and similar high achievers. The aim is to allow women who would otherwise be unable to have a family to choose a father for their children from among the most talented, intelligent people in the world.

There are many difficulties with the new discoveries. One is that 'IVF' (in-vitro fertilization) is not a sure-fire guarantee of successful birth. The highest level of success which can be expected is likely to be around 30–35 per cent.

Another problem is that projects like the 'Repository for Germinal Choice' assume that intelligence and creativity are all that matter in creating a 'successful' child. The importance of close, natural, loving family relationships can be forgotten, and the technique can be misused to produce children without a normal family and social network to support them in their growing up.

Even more controversial, the technique used for extracting eggs usually leaves a few 'spare embryos', fertilized but unwanted, at the end of the process. Should these be destroyed? Or should they be used (as has often happened) for further research? If so, are you annihilating or experimenting with a potential human being?

There are many problems to be solved. But it cannot be denied that 'IVF' has brought new hope to many childless couples, and can be a tremendous force for good if used responsibly.

There is a story (probably apocryphal) that Albert Einstein did not utter a word until he was four years old. Then at dinner one day he suddenly remarked, 'This soup is too cold'. His parents were delighted and relieved to find their child talking at last, and asked him why he had said nothing before. He replied, 'Everything has always been all right until now.'

Another stubborn non-talker was poet Alfred Lord Tennyson, who remained silent until one day a maid spilled some boiling water over his foot. As she tried to clear up the mess and bandage his foot, the infant Tennyson is supposed to have said coldly, 'You may desist from your applications. The pain is now considerably abated.'

It sounds too good a story to be true—and perhaps it is. But it serves to remind us that children grow up at different speeds and in different ways. And certainly a toddler can understand a lot more than it can say. For most children, however, talking will begin somewhere between eight and twenty months. This provides another source of power, a new medium through which to assert our will. Which is why the first words each of us learned included 'No!', 'Don't!', and 'Mine!'.

Becoming aware of ourselves means becoming aware of others, too. We start to find that other people have wishes and desires which sometimes conflict with our own; the toddler's big problem is how to assert his or her new sense of individuality and autonomy without conflicting too much with the wishes of others, and so ending up with a smacked bottom. Until the age of two, most children play alone. After that, they begin to let other children into their games, although cautiously at first, and only one at a time. Not until they are five will most children play with several others. Social relationships are tricky; they need to be built slowly.

Digging like dad, wearing dad's jumper — children model themselves on parents in their play, for good or ill!

Developing into childhood

From the age of five onwards, play becomes much more important. The child's imagination suddenly starts to develop in a wild, fantastic way. Children at this stage often make up stories about fictional things they have done, invent imaginary playmates, devour fairy tales and story books of all sorts. The boundaries of fantasy and reality often seem quite blurred in the child's mind, but the imaginative expansion which is going on is just another way of trying out our newly-found identity against the real world. Play has been described as 'moving from the known to the untried and unknown'. The little girl who pretends to be running a sweet shop is trying out social skills she may need in future. The boy who pretends to be doing woodwork like his daddy is imaginatively putting himself into an adult situation and 'trying it on for size'.

Relationships with other children become more complex. Likes and dislikes begin to emerge; children begin to feel some responsibility for those younger than themselves, and often enjoy looking after little brothers and

sisters. Most importantly, the increased knowledge of other people and their reactions is making the child aware of 'what will happen to me if...' *If* I make a mess of my bedroom, Mummy will shout at me. *If* I eat up all my dinner without making a fuss, she will be pleased. Instead of just acting on impulse and then waiting to be praised or smacked, the child starts to realize that it can prevent the smackings by choosing to behave in a certain kind of way!

In other words, the child has now begun to appreciate what the value systems of others are, and how to apply them to its own conduct. Instead of others being in control she or he realizes the possibility of controlling his or her own conduct. This child has begun to have a conscience.

The age of learning

Beginning school is a milestone in a child's life. Suddenly a new source of authority comes into being—the teacher. And now, with a whole class of other children to relate to, the child's social circle all at once becomes much broader. Life changes dramatically.

School helps to satisfy two major needs which emerge in a child's development between the ages of six and twelve.

- One is to learn practical skills: children soon become bored with purposeless play, and start wanting to do something useful and productive. The ability to complete an activity with a purpose—adding up a sum, weighing flour for cakes, or making Christmas decorations for the classroom—gives a sense of participating in the real world.
- The other is to adapt to other people socially. Children need to leave the cosy, restricted circle of their own family and closest playmates, and start to meet a variety of new people in a wider group. School provides the place where all the social experiments—gangs, best friends, rivalries and jealousies—can be worked out. Children at this stage are often extremely cruel to those who are different: those who look unusual, talk with a different accent, are too slow at lessons (or too good at lessons). It is all part of the social experimentation which is going on.

And children can be marked for the rest of their lives by the impact of injuries received at this stage. Philosopher Søren Kierkegaard had a lonely, gloomy childhood with little love and friendship. Later in life, he was distrustful of relationships and constantly hurt by the attacks of others; he backed away from marriage to a girl whom he sincerely loved, afraid that intimacy would destroy them both. And on his deathbed he refused communion from a minister who was his oldest friend.

J.M. Barrie, author of *Peter Pan*, grew up desperately trying to please his mother, knowing that he was just a poor substitute for the son she had really loved—his brother David, killed in an accident when Barrie was six. And so Barrie's adult personality was marked by fantastic gestures of generosity in the quest to win friends, by pathological possessiveness and crippling jealousy. In his books he idealized childhood in an unreal, sentimental way, and he was incapable of adult sexual relations.

But these are exceptional cases. Most children get through the later years of their childhood pretty much unscathed. John J. Mitchell has written:

For many children the year which produces the least difficulty, whether it be psychological or social, internal or external, is the tenth year. On the whole, Ten is rather well-adjusted to himself, his family, and his limited community... His personal and social harmony are much more conspicuous trademarks in his daily life than are their opposites.

And then everything changes.

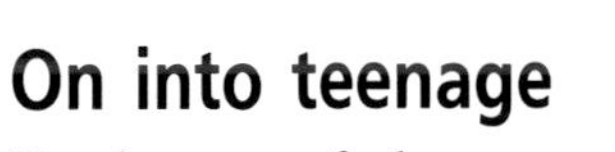

On into teenage

By the age of eleven or so, we have more or less settled down in our world. We have a fairly clear idea of who we are, how we are supposed to behave, and how we fit in with other people. Then begins an epic upheaval.

Most noticeable are the physical changes. Girls begin to menstruate, boys to have broken voices. In both sexes there are rapid alterations in size and shape. A boy's muscles double in size between his twelfth birthday and his sixteenth birthday.

There is some evidence that as the years go by these physical changes are taking place earlier and earlier in life. Between 1830 and 1960 the average age of puberty crept forward by four months every decade. But there can be wide differences between individuals, and this causes even more bewilderment and insecurity. It is no fun to be the last boy in the class to develop adult sexual organs, or to be a prematurely full-breasted girl.

There are other changes in teenagers, too. The sex drive becomes a much more prominent part of life. Freud showed that our sexual drive is already there from birth, but it is not until our genitals begin to develop fully that sexual impulses become a strongly-felt part of our experience. It has been claimed that the average nineteen-year-old thinks about sex once every twenty-five seconds, though it is hard to see how this could be tested! But certainly sex occupies much more of his thoughts than it did when he was eleven!

Adolescent friendships often go through four phases of development:

- At first young people will make friends with other members of the same sex only, and hang around in single-sex groups.
- Then one special friend of the same sex will emerge as more important than the rest of the group, and an especially close relationship will form.
- In the next phase boys and girls start to mix socially in groups of friends.
- Eventually one boy and one girl will single each other out for a close relationship. It is as if the single-sex friendship of the second phase is a 'trial run' for the life partnership which will take place later on.

This pattern is often obscured in our society by the attention which is focused on love and romance, the prestige attached to having a romantic relationship, and the pressure on boys and girls in some groups to 'pair off' earlier and earlier. But the basic pattern of the four phases remains the same.

The changes taking place in a teenager's life leave a deep uncertainty about questions such as 'Who am I really?' and 'What am I supposed to do with my life?' In our mid-teens we develop our intellectual skills: now we are able

IS THERE REALLY A 'GENERATION GAP'?

Mark Twain once commented that when he was seventeen he was amazed at how little his father knew. When he was twenty-one, he realized how much the old man had learnt in four years.

Young people and older people have always been prone to write one another off. 'The young people of today think of nothing except themselves,' wrote Peter the Hermit. 'They have no reverence for parents or old age. They are impatient of all restraint. They talk as if they know everything, and what passes for wisdom with us is foolishness to them.' It may have an oddly contemporary ring, but this statement was made in 1274.

Even further back, three hundred years before Christ, Aristotle wrote, 'When I look at the younger generation, I despair of the future of civilization.'

The natural misunderstandings which can exist between the generations have never been so much talked about as in the years since the Second World War, when the phrase 'generation gap' became popular to describe the gulf between adolescents and parents. The reason for this is really commercial. In the lean years of austerity which followed 1945, not many adults had a great deal of cash to spare; but manufacturers and advertisers soon realized that unmarried young people were a ready and lucrative market, if only they could be made to feel important. And so 'teen culture' came about. Whereas in 1948 a BBC radio discussion programme found that most young men aimed to dress like their fathers, five years later there were distinctive teen fashions, teen music, teenage meeting places and leisure activities. Youngsters started to pride themselves on having created a private world into which adults were not invited, a Teenage Heaven which reflected *their* individuality and *their* sense of self-worth. Most importantly, there was rock'n'roll, a new music which upset adults and offered a way of expressing adolescent feelings vividly:

Take out the papers and the trash
Or you don't get no spending cash.
If you don't scrub that kitchen floor
You ain't gonna rock'n'roll no more.
Yakety yak. Don't talk back.

Since those early days there have been many changes in 'youth culture', following a pattern which George Melly has described as 'revolt into style'. A new movement comes along (punk, Merseybeat, heavy metal) which sparks off a fresh revolt against the status quo; this trend is captured by the business entrepreneurs, marketed commercially and turned into a slick product; then it continues to exist merely as a meaningless style, but a fresh revolt is called for. And so on.

It might have been expected that 'youth culture' would widen the gap between adults and teenagers more than ever before, but that does not seem to be happening. Some of the latest studies by sociologists show that today's generation of teenagers feel closer to their parents than their parents did to their mothers and fathers. Parents still constitute one of the most important sources of advice and strength in the life of most teenagers, and it has been shown that while teenagers are enormously influenced by their peer group on minor issues—fashion, spending patterns, and so on—for the big decisions in life they are liable to follow their parents' lead.

There is a 'generation gap'. But it is not as wide as commercial propaganda would like to make us think.

to think systematically about ideas, hypothesize, conjecture. We become aware of all sorts of possibilities we never considered before.

And so teenagers can spend a lot of time thinking and even worrying about themselves. They are especially sensitive to criticism from their own peer group, and in an attempt to find their own identity are often prone to identify themselves closely with various 'images', or people they admire. Some wear outlandish clothes in imitation of rock heroes; some try to be like a deeply-admired teacher or youth leader; some fervently espouse causes ranging from Animal Liberation to the legalization of cannabis. In each case, a certain style is being 'tried on', so that the teenager can examine how well it fits and decide how much of it reflects what he or she is really about.

It is all complicated by the fact that our emotional awareness reaches its lifetime peak during adolescence. We feel things more keenly than we ever will again. The heights of exultation, the depths of misery—no one experiences them more dramatically (or savours them more curiously!) than a teenager. This is why a book about teenage emotions, such as *The Growing Pains of Adrian Mole*, can be so comic:

3 a.m I have used a whole Andrex toilet roll to mop up my tears. I haven't cried so much since the wind blew my candy floss away at Cleethorpes.
5 a.m. I slept fitfully, then got out of bed to watch the dawn break. The world is no longer exciting and colourful. It is grey and full of heartbreak. I thought of doing myself in, but it's not really fair on the people you leave behind.

It is not surprising that the majority of us make our basic decisions about what we will believe for the rest of our lives during the time we are teenagers. Religious conversion, adherence to Marxism, despair of ever making sense of it all—whatever we end up believing, the mid-teenage years are likely to fix it in place for us.

Young adulthood

One of the problems of being a teenager in our society is that there is no indicator to mark exactly when someone becomes an adult. Many primitive societies have 'rites of passage' which take individuals from childhood to adulthood in one clearly-definable step, but 'developed' societies allow teenagers admission to different aspects of adult society at different ages. When are you *really* grown up? When they let you get married? Or vote? Or drive a car? Or drink and smoke legally? Or join the army and kill people? Young people exist in an uncertain borderline area on the fringes of adult life.

Round about twenty, however, we are indisputably through the border at last and on to the next stage: young adulthood. Robert Wrenn and Reed Mencke have described it:

This may be a lonely stage. Young adults are usually 'between families' during part of this time. They are often on their own for the first time or living with someone who may or may not be particularly supportive. A number of events take place in this stage and major decisions are made for which little or no training has been given—for example, buying a house, deciding on marriage, or having a child.

Developmental psychologist Robert Havighurst comments that at this time we are moving from an 'age-graded' society to a 'status-graded' one. In other words, where throughout school and college our place in society tended to be fixed by the year group we belonged to, now in the wider world we find that our job throws us into contact with people widely different from us in age. And that gives us the problem of working out where we slot in and what behaviour is appropriate to which relationship (you don't talk to the boss's wife as you would to the cleaning lady).

Indeed, the main problem for a young adult is to work out the patterns of relationships and responsibilities on which the rest of life will be founded. Work relationships, social ties, marriage and parental responsibilities—now there is a much more complex web of duties and obligations than at any stage of life so far.

Many people find, in the course of sorting all this out, that their tastes, likes and dislikes become more firmly fixed than ever before. Suddenly they become aware that the music they really like best is not the latest hit records, but much more their old favourites from their mid-teens. They find less and less time for keeping up with each twist and turn of fashion. The ground is being prepared for the day when their teenage offspring will start complaining, 'Oh, Mum, you're so dated. . .'

Other interests may start to loom larger than before. Many young adults discover an increasing interest in politics and a greater awareness of world issues. Suddenly the world no longer belongs to the previous generation: we wake up to the fact that responsibility for it belongs to us as well.

One man studied by a group of American psychologists reflected, 'At twenty to thirty I think I learned to get along with my wife. From thirty to forty I learned how to be a success at the job. And at forty to fifty I worried less about myself and more about the children.' He had followed a typical pattern.

Often young adults go through a time of re-evaluation around the age of thirty. Suddenly, it seems, we realize that three decades of life are now behind us, and the word 'young' doesn't fit us quite as well as it used to. And so we ask ourselves some questions. What have I achieved so far? Where am I going from here?

And we try to sort out the contribution we want our life to make in the public world of jobs and achievements.

It is interesting to trace how many great people took a vital step in their careers not long after their thirtieth birthday. Marx wrote the *Communist Manifesto* at thirty. De Gaulle founded the Free French movement. Werner von Braun built the first true missile in history. Augustine of Hippo embarked on a spiritual journey which was not to end for another three years; Martin Luther did the same thing, but did not resolve his thinking until he was thirty-six. At thirty-two William Blake wrote his first great collection, *Songs of Innocence*, Fidel Castro attained power in Cuba, Herman Melville wrote *Moby Dick*.

'The various decisions that were made in one's twenties do take their toll.' remarks Robert Wrenn. 'During the thirties divorces are high, careers are derailed, and accidents and suicides occur with great frequency.' Many couples who married in their twenties experience a 'seven-year itch', when they feel a sudden impulse to break free. But the most significant crisis—especially for men—usually comes ten years later.

Middle age

Somewhere between forty and forty-five, many people—especially men—begin to question the effectiveness and purpose of their lives. Many realize that they are at the pivotal point of their careers; they have not many years left; from here on it will be up, or down, all the way. H.C. Lehman's work on creativity reveals that we are at our most creative between thirty and thirty-four, then fall to only 47 per cent of maximum rate by our late forties, and reach nearly zero after seventy. Men in the mid-life crisis often sense the downward curve of their powers of creativity, and start to worry.

Energy diminishes, too. After years of vigorously establishing ourselves in society and working to bring up a family, it is easy to suddenly feel overwhelmingly tired. Some people have not achieved much by their forties, and so have to push themselves harder. Others have made their mark, but find that now they have to work more strenuously to maintain their position.

The dissatisfaction with oneself, and the determination to make a mark in the world, can lead to some remarkable achievements. It was in the forties that Marie Curie isolated pure radium. Marcel Proust wrote *A la Recherche du Temps Perdu*, Scott reached the South Pole and Nelson won Trafalgar. All George Eliot's great novels were written between forty and fifty-three, while Sir Walter Scott had not written any prose fiction before he was forty-three. Einstein finally produced his general theory of relativity at the end of his forties.

For both sexes, during this period, there are unmistakable signals of the passage of time. Children grow up and leave home—and the unaccustomed silence brings many couples to a sudden bleak feeling of emptiness in their married life. Parents become old and infirm, and often depend on their children for attention and help. And every glance at the mirror reveals more evidence of advancing years.

A face pack — one weapon in the war against wrinkles. As the years pass by some people become disturbingly conscious of good things being lost. But are other good things being gained?

'Middle-age spread' develops as body fat increases to form 20 per cent of total body weight (during adolescence it was only 10 per cent).

To some people, these things are the cause of grave discontent. It is not uncommon for men who have been married, seemingly happily, for years, suddenly to leave their wives for someone much younger, in a subconscious

effort to deny the reality of advancing age. Or for a woman to try with increasing desperation to prolong her youth artificially by her choice of clothes and hairstyle. The reason for such uncharacteristic behaviour lies in the mid-forties feeling that something vital has been missed out of life and could easily slip away for ever.

Psychologist Carl Gustav Jung said, 'We overlook the essential fact that the achievements which society rewards are won at the cost of a diminution of personality. Many aspects of life which should have been experienced lie in the lumber room of dusty memories.' Quoting these sentences, Rabbi Harold Kushner commented:

I looked at that sentence when I had read it and had the feeling of confronting a truth I had always known and had worked hard at not admitting to myself. Only now, in my late forties, was I prepared to face it. Like so many people, I had become very good at certain aspects of my work, but at the cost of distorting my personality. My family, my own sense of wholeness had paid the price, but society at large was so appreciative of the imbalance that I managed not to notice what I was doing.

HOW LONG DO PEOPLE LIVE?

Today in the Western world human beings can expect to live—barring accidents—for about seventy years. But it hasn't always been that way; nor is it like that in many other parts of the world.

Our ancestors seem to have lived much shorter lives than we do. The life expectancy of people in the Bronze Age is estimated to have been around eighteen years. By medieval times it had risen to only thirty-seven, and even in the year 1900 life lasted on average for about fifty years.

It has to be remembered, however, that these figures are influenced by a very high rate of infant mortality. Professor Carlo Cipolla describes an agricultural society of the past:

Of 1,000 newborn children, 200 to 500 usually died within a year. Many of the remaining ones died before reaching the age of seven. A famous sixteenth-century physician, Jerome Cardano of Pavia, used to maintain that he could cure anyone on condition that the patient was not younger than seven or older than seventy.

The high life expectancy we now enjoy is not shared by poorer countries. In 'middle-income' countries such as Kenya, Morocco and Peru, health spending is only an average $15 per person per year—compared to $235

Psychologist Erik Erikson says that the challenge of the middle years is to choose between 'generativity' and 'stagnation', between continuing to make an impact and nervously filling in time until death. One of the most creative and fulfilling ways in which middle-aged people can make an impact is by passing on some of their experience and skills to other, younger, people. Daniel Levinson highlights the potential:

Being a mentor with young adults is one of the most significant relationships available to a man in middle adulthood. The distinctive satisfaction of the mentor lies in furthering the development of young men and women, facilitating their efforts to form and live out their dreams. . . More than altruism is involved: the mentor is doing something for himself. He is making productive use of his own knowledge

Developed world: more old people

Developing world: more young people

in industrialized countries. Not surprisingly, life expectancy is only sixty years. And in low-income countries, with an average health spending of only $1 per year, average life expectancy is forty-eight.

The fact that people now live longer in Western society has produced several new social problems. For one thing, it means that our population is increasingly dominated by older people, and this increases the burden upon medical services. Also, marriage now lasts much longer. In Shakespeare's day a couple who married could expect thirty or so years together; today a lifelong marriage could last for twice that time. This is probably one reason why divorce has become much more common.

and skill in middle age. He is learning in ways not otherwise possible.

Middle age can be rewarding and satisfying. It all depends on our attitude. Do we become excessively preoccupied with ourselves, the extent of our own achievements, the time still remaining to us, our health, popularity and capacity for enjoyment? Or do we set out to make a difference to others instead?

The final stages

In the United States, 50 per cent of all suicides are committed by people over forty-five—and 25 per cent by those over sixty-five. Our society has placed a high premium on the attractiveness of youth and the importance of looking young. When people just cannot manage to appear youthful any more, many decide they have nothing left to live for.

This is sad. Certainly old people have reached a stage in life where there are many problems. Friends and acquaintances begin to die, and the social circle shrinks. Loss of energy and reduced mobility make it hard to find new friends. Physically, illnesses become a more persistent problem, and mentally, slower reactions and failing memory can cause great frustration. It is easy to lose sympathy with a brash young world in which one seems not to fit any longer, and shrink back into constant daydreaming about 'the good old days'. Financially, too, life can be hard, since expenses can rise but retirement from work and a fixed income reduce the money available.

The death of a spouse can be traumatic. Men tend to die a little younger than women. But whichever partner goes first, facing a life bereft of one's 'other half', deciding whether to continue living alone or to move in with someone else, involves a colossal emotional upheaval. No wonder that many elderly people die soon after their partners.

Bernice Neugarten has studied the personality attributes of over 2,000 elderly people. She

IS THE HUMAN RACE COSMICALLY SIGNIFICANT?

Suppose you had a spaceship which could travel from London to New York in three seconds. And suppose you wanted to travel right across the solar system in it. The journey would take three-and-a-half monotonous weeks.

Then suppose you decided to travel to the next closest star to earth after the sun. How long would it take? The answer is staggering: 430 years!

Just how big is the galaxy we live in? Two American astronomers put it like this.

Let the sun be the size of an orange; on that scale the earth is a grain of sand circling in orbit around the sun at a distance of thirty feet. Jupiter, eleven times larger than the earth, is a cherry pit revolving at a distance of 200 feet or one city block from the sun. The galaxy on this scale is 100 billion oranges, each orange separated from its neighbours by an average distance of 1,000 miles.

And if this were not humbling enough, our galaxy is only one of innumerable galaxies which exist in the immensity of the universe. The most distant one that we know about (but there could be others) is no less than 5,000 million light years away from us. And the diameter of the entire universe—as far as we can calculate it—could be 26,000 million light years.

This means that for our spaceship to cross the entire universe would take a full 2,600,000 *million* years. And, remember, it is travelling constantly at 3,600 times the speed of Concorde!

In the vastness of the universe, human beings are very small indeed. We are just the inhabitants of a tiny planet circling around a medium-sized star in a fairly ordinary galaxy. (Some of the larger stars are 1,220 times the size of the sun in diameter.) Does it really make sense to believe that human life has any significance?

Again, if scientists are correct in their guesses about the age of the earth, human beings have been here for a very short time indeed in the history of this planet. Nobel Prize-winning biologist Francis Crick claims that if the age of the earth were only a week. . .

. . .on such a scale the age of the universe, since the Big Bang, would be about two or three weeks. The oldest macroscopic fossils (those from the start of the Cambrian) would have been alive just one day ago. Modern man would have appeared in the last ten seconds and agriculture in the last one or two. Odysseus would have lived only half a second before the present time.

And the future of the earth? Unless we succeed in blowing it up, say the scientists, it could last for another 10,000 million years. We live on quite a young planet.

When we are confronted with facts like these, can we still maintain that humanity is significant? And is it still possible to believe in a God who has a special concern for human beings? Many scientists who are Christians maintain that all they have discovered has only strengthened their faith. Says Dr Donald Carr, a specialist in geological-age determination:

Speaking of my own particular branch of science, the study of geochemistry teaches one to look at things on a vast scale; to think of time in units of billions of years of earth history, of space in terms

claims to have found four major personality types:

- The integrated, who manage to continue in sturdy psychological health;
- The defended, who face life with determination, shopping obsessively for just the right foods, and being ultra-careful of their health;
- The passive dependent, who make themselves depend on the care and attention of other people;
- And the disintegrated, a final small group, unable to cope alone, who are disorganized and psychologically unwell.

Neugarten points out that 75 per cent of those studied claimed to be satisfied with their lives since retirement. And this points to the fact that there can be tremendous compensations in old age, alongside the difficulties. The physical slowing-down can provide the first chance in years to reflect on the varied experiences of life, and grow in wisdom. If the short-term memory does not function so well as formerly, the long-term memory is often improved. And sexuality does not come to an end. Physical relationships may be less frequent and more gentle, but the expression of love and

that encompass the universe, of processes that involve world-wide cycles. The vastness of it all leads one inevitably to a new appreciation of the majesty of God.

It is sometimes thought that people in earlier ages managed to believe in God only because they saw the universe as a very small, cosy affair with the earth at the centre of everything. But C.S. Lewis pointed out that this was not the case at all.

People usually think the problem is how to reconcile what we now know about the size of the universe with our traditional ideas of religion. That turns out not to be the problem at all. The real problem is this. The enormous size of the universe and the insignificance of the earth were known for centuries, and no one ever dreamed that they had any bearing on the religious question. Then, less than a hundred years ago, they are suddenly trotted out as an argument against Christianity. And the people who trot them out carefully hush up the fact that they were known long ago. Don't you think that all you atheists are strangely unsuspicious people?

companionship between older couples can remain an important part of life.

Death is closer. But oddly enough the terror of it does not necessarily increase. It is the middle aged who are more likely to be scared by the prospect of their own end. Older people, living constantly with the possibility of death, are often more objective about it. Said the philosopher Lao-Tze, 'Who dies and, dying, does not protest his death—he has known a true old age.'

What it was all about

You may, of course, be a visiting astronaut from another planet who has picked this book up out of curiosity. But I suspect that like most readers you are a human being yourself—and so can place yourself somewhere on the journey we have sketched out over the last few pages.

Human life is the richest, most complex phenomenon we know about anywhere. But we are all part of it, and moving through it rapidly—more rapidly than often we would like. What is it really all about? When the end comes, and the notice of our funeral appears in the local paper—what will it have been for? Harold Kushner again:

I am convinced that it is not the fear of death, of our lives ending, that haunts our sleep so much as the fear that our lives will not have mattered, that as far as the world is concerned, we might as well never have lived. What we miss in our lives, no matter how much we have, is that sense of meaning.

I believe Kushner is right. And the rest of this book is designed to help you look at these questions. Who am I? Does it matter?

WHAT MAKES EACH INDIVIDUAL UNIQUE?

When two baby boys were born in an Irish hospital, the nursing staff made a terrible mistake. They mixed them up. And so two mothers were each presented with the wrong child—an error which took ten days to sort out. Eventually blood tests proved conclusively which baby was which. But the case made headline news in the newspapers of several countries, and one of the mothers was most reluctant to give up the baby to which she had already grown attached.

Why was this a 'terrible mistake'? Why were the newspapers so interested? Why was it so important to sort out which baby was which, and why did it matter to the aggrieved mother which baby she had? After all, both mothers ended up with exactly what they had to begin with: a healthy baby boy.

The answer, obviously, is that human beings are not transferable. Any baby wouldn't do. We treat human beings as having a worth and a unique identity of their own; you can't switch them around like packets of sausages, or even like pet gerbils.

This is why we are so shocked by mass brutality, such as the extermination of Jews in the Second World War, or the horrific genocide in Kampuchea in the 1970s. Every person who dies is an individual, with a specific history, a unique personality, his unique personal importance. We resent being treated as statistics or code numbers by government departments because we believe in our own individual significance. I am not just a specimen of a certain biological phenomenon, *homo sapiens*; I am *me.*

This is all obvious. We think like this from our earliest years. But *why* do we assume human beings are unique and valuable? Is our claim of 'uniqueness' real, or is it just a delusion? And if we are 'unique'—does it matter? Is this special value something which gives meaning to life, or does our uniqueness perish with us when we die?

Our sense of personal identity is one of our strongest natural instincts. We may go through all sorts of changes in our lives—violent swings in our opinions and attitudes, startling new discoveries which transform the way we see life, physical alterations even to the extent of changing our sex—and yet, despite everything which happens to us, we retain a stubborn sense of being the same person. The physical materials of our body are constantly changing, and will alter completely ten times or so in the course of an average life span; but we are convinced that 'the real me' hasn't changed, that there is some sort of continuity between what I was at age five and what I will be at age eighty.

'Although we cannot understand this mystery of identity,' comments Professor M.V.C. Jeffreys, 'we accept it, we expect it and count upon it. Indeed, if the tough cord of continuity is broken, we immediately assume some mental disorder.' Every so often a person suffering from amnesia will wander into a police station and plead for help, explaining shamefacedly that all memory of who he or she is has been lost. Yet such people are not in any doubt that they are somebody, even if they have no memories of past experiences to back up the feeling.

The philosopher David Hume thought at one stage that our sense of 'ourselves' was composed of nothing more than our jumble of past experiences:

When I enter most intimately into what I call myself *I always stumble on some particular perception or other, of heat or cold, light or shade, love or hatred, pain or pleasure. I can never catch* myself *at any time without a perception, and never can observe anything but the perception.*

But this is too neat (and Hume later changed his mind). It doesn't help us much with the amnesiac in the police station. And other questions arise. Can thoughts exist without someone to think them? And if we define 'ourselves' simply as a jumble of thoughts and experiences, what differentiates my thoughts from your thoughts? Our thoughts and experiences are certainly intimately associated with our sense of being unique, but they do not constitute the whole story.

How it all begins

Psychologists have explored the tricky question of how our sense of uniqueness and identity develops. When a child is born, it has no clear idea of where 'myself' ends and 'the external world' begins. It takes a while before the limits are established. And not until the age of two will a child begin to lose its preoccupation with itself, and start to become interested in other people. It is at this time that pronouns begin to appear in its vocabulary—'my', 'me', 'you', 'I', usually in that order. And while the child is two it goes through a stage of rebelliousness and wilfulness in which it suddenly becomes domineering, endlessly inquisitive, and impatient when its wishes are not gratified straightaway. The child seems to be waking up to the fact that it has an identity of its own which needs to

HOW MUCH DO WE INHERIT FROM OUR PARENTS?

Are you overweight? If you are, and you marry another overweight person, your poor children stand three chances in four of being fairly portly themselves. On the other hand, if neither Mother nor Dad are too heavy, there is less than one chance in ten that the children will be.

We all inherit all sorts of characteristics from our parents. How does it happen?

The answer is: through our genes. These are the small units inside a cell which determine what a new human being is going to be like. It is difficult to tell how many we have; one estimate is that each parent contributes 10,000 or so. At fertilization each of the genes 'pairs up' with another from the other parent, and it is these pairings which decide the size, weight, colouring, and much else, of the future person. Some genes are 'dominant' and some 'recessive'. In other words, some have more power to express themselves than others. For example, if a blue-eye gene from the father pairs up with a brown-eye gene from the mother, brown is dominant to blue, and so the baby will have brown eyes. Its only chance of blue eyes should be if two blue-eye genes come together.

I have just written 'should be', because in reality things are a little more complicated! Many of our features are caused not by one gene, but by several. And so, in just one case in fifty, two blue-eyed parents will in fact produce brown-eyed children—because as many as three pairs of genes can be involved. The same complex situation is true of qualities such as height, colour and physical build. For a complicated organ such as the eye, there may be hundreds of genes all playing a part.

The number of genes, and the interplay between them, means that we are all truly individuals. No one quite the same as you has ever been born before—and if

fit in alongside the identities of other people, and is simply testing out the limits of its powers and freedoms.

When this subsides, the child goes into a phase in which it gradually picks up the attitudes and responses of its parents, and starts to copy them. Imitating adults is one way of finding out about oneself. But gradually the imitation becomes less necessary. The child scraps the imitation but keeps the character which results, and this now becomes a part of his own personality. No longer does he say, 'I'm a brave boy *like Daddy*', but, having incorporated his father's standards of behaviour, says, 'I'm a brave boy.' He has now established within himself a guiding principle of life by which he can control and direct all his native impulses, and so harmonize his personality. The centre of gravity of his behaviour has shifted from the other person to within himself.

This transition brings a lot of changes to the child's personality. A little girl who at two years old would chatter away quite happily to strangers who had come to tea, becomes shy and tongue-tied at age four, and hangs her head when addressed by someone she does not know. She has become 'self-conscious'—aware of herself as a person. There is now a part of her mind which is observing the other part of her mind, watching critically how she behaves and responds, and throwing her into embarrassment and confusion.

It is at this stage, too, that we become conscious of a gap between the way we behave and the way we would like to behave! We start to realize that sometimes our instinctive impulses are not good ones. We may feel like attacking the child who has just wandered off with one of our favourite toys—and at two years old we would have bashed him quite cheerfully without thinking twice about it. But by now we have made the discovery that hitting other children has social consequences—we do not want our own bottom smacked—and we have taken on board enough of our parents' attitudes to feel, 'This is something I shouldn't do.' Thus we start experiencing the tug-of-war between 'what I want to do' and 'what I ought to do' which will continue for the rest of our lives.

And so at around the age of three or four we start to take responsibility for our own moral

someone exactly like you should emerge in the future, it will be a fantastic fluke. You are not a carbon copy of either of your parents, but an incredible, haphazard mixture of genetic material from both of them.

Another factor that has to be remembered is 'regression towards the mean'. When two sets of super-intelligent parents each have super-intelligent children, and these children marry one another, it does not follow that their children will be even more intelligent yet, and so on for ever. In fact, in a family where the level of intelligence has steadily been increasing for a few generations, there will sooner or later be a down-swing again—in the direction of the average intelligence level of the population. The same thing happens with height. Two tall parents will have tall children, but probably their children will be not quite as tall as Mother and Father. Similarly, short parents will have diminutive children who are nonetheless just a bit taller than themselves. . .

Inheritance is an intricate business. And it doesn't *determine* us, by locking us in to one inescapable future: we are still responsible for the kind of people we become. As the geneticist Theodosius Dobhzhansky put it, 'The genes do not determine "characters". . . the genes determine the reactions of the organism to its environment.' We cannot blame our behaviour on our genes.

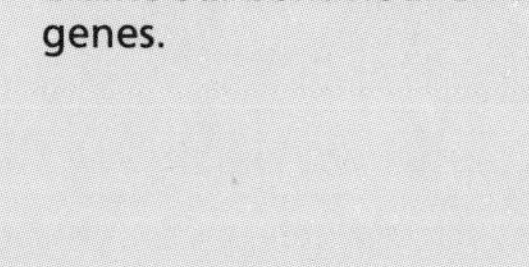

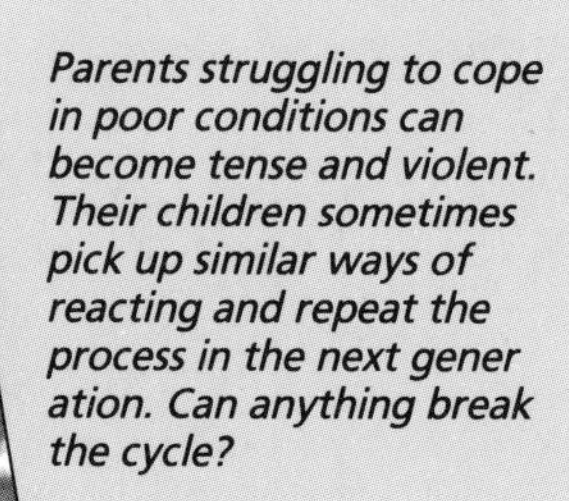

Parents struggling to cope in poor conditions can become tense and violent. Their children sometimes pick up similar ways of reacting and repeat the process in the next gener ation. Can anything break the cycle?

choices, to look at ourselves and criticize our own conduct, to gain a view of ourselves as individual, unique beings. This is what happens. But *why* does it happen? There is no logical necessity for it, says Gordon Rattray Taylor:

It is so surprising. If the mind is machinery, merely, one would not expect it. Robots are not seen as having an identity. Machinery does sometimes acquire a certain identity with the passage of time, as seen by its users (one thinks particularly of cars and boats). But it does not demand identity as a condition of its own effective functioning.

Does our identity have a purpose? Or is it just an illusory psychological by-product?

The mystery of identity

Over the last century, several things have happened to make this a vitally important question for human beings to answer. For example, there has been a massive growth in personal freedom to choose—at least in the Western world. Centuries ago the inhabitants of a village in Central Europe would have had the main contours of their lives already determined before they were born: their occupation, their diet, their clothes, their religious understanding, their spare-time occupations. They would not have been able to travel very far, and so their choices of marriage partner would have been very limited. Their understanding of other cultures and other possible ways of life would have been minimal. They would have lived a life very like that of their parents, their grandparents, and their great-grandparents. And they would have had very little say in the matter.

But nowadays our culture presents us with a bewildering variety of choices to make—ranging from our career ambitions to our favourite brand of toothpaste. We can change our religious views and political affiliations as often as we like. We can move house frequently or

WHERE DO OUR IDEAS OF RIGHT AND WRONG COME FROM?

It is a curious fact that widely different human societies have all tended to come up with the same basic code of morality. C.S. Lewis once wrote about 'the triumphant monotony of the same indispensable platitudes which meet us in culture after culture'. Why is this?

Obviously, some of our moral ideas come from **sheer common sense.** It is not difficult for human beings, wherever they live, to see that they cannot have a stable society unless they can trust one another, and respect property that belongs to others. So lying and stealing are obviously bad things to encourage.

But morality is not just a matter of logic. There is a kind of inbuilt **moral intuition** in all of us too, which makes us take certain directions. We fume when we hear of injustices. We automatically feel pity for the underdog. And this instinctive reaction exists quite apart from our rational calculations, or our religious beliefs.

Where did it all begin? One famous suggestion is that morality developed from an act of prehistoric parricide. One of our pre-human ancestors killed his father and felt guilty about it, and so started to evolve an idea that there were things one should do and things one shouldn't. But as C.S. Lewis pointed out, 'If the parricide produced a sense of guilt, that was because men felt they ought not to have committed it.' And if they felt they 'ought not', clearly they already *had* some sort of moral framework.

More recently Konrad Lorenz has suggested that our adherence to moral codes is 'caused by creature habit and by animal fear at their infraction'. In other words, we developed morals as inhibitory mechanisms which helped the species to survive, and now we cannot shake them off. E.O. Wilson says much the same, except that he sees morality as something which derives from our genetic conditioning: 'Beliefs are really enabling mechanisms for survival. . . thus does ideology bow to its hidden masters the genes.'

Ideas like this have an inbuilt contradiction. On the one hand, they are saying, 'We're stuck; we're conditioned. This is how we have to be.' And then on the other hand they are adding, 'So let's realize it and become different.' (Wilson, for stay in the same town for the whole of our lives. And all of this, say the sociologists, makes the question 'Who am I?' much more important than ever before.

It is possible for an individual to picture himself or herself as having different biographies, each carrying its own separate identity. And the more one can choose one's 'biography' for oneself, the more anxious one is likely to become. 'Am I doing this right? Have I taken the best decisions? Did I take a wrong turning two years ago? Have I got the right job, and the right marriage partner, to fulfil the needs of my personality? What is my personality anyway? What is unique about being me? Who am I?'

But there is another side to this question of individual identity. We have become much more conscious of our own insignificance this century, as we have realized how many people actually live on this planet, and how many different civilizations there have been. We have also come to appreciate how humblingly small we are in such an immense universe. Does the

example, says, 'The time has come for ethics to be removed temporarily from the hands of the philosopher and biologicized.') But if morality is not a rational, purposive phenomenon at all—if it is simply a survival mechanism—what point is there in continuing to speak of a 'reasonable' or 'fair' morality?

Religion has always been closely connected with morality, so can Christianity suggest anything better than the 'survival' mechanism theory? Christians say that God is the origin of human moral ideas, and that humans have a natural moral sense because they bear the image of their Creator. Paul wrote that even those who have never read the Bible can still show evidence that the law of God is 'written on their hearts'.

And so all human beings have an instinctive moral sense which, in culture after culture, tends in the same direction. Christians do not follow their particular faith because they feel that they have a moral code which is completely different and superior to everyone else's. Their motive is rather that they see in Jesus Christ a possibility of gaining the power to live up to the moral aspirations which human beings have always had, but could never realize on their own.

Amin, Hitler, Himmler... Millions have suffered and died because of the peculiarly evil men thrown up by this century, and every previous one. Are we all capable of similar evil, given the same circumstances? Or can we choose to go another way?

Which one is Marilyn Monroe? Two people may share identical physical appearance, but never the same identity. We are all uniquely ourselves.

individual really matter?

To make this question even tougher, some of the most important developments in the realm of thought have chipped away at our sense of uniqueness and importance. Charles Darwin caused a revolution in biology by demonstrating links between human life and the rest of creation. How many of the decisions I take are really an expression of my own free, unique mind, and how many are really just a pre-programmed survival of animal behaviour?

Karl Marx, whose theories now influence the political destiny of almost half the world, based his view of human life on the claim that our behaviour is dictated by our economic circumstances. In Marx's teaching, humans are not free agents, as they like to think, but are the puppets of the forces at work on them in society. If this is true, what does it mean for human dignity? Is there any point in treating individual human beings as if they matter? It was within a year of the Russian Revolution that Lenin began the Gulag Archipelago—the cynical, dehumanizing system of slave labour in

Russia which Alexander Solzhenitsyn claims has killed millions more than Hitler ever destroyed.

And when psychology became a respected discipline at the start of the twentieth century, human self-confidence had to take another knock. Sigmund Freud showed that a lot of human behaviour was related, not to free choices by unique individual minds, but to murky drives and compulsions buried deep in the subconscious. Behaviourist psychologists such as J.B. Watson went even further and denied that human ideas, intentions and perceptions had any real value. Human beings were just predictable machines. Change their environment, and the machines would function differently. Choice and purpose had nothing to do with it; as one behaviourist put it, there was no difference between a man training for a race and a man racing for a train.

And yet, despite all this evidence against individuality, we still cling to our own uniqueness. What *is* personal identity? To answer this question, we need to look at several other questions first.

The body and the self

The first (and most mysterious) question is: what exactly is the relationship between 'myself' and my body? Because obviously there is a very close link indeed.

If I have an accident in which my brain is damaged, my whole personality may alter. A well-known case of this kind of personality change is the Russian sub-lieutenant Zasetsky, who was hit in the head by a German bullet at the Battle of Smolensk, and suffered irreversible damage to part of his brain. He described his condition like this:

Again and again I tell people I've become a totally different person since my injury, that I was killed on 2 March 1943, but because of some vital power of my organism, I miraculously remained alive... I always feel as if I'm living out a hideous, fiendish nightmare— that I'm not a man but a shadow, some creature that's fit for nothing.

Antidepressant drugs and electroconvulsive therapy can have an equally radical effect. And brain surgery such as lobotomy (an operation to sever the frontal lobes from the rest of the brain, popular in the 1940s and 50s but now less commonly practised) has led to dramatic changes of personality. This means that the brain surgeon has awesome responsibilities—and terrifying moral problems to solve. It has often been asked whether such operations are equivalent to terminating the life of one individual and introducing another, quite alien personality.

In the light of this, another question arises. Our sense of identity seems to be perilously dependent on the healthy working of the brain. Does that mean that identity is just a chance by-product of the brain, with no independent existence of its own? That my sense of being 'me' is just a psychological trick which my own brain has foisted on me? That really I *am* just a machine?

Obviously, if this were true, there would be no such thing as immortality. If my brain is totally responsible for generating my sense of identity, then I will stop when my brain stops—at death. Any ideas about heaven, the spirit world or reincarnation are all equally impossible scientifically.

But in fact there is no need to be so gloomy about our potential. There is plenty of evidence to suggest that our personalities are not simply a casual spin-off from the workings of the human machine. One of the most bizarre pieces of evidence is the odd phenomenon known as 'multiple personality'.

Very occasionally a human being suddenly loses all recollection of the past and takes on a completely different personality. The new personality will often do things which are out of character with the former 'self'. One celebrated case this century was a lady named Chris Sizemore, who alternated between being a demure, teetotal, churchgoing housewife, and a malevolent, whisky-drinking party-goer prone to rush into completely unsuitable liaisons with strange men. The physical characteristics of the two personalities (which would switch themselves on and off with bewildering unpredictability) were different too. The 'bad girl' was allergic to nylon, which brought her legs out in blotches; the 'good girl' had no such problems, and the blotches faded when she took over. If a doctor anaesthetized one of the personalities, and 'she' started to fall asleep, the other personality might take over—and show no signs of being affected by the anaesthetic.

Flora Rheta Schreiber has reported that in one case of multiple personality, each of four 'selves' demonstrated different brainwave patterns and responded differently to word-association tests. Colin Wilson comments:

If the personalities are really just chips off one original block, then they ought to have the same brainwave patterns and the same word-association responses. In fact, such cases look far more like the medieval concept of possession. It is just as if the same body is literally taken over by a series of different people, each with their own personality.

And this, he says, suggests that whatever the 'self' turns out to be, it cannot simply be explained away as the by-product of the brain. 'We shall have to replace the old mechanical models,' he argues, 'with a model in which the brain and body are the puppet, and the "ego" is the puppet master.'

Wilson mentions 'possession' as a 'medieval concept', but in fact there are still plenty of cases today where one personality seems to be invaded by another—something which is extremely difficult to explain in terms of 'mechanical models'.

The studies of the subject are all clear: what is being spoken about is not just changing behaviour. The 'possessed' condition is a radical change for the worse from normal, of which the best available analogy is of an invasion by something previously external, and which has to be made external again to restore normality.

Perhaps, then, we need to ask a different sort of question. How *independent* is our personality of our body? Is it possible for our sense of identity to exist outside of a body? Is the self permanently tied to the workings of the brain—or could it express itself in some other form? Professor Paul Davies sees no reason why this could not be the case:

The essential ingredient of mind is information. *It is the pattern inside the brain, not the brain itself, that makes us what we are. Just as Beethoven's Fifth Symphony does not cease to exist when the orchestra has finished playing, so the mind may endure by transfer of the information elsewhere. . . Rather than 'ghosts in machines', we are more like 'messages in circuitry', and the message itself transcends the means of its expression.*

If the brain and the self do have this kind of relationship—a bit like the difference between 'hardware' and 'software' in the world of

INTELLIGENCE AND HOW TO MEASURE IT

'The whole theory of learning and intelligence is in confusion,' wrote psychologist Harold Lashley. 'We know at present nothing of the organic basis of these functions.' Lashley was writing some sixty years ago, but still today many researchers would agree with his analysis of the situation. We all like to think we are 'intelligent'. Yet there is no generally agreed definition of what 'intelligence' is. . . or how it is caused.

The problem is that intelligence is actually a mixture of different kinds of skills, including the sorting of new information in the brain, the ability to discern relationships between the new information and what is already stored there, and the power of making good decisions quickly on the basis of all this. Canadian neurologist D.O. Hebb also distinguishes between 'Intelligence A'—the mental capacity we are born with—and 'Intelligence B'—the mental capacity which develops within us as we respond to the stimulus of our surroundings and grow up from babyhood.

computers—there is no reason to suppose that the 'programme' (myself) could not be run on a different machine (for example, a different kind of body after death—what the apostle Paul described as the 'resurrection body') without the loss of anything vital. And just as a defective computer will sometimes make a mess of a programme which is run through it, we could expect a defective brain (after brain damage, or contamination with drugs) to distort the personality which it expresses. Computer users soon learn to keep a back-up copy of any important programme, just in case of accidents, because the fouling up of one copy doesn't necessarily mean the end of the programme. Similarly, the distortion or even death of human personality through brain damage does not necessarily mean the end of that human being; if there is a Creator who possesses the master copy of the programme, perhaps it can be run again in a different form.

It is hard to measure 'Intelligence A', since by the time a child is old enough to take some form of intelligence test, 'Intelligence B' has had a good length of time to develop! So is it the case that intelligence testing actually measures a combination of Intelligence A and Intelligence B? Perhaps. But some scientists claim that such tests are actually a measure of 'Intelligence C'—our ability to respond appropriately to the kind of behaviour our society expects from us. In other words, problem-solving, logic-based challenges are highly valued in our Western society, and so people with a lot of 'Intelligence C' can cope with them well. But it would be possible for someone to have a lot of natural intelligence (A) and to be developing impressively (B), yet still do very badly in an intelligence test! Whether this is true or not, it shows how complicated the whole subject can become.

It seems likely that Intelligence A accounts for 80 per cent of our total intelligence. What we inherit from our parents is more important than the circumstances of our upbringing and education. Identical twins show little difference in intelligence, even when one is brought up in a cultured family and the other grows up in a slum. The intelligence of adopted children is closer to their real mother's than to that of their adoptive mother. This is not to say that upbringing doesn't matter; 20 per cent is still quite a chunk of the total, and a supportive, stimulating environment which encourages Intelligence B can be enormously important to a child's development.

Yet it must be remembered that intelligence is not all that matters in life. Tests can measure our logical and mathematical skills; they cannot measure artistic sensitivity, maturity in relationships or practical wisdom. Philip Mason points out, 'We do not automatically make the man with the highest IQ the Prime Minister or the President: we wait to see what other qualities he will develop. We judge him by his total response to the situation in which he finds himself.'

Schoolgirls grapple with a computer. The new information technology requires a mental ability rather different from the traditional academic mind.

Four views of our identity

Philosophers who have wrestled with the problem of human identity have developed four main theories about it. Some are **materialists,** believing that ideas such as 'mind' and 'self' and 'identity' are really illusory. Ultimately the human brain works in a mechanical way, which determines our actions and choices in advance, and so we have no genuine freedom. As we have just seen, this view does not seem to cover all the evidence.

Further, it involves us in insisting that the most memorable experiences of life—love, beauty, creativity, ambition—are totally without meaning. It may just be possible to believe this. But it is certainly not possible to live in such a way. We have to act *as if* our opinions matter, *as if* we are free to choose, *as if* other people are responsible individuals with a say in their own destiny. To be a materialist we have to disregard the most basic data that our minds receive from the world around us.

We do not *seem* to be 'just machines'. Gordon Rattray Taylor has written about the difference between our mental processes and the workings of a computer:

Within our skulls there are complex circuits. . .The equipment analyzes input from the world around and then selects and executes some behavioural response. Nothing odd in that; a computer, in its crude way, can do much the same. But in our case there is a seemingly superfluous miracle: we see a brilliantly coloured scene. . . we have the sensation

This robot-man is fantasy. Human beings do not respond to artificial programming. We have at least some degree of freedom over how we react to what happens to us.

of falling in love. . . we recall events from the past and even, as some would claim, from the future. The humble electrochemistry has given rise to a vivid personal experience.

If we are just machines, something inside us is trying very hard to deceive us about it.

Other thinkers are **idealists,** so called after Plato's notion that every object has an ideal form. They theorize that since our knowledge of the world comes only from the impressions we receive mentally, our *perceptions* must be real, but we cannot be sure about the physical world! This philosophy is just as hard to live by. It hits the same problem: we have to behave *as if* the physical world is real. And idealism logically leads to doubting the existence of everything—and everybody—outside ourselves. How can we be sure of anything, if what constantly presents itself to us as real actually isn't?

Both materialism and idealism are attempting to get rid of half of the evidence—the physical reality of the brain, or the mental reality of our perceptions—in order to maintain that the *other* half is real. It seems more true to our experience to say, 'Both are real.' This has led to the other two theories: 'dualism' and 'holism'.

Dualism is often thought to be the Christian view, and in fact many Christians have maintained it. But it is not the Bible's teaching and really came into Christian thinking only when some well-meaning church leaders tried to incorporate the best insights of Greek philosophy into Christianity. So ultimately dualism comes from a Greek view of reality.

The philosophers of ancient Greece tended to see 'the soul' as an intangible, spiritual part of humanity which was unhappily imprisoned inside the body. The most important aim of life was to cultivate the soul and allow it to grow in importance, so that one day it could fly from its prison to freedom and fulfilment. Thus human beings were composed of two parts: a physical component and a spiritual one.

Following this idea, Christians have often talked about 'the soul' as an intangible essence which somehow lived undetected inside the body, the 'ghost in the machine'. The philosopher Descartes suggested that the soul and body were joined to one another through the 'pineal gland'. The idea was that soul and body were two distinct substances, which could be sharply differentiated.

This war cemetery at Verdun, France, reminds us that death awaits us all. But is death the end? If not, what comes after?

But this is not the Bible's view at all. In the Bible the 'soul' is not a special bit of human life, which can be separated from the rest. The term stands for the *whole* of a human life, seen from the point of view of its meaning and uniqueness. And when we humans die, it is not merely our 'souls' which drift off, disembodied, to sit on a cloud somewhere playing harps. The Bible talks of a day when all the dimensions of human life—the body as well as the soul—will be brought together again. In the Christian view, every part of a human being has its own importance—not just a ghostly substance called 'soul'.

And so the Christian view is a *holistic* one. Holism means recognizing that the final truth about something cannot be known until it is considered *as a whole*, with every bit of evidence brought into consideration. To say that human beings are 'nothing but machines', or 'nothing but perceptions', is to miss out most of the truth; and even to say that we consist of two 'kinds of stuff' is to divide up what should be held together. Seen from one point of view, human beings are sophisticated computers; seen from another, they are biologically efficient forms of animal life; seen from another, they are unique individuals, with personalities and life histories of their own, and an importance in God's plans. And *all* of these different descriptions are complementary parts of the same truth.

The meaning of people

This brings us to the most important question of all. If people really are individuals, and there is something uniquely personal about them—does it matter? What is the meaning of our individual identity?

Many writers this century have argued that there *is* no ultimate meaning—that identity is

Does the yuppie matter more than the drop-out? Do people's value and importance depend at all on their position in society?

something we must merely accept and respect. Professor Morton Hunt ends his book about the human mind with these words:

Now that we know so much about our minds, we have reason to appreciate and value ourselves after all. And if we truly value ourselves, if we appraise the human difference at its real worth, how can we then, except in self-defence or the defence of others, treat any other person or people as less than precious?

On the face of it, this seems perfectly reasonable. It gives us a reason for taking care of one another and honouring human life, without bothering too much about questions of ultimate value and meaning. But some worrying questions arise.

First, if the 'human difference' came about simply as some kind of cosmic accident, have we really any reason to be so proud of ourselves? Why should we exalt our own species above others which just didn't have the evolutionary luck to develop quite so advantageously? Is it fair to treat humans as more valuable than dogs and cats just because we had all the breaks?

Second, if what we value in human beings is our stunning mental performance, how does that mean we grade people? As less or more worthy, depending on their ability to perform? If we come across examples of humanity which are no better than lower forms of life—people who are 'human vegetables', for example—are we free to take away respect from them and dispose of them? And if the answer is no—why ever not?

Most crucially, we may agree that the 'human difference' demands that we treat one another as 'precious'. But how far does that mean we should go for one another? Does it make sense to die for someone else? If a situation arises in which the rights of one individual are at stake, do we defend that person's rights even if it means the community has to suffer? Or do we allow that one to be deprived so that the majority can benefit? If you apply this policy consistently, you may well end up by bringing about another Gulag Archipelago!

Obviously we need something more. We need to know that individual human beings have a value and a meaning which does not depend simply upon their ability to perform more feats than the rest of the animal creation. And one of the most agonizing problems for many twentieth-century thinkers has been that they could not see any genuine source of value for human life.

If death ends all, what am I here for? What can justify me in adopting this or that value or scale of values?

Thus a great deal of twentieth-century thinking ends up by going round and round in despairing circles. There has to be a value in the individual human life, to make the business of living sensible. But where can we get it from?

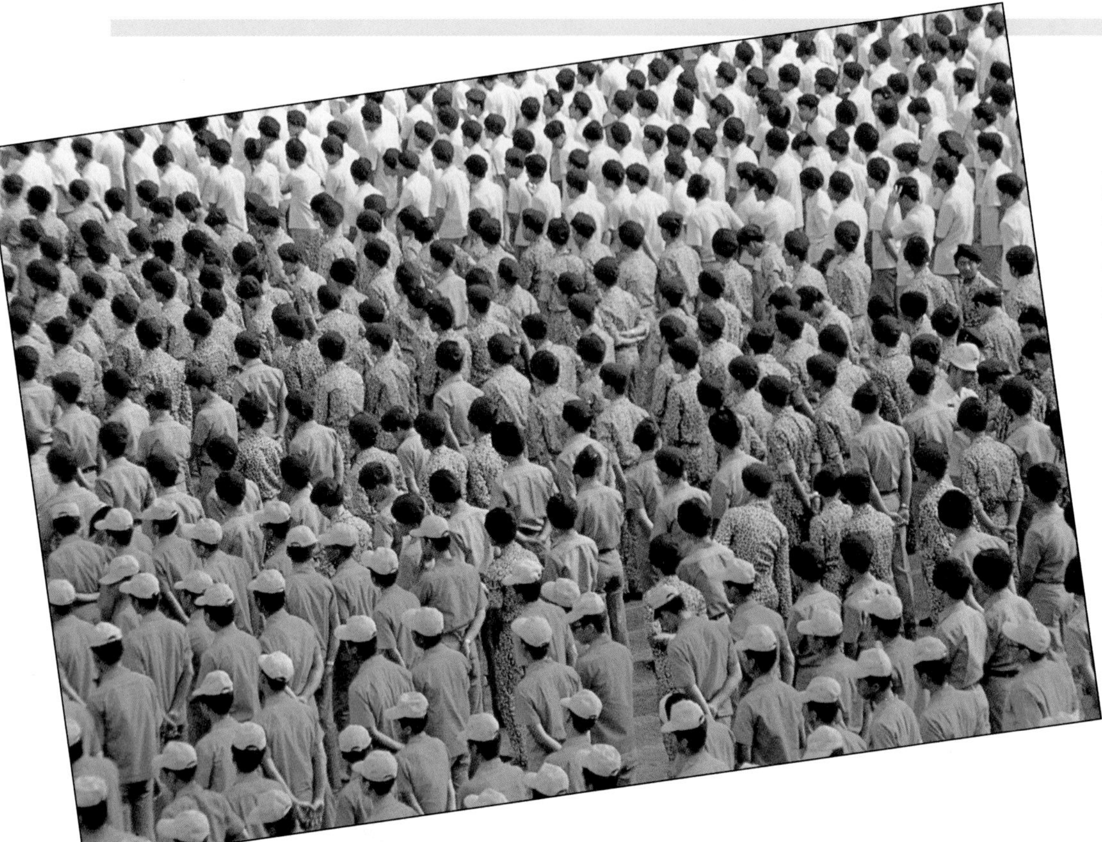

People in the mass can seem to lose their individual identity. But each of these Korean schoolboys has his own sense of being himself, and his own way of understanding what is going on.

Discussions of 'human rights' tend as a result to be imprecise and unsatisfactory, for how can you define the rights of human beings without first defining what human beings are? In an attempt to give a fuller account of the non-mechanical side of human life, some psychologists devised 'humanistic psychology' to replace the older schools of Freudian psychoanalysis and behaviourist materialism. But its great weakness proved to be that none of its exponents could define very clearly what a human being really meant. As a result a fourth school, 'transpersonal psychology', has been formed to seek for the true meaning of humanity in some kind of spiritual or mystical experience.

The 'human difference', then, consists in something much more far-reaching than an advantageous evolutionary development. And this is where Christian teaching has an important dimension to add. Christians insist that human identity and human uniqueness make sense only if we see people as the deliberate creations of a God who loves them and has a purpose for their lives. Without this dimension of reality, the others are incomplete.

Without a God, the miracle of human consciousness, the inbuilt sense of identity which we all possess, has no explanation and no value. But if God exists, our uniqueness ceases to be an unanswerable puzzle. It becomes a pointer to the source of life itself.

Part II

The Potential of Human Beings

PEOPLE: LIKE AND UNLIKE THE ANIMAL KINGDOM

Human beings are animals. That's why we flock to zoos: it isn't just that we are fascinated with the variety of other species in the world, but that they tell us something about ourselves. It's always the animals which are most human in appearance that draw the biggest crowds of spectators—the monkeys and apes, the penguins walking upright. And shows which feature animals doing human-like things (menageries, dolphinariums, circuses) have fascinated *homo sapiens* for centuries. We are like them. We are animals too. And yet—there is a difference.

It would be obvious to any casual visitor to earth that human beings are quite unlike any other life form here. For one thing, there are more of us, and we live in many more kinds of environment than any other animal. We are the only creatures who can travel so easily around the world—and even out of it to other planets. The marks of human domination can be seen all over the planet. We're the most aggressive of animals, too (as we shall see in another chapter), and that makes it serious that we are the only animals capable of destroying the entire earth.

What is the one essential difference between

humans and other animals? Many attempts have been made to answer this question. It used to be said, for instance, that only human beings use tools. But this is incorrect; we know now of some animals who employ sticks and stones for certain tasks. Perhaps humans are the only tool-*making* animals, then? No; some chimpanzees in the wild make crude tools. Are we the only ones to communicate by language? The only ones to cook our food? Peter Farb comments:

The search for such a single unique trait is futile. Scientists now know that the chasm separating humans from animals is not so wide as it once appeared. Some animal species have evolved a rich communication system, while others make and use tools, solve difficult problems, educate their young, live in complex social organizations, and apparently possess an aesthetic sense. On the other hand, no other species even approaches the human one in the scope and intensity of these behaviours... So any definition of human uniqueness obviously would have to be based on differences in degree. Humans exhibit more of certain behaviours than other animals.

Most of the physical abilities of human beings are not as impressive as those of other species. A man can run at 27 miles (43.5 kilometers) per hour on an even surface, but even ponderous creatures like rhinos and hippos can better that time. A man who is really good at high jump can clear well over two metres; but that's nothing to a kangaroo, or even a tiny bushbaby. And what gymnast or trapeze artist can equal the feats of a monkey in the tree-tops?

Part of the flexibility comes from the fact that we walk upright. We pay quite a price for this accomplishment: humans wouldn't suffer so many back problems and hernias if we walked on all fours, and the narrowing of the pelvic outlet means that childbirth is much more painful for a woman than for the female of any similar species. We would be cleaner, too, if we didn't walk upright: our buttocks are designed (like those of other primates) so that waste matter drops away quite cleanly when we move on all fours. Obviously walking upright is not the most obvious way for human beings to behave. Why did we do it?

One obvious answer is that walking upright leaves us free to use our hands for other purposes. With our hands we can touch, probe, manipulate, gesture, signal, manufacture. We can start to shape our environment, communicate with one another, experiment with technology. None of the most important human activities would be possible if it were not for the fact that we have freed our hands of the responsibility for propelling us around.

It also helps that human beings have a longer period of infancy and childhood than other species. The young of some animals are able to function like their parents almost from the day of birth. But it takes years to become a

fully-fledged member of adult human society. At birth a rhesus monkey has a brain which is 65 per cent of the maximum size it will finally grow to. A new-born chimp's brain is 40.5 per cent of its normal size. But a human being has only 23 per cent of the brain size he or she will one day achieve.

Human teeth come later. Sexual maturity arrives later. The skeleton develops to its final form later than in any monkey or ape. W.M. Krogman, an expert in child growth, claims, 'Man has absolutely the most protracted period of infancy, childhood and juvenility of all forms of life. . . nearly 30 per cent of his entire life-span is devoted to growing.'

And all of this helps us become the clever animal we are, argues evolutionary theorist Stephen Jay Gould:

But what is the adaptive significance of retarded development itself? The answer to this question probably lies in our social evolution. We are pre-eminently a learning animal. We are not particularly strong, swift, or well designed; we do not reproduce rapidly. Our advantage lies in our brain, with its remarkable capacity for learning by experience. To enhance our learning, we have lengthened our childhood by delaying sexual maturation with its adolescent yearning for independence. Our children are tied for longer periods to their parents, thus increasing their own time of learning and strengthening family ties as well.

WHAT DOES STRESS DO TO US?

Why is it that company directors are seven times more likely to die from coronary disease than miners? Why do they have twenty times as many fatal strokes as clergymen? Why do so many elderly married men die very soon after the death of their wives, and why is it often a bad idea for retired couples to move to a dream bungalow in an unfamiliar area?

The answer to all of these questions is one word: stress. This is the name we give to the way the body reacts to change—especially worrying change. Stress can have profound effects on our health and even on the length of our lives.

'Stress is not defined by what causes it,' explains Dr Peter Tyrer, 'but by a person's reaction to the cause, technically called the stressor.' Some of the things which I would find incredibly stressful (for example, free-fall parachute jumping, or working for the Inland Revenue) may not bother you at all. The similarity is not in the cause, but in the effects.

But some events do tend

Just how important are 'family ties'? Does a human being need other humans in order to develop properly? All infant animals need

Sometimes the body's formation goes wrong, for genetic reasons, through damage before or during birth, sometimes as infants develop. Modern technology can come to the help of the handicapped.

to be more stressful than others, for all of us; and in 1967 the *Journal of Psychosomatic Research* published a league table of the most common causes of stress. Top of the list was 'Death of spouse', followed by 'Divorce', then 'Marital separation', 'Imprisonment', 'Death of close relative', 'Personal injury or illness', and 'Marriage'. This last item demonstrates one very important fact: that *all* change can be a cause of stress—not just unpleasant, unwanted changes. That is why the retirement bungalow may prove to be too much for the health of people who go to live there.

What are the effects of stress? When we feel threatened by change, the 'autonomic nervous system' gets to work straightaway. It makes our lungs breathe more quickly, our heart pump blood faster, our muscles tense up and our mouth go dry. This is so that more blood can be diverted to the muscles immediately—in case the 'emergency' we have encountered requires us to fight, or run away. All of this happens without our even thinking about it.

When the crisis is over, the 'parasympathetic system' of the body—responsible for rest, sleep, digestion, and overall regulation of the body's processes—will get to work to restore the balance. Stress begins to *harm* us when the parasympathetic system is not given enough time to repair the damage: for example, when we go on working long hours without taking adequate rest, or when we keep exposing ourselves to anxiety-producing situations. A study of the blood samples of racing drivers showed that their blood was almost milky in consistency—because their breakneck driving resulted in quantities of cholesterol being pumped into their bloodstreams, ready for a burst of violent physical energy. But there was no burst of energy (none is needed in driving), and the cholesterol remained suspended in their blood.

The autonomic nervous system works with amazing efficiency. But we misuse it at our peril!

Racing drivers work under great stress, but cannot undertake the physical activity which stress demands.

stimulation to develop properly. In an experiment on white rats, one group was given extensive handling, another was subjected to mild electric shocks, and a third group was simply left alone. The group that fared worst was the ignored one.

Throughout history there have been just one or two cases of children deprived of any normal social development. For instance, in 1938 a ten-year-old girl was discovered in a loft of an American farmhouse. She had been imprisoned there since birth, with no human interaction whatsoever; she had no idea how to talk, no concept of normal human behaviour; she was the child of an incestuous relationship, and the family had been so ashamed of her that they had kept her alive but simply pushed her out of sight. Studies of such children as these show that association with other human beings is vitally necessary if infants are to become fully human. We are born with human physical equipment and a few reflexes, such as sucking, grasping, and so on; but unlike some other animals we do not inherit many of our patterns of behaviour. Human behaviour needs to be learned.

Culture and symbols

This means that humans are much more social beings than most animals. Not many mammals form organized, long-lasting societies; but human beings invariably do. And societies develop another uniquely human product, 'culture': a store of values, ideas, information, viewpoints and customs which can be transmitted from generation to generation. Culture means that human babies do not have to re-learn everything about life by painful experience. Their ancestors have heaped up a collection of facts and rules to get them started. In turn, when they die, they will leave the store behind for those who come after them—slightly increased and altered by the discoveries that have been made during their own lifetime.

Cultures vary from society to society, but human culture in general is one of the most important advantages we have over the rest of the animal kingdom. We are not restricted to following the patterns remorselessly dictated by our instincts. We can learn new and more effective ways of behaving. We can try out different forms of organization in society. We can assert our individuality by making our behaviour a little different from what our culture expects from us. The rich variety of human life, the colour and imaginative abundance which characterizes no other species—all of this comes from culture.

And culture depends, in turn, on the ability humans have to construct 'symbols'. A symbol is something which we experience which reminds us of something else we have experienced. Thus when I look at the *Mona Lisa*, I experience a vision of bits of paint on a canvas background; but I hardly even notice the paint. Instead it makes me think about a beautiful woman. When you say the word 'Laura' to me, I experience your voice making certain noises; but it makes me think about my daughter. This ability to make symbols—to produce objects, sounds and marks that remind us of something else—has extended human behaviour and made it more complex than the most intelligent animal could understand. No other animal could make sense of a football match, a religious service, a comedy programme. No dolphin or gorilla could appreciate the importance of queuing at a bus stop or saluting a flag.

The most widespread and valuable way of making symbols, awesomely simple and effective, is human language. Again, this is something that other animals cannot copy. Or so think most scientists, though Carl Sagan, for one, disagrees. In a book about human and animal intelligence, he wrote:

Although a few years ago it would have seemed the most implausible science fiction, it does not appear to me out of the question that, after a few generations in such a verbal chimpanzee community, i.e. where chimps have learned a vocabulary of around 100 words as some have been trained to do, there might emerge the memoirs of the natural history and mental life of a chimpanzee, published in English or Japanese. . .

Of what value are our bodies? Of great value, because they express our selves. The solemn funeral rites of different cultures show this connection, as in a funeral pyre at Varanasi, a procession in Rajasthan, and a Mayan-influenced Christian cemetery on Yucatan peninsula.

What are the facts? In 1966 two American psychologists, Beatrice and Robert Gardner, embarked on an experiment to teach Ameslan (American sign language) to two chimpanzees, Washoe and Lucy. Their pupils proved able to learn an impressive number of gestural signs—Washoe managed 200 in the first four years—and to employ them in sentences. They even created new expressions for phenomena they had not seen before: 'water bird' for duck; 'drink fruit' for watermelon; 'cry hurt food' for radish (after Lucy had burned her mouth on one).

Lana, a chimpanzee in Georgia, has been taught to type out sentences using a specially-designed computer language, and to monitor the results on a display screen. One day her trainer, using a separate computer console in the same room, began spoiling her sentences by interposing a nonsense word in the middle of them. Lana suddenly realized what was happening, and composed a new sentence: 'Please, Tim, leave room.'

When chimps can understand complex sentences ('If red on green then Sarah take red'; 'Sarah insert banana in pail, apple in dish'), invent new terms, and even swear at their trainers, can we really say that human abilities are that much different? Isn't it simply a matter of time until they catch up with us?

No, says psychologist Herbert Terrace. 'Apes can learn many isolated symbols (as can dogs, horses, and other non-human species), but they show no unequivocal evidence of mastering the conversational, semantic, or syntactic organization of language.' A trained adult chimp and a child of two may have roughly the same vocabulary size, but children will develop a grasp of more and more complex structures, enabling them to express finer and finer shades of meaning. Chimps will stay exactly where they are.

Another problem for chimpanzees is their physical construction. To quote Peter Farb again:

It is impossible for apes to speak because their vocal tracts are so constructed as to prevent them from sounding important vowels. This lack is not so trivial as it might seem... Humans can count rapid pulses of sound made by certain electronic machines at rates up to ten per second. Beyond that the pulses fuse and are heard as one continuous tone. Humans, though, speak at a rate of about twenty pulses per second—and these do not fuse. It is the vowels attached to consonants that allow us to decode the sounds as speech signals; these vowel sounds are the very ones that the vocal tracts of the apes are unable to produce.

Society, culture and language make it possible for human beings to enjoy more complicated relationships with one another than the rest of the animal kingdom. Human sexual development has helped here too.

Most animals follow the rule of the oestrous cycle—they have a mating season. Humans are one of the few species where mating can continue throughout the entire year (and usually does, according to all the surveys of human sexual behaviour). With other animals the sexual act is often very brief (a few seconds for a bull or ram, under ten seconds for a chimpanzee; less than thirty for an elephant). Human beings can vary the length of it, and usually take at least a few minutes. Human females can experience orgasm, too, which is unknown among other animals. And humans are the only mammals who prefer making love in a face-to-face position (although they are capable of wild experimentation, also unlike other species).

All of these factors combine to make sex among humans a much more intense, personal, emotion-laden kind of thing than it is among other animals. It is not just a physical function but a means of communicating with another human. And it is capable of becoming a rich language, with infinite subtleties and variations of expression, between two partners who learn to use it in lasting commitment to one another—another human trait which doesn't appear very often in other species.

Humankind, then, is much more than 'the naked ape'—as the title of Desmond Morris' popular book once suggested. (We aren't descended from apes anyway, as zoologists are constantly pointing out. We represent a different branch of the *Hominoidea* superfamily.) By any standard there is an awesome gulf between even the most advanced of other animals and ourselves. It prompts a question. Is this simply chance, a random development? Or, to quote Sir Bernard Lovell, a well-known astronomer, 'Is the universe the way it is, because it was necessary for the existence of man?'

The apostle Paul, at least, had no doubt:

The God who made the world and everything in it is the Lord of heaven and earth... From one man he made every nation of men, that they should inhabit the whole earth; and he determined the times set for them and the exact places where they should live. God did this so that men would seek him and perhaps reach out for him and find him, though he is not far from each one of us.

The human body

What are humans made of? Let's assume you weigh around ten stone (70 kilograms). If we could separate you out into your constituent elements, this is what we would find: 100lb (45.4kg) of oxygen; 28lb (12.7kg) of carbon; 15lb (6.8kg) of hydrogen; 4.6lb (2kg) of nitrogen; 2.3lb (1kg) of calcium; 1.6lb (0.7kg) of phosphorus; a few grams of potassium, sulphur, sodium, chlorine, magnesium, iron and zinc; and traces of copper, manganese molybdenum, cobalt, selenium.

Clearly this is not the whole story (it is often commented that a chemist would give you one pound sterling for the lot). The importance of the human body is not in the rare and precious things it is made of, but in the intricate way in which it uses these building materials. And as we shall see, there are few things in nature more awesome than the efficient complexity of the human body.

Very little in the human body seems to be superfluous. Biologists have often been puzzled by seemingly meaningless parts of the body, only to find later that they do serve an important function. Take the thymus, for example. Until quite recently it was dismissed as a useless survival of an earlier stage of development, but now it is known to be the control centre of the body's defence system against germs. Tonsils and adenoids were often removed from children, because they were thought to serve no function. Now we realize they help to protect the throat and nose against infection.

We all have a strange organ known as an appendix, the cause of a lot of sudden operations when it becomes inflamed; in England and Wales, says Anthony Smith, 'at any time, one in fifty of the general hospital beds is occupied by someone who has every reason to wonder what on earth the human appendix is all about'. However, we may be about to discover the answer. The appendix may be part of our lymphatic system.

Before looking at the various 'bits' of the body—the bones, muscles, organs and so on—we ought to look at the building-blocks of which they are all constructed. These are the cells. A human body contains about sixty billion cells, shaped slightly differently depending on the job they have to do. (Red blood cells are saucer-shaped, and liver cells square-shaped, for example; while nerve cells have long extensions on the end.) All of these cells trace their origin back to one original cell—the one that was formed when an ovum from the mother was penetrated by a sperm cell from the father. Every one of the sixty billion cells is potentially capable of forming a complete human on its own; it contains all the information necessary (except for the red blood cells, that is, which have no nucleus).

In the human body cells are grouped together to form specialized units. Each unit is called a 'tissue'. Tissues are grouped into organs, and encased in a watery substance known as tissue fluid. Actually, water is a very large component of the human body: it accounts for about 60 per cent of a man's body weight, and 50 per cent of a woman's. The average male body contains about nine gallons of water.

Inside a cell, among a quite complex set of components, is the nucleus, which contains twenty-three pairs of chromosomes. These chromosomes contain the blueprints for a human being's life: whether that person will be male or female, have blue eyes, grow tall or

short. And, remember, there are 60 billion production plants like this in your body.

Cells produce proteins. And this is important because proteins (amounting to 12 per cent of your body weight) are the agents that act on the orders of the chromosomes. They work to shape the characteristics of the individual cells, fitting them for the job they have to do in the body, and control the changes that take place within them. They form 'hormones' (the chemical messengers inside us which direct our growth, our 'biological clock', our basic drives and emotions) and 'enzymes', which help to precipitate biochemical reactions in the body.

The body's framework

'As a chassis,' claim Christian Barnard and John Illman, 'the skeleton is unique. It twists and bends to permit a wide range of movement

TWINS

In June 1979 James Lewis, a security guard in Lima, Ohio, finally succeeded in tracing his twin, James Springer. He had not seen his brother for thirty-nine years; both boys had been adopted at the age of five by different families.

The two found they had the same sleeping problems, migraines and haemorrhoids; they had both had two confirmed or suspected heart attacks; both liked

maths but had trouble with spelling. But there was more.

Each twin had married a wife called Linda. Each had divorced his Linda and married a girl called Betty instead. Each had owned a dog called Toy, had worked as a deputy sherriff and had also been employed by Macdonalds. Each had had a spell as a petrol-pump attendant. Lewis's eldest son was called James Alan; Springer's was James Allan!

These coincidences are quite unusual, even for identical twins. But they show that, even when brought up quite differently, identical twins will exhibit a significant amount of behavioural similarity. If one twin is alcoholic, for example, there is a 65 per cent chance that the other will be. For male homosexuality, there is a 98 per cent correlation; for schizophrenia 86 per cent. Why is this?

'Identical' twins and 'similar' twins come to birth in quite different ways. When an egg cell is fertilized by a sperm cell, it usually starts multiplying into a cluster of cells and developing into one new human being. But just occasionally it will split into two eggs, which then start growing side by side in the womb. (Sometimes the splitting process doesn't happen *quite* in this way, but takes place after the egg has already become implanted in the uterus; however, the process is very similar.) This phenomenon produces two children (of the same sex, except in very unusual circumstances) who share the closest possible genetic matching. It happens about twice or three times in every thousand human births. It does not run in families.

The ability to have 'dissimilar' twins does run in families, however. This is because the female hormones which release eggs at the time of ovulation each month are controlled by genes—and some people inherit genes which in some months permit two eggs to be released, instead of the usual one. And so two eggs can be fertilized by quite separate sperm cells. (In fact, if the woman has been sleeping with more than one man, it is just possible that the sperm cells will come from different donors, with the result that twins are born who have different fathers!) Obviously, with this type of twin, there will not be nearly so much close matching, because the twins are quite separate individuals with slightly different genetic mixes, who just happen to be inhabiting the same womb at the same time.

The number of 'dissimilar' twins born tends to vary from society to society. Food, health, age of parenthood and genetic inheritance all have something to do with whether the rate is low or high. Much less common, however, are triplets, quadruplets and quintuplets; in fact, it almost never happens that more than four babies are born simultaneously, unless the mother has been receiving hormonal treatment.

The strangest case of multiple birth is 'Siamese twins', when a single egg divides to form twins, but never quite completes the job. The result is that two individuals are born whose bodies are fused together at one or more particular points. The phrase 'Siamese twins' comes from a celebrated pair, Chang and Eng, who were born in 1811 (but weren't actually Siamese!) and were exhibited as a circus curiosity by P.T. Barnum. Later they became farmers in North Carolina, married two sisters and had over twenty normal children. No other pair has ever lived so long. But at least this century scientists have become able occasionally to separate some 'Siamese twins', so that the two can lead independent lives.

unequalled by any man-made machine.' Part of the supremacy of human beings over other animals has got to be due to the tremendous range of things their bone structure allows them to do.

There are just over 200 bones in the adult body. They account for only 14 per cent of our total weight; steel bars of the same size would weigh more than four times as much. But they are very strong, because of their structural design. The thigh bone, which is really a hollow cylinder, is capable of withstanding a pressure of 1,200 pounds per square inch whenever we walk. Bones contain a tough protein fibre called 'collagen' on which calcium and mineral salts are deposited, creating hardness and strength. The total effect is to supply all the strength of reinforced concrete.

We do not have the same number of bones throughout our lives. A new-born baby has 300 bones, but some of them fuse together after a while. There can also be differences between individuals: something like one person in twenty is born with a thirteenth pair of ribs.

Can bones lose their size and density through under-use? That seems to be the experience of Apollo and Gemini astronauts. Weightless floating was producing a loss of bone structure of four grams of calcium per month. At that rate, twelve years of weightlessness would have removed half the calcium from their bodies. If humans are to exist for long periods in space, this is one of the unexpected problems they will have to face.

Different bones have widely divergent functions. The skull is the most important protective device in the body. It contains twenty-nine bones, including the six smallest ones we possess: three in each middle ear, which are crucial to our sense of hearing. They convey sound vibrations from a membrane in the outer ear, which receives them, to an organ further inside which turns them into nerve impulses and then transfers them to the brain for decoding.

Moving further down, the skull is supported by the spine—twenty-six bones called vertebrae, separated by flat discs of cartilage, which is a flexible white tissue. The discs are extremely important. They act as shock absorbers (so that our spine is protected when, for instance, we jump off a wall) and allow movement so that the spine can bend and rotate. It is curious how similar the skeletons of mammals can be. A long-necked giraffe has the same number of cervical vertebrae as a man—seven; and so does the whale, which has no neck at all.

Our bodies are capable of remarkable feats of strength and elasticity when we exercise and train with enough determination.

More than half of our bones are in our arms and legs (thirty-two in each arm, thirty-one in each leg). Of this collection of 126 bones, 112 are in our extremities—hands and feet, wrists and ankles. This arrangement allows us a degree of flexibility in the use of our hands and feet which is vital for the tasks we have chosen to perform.

Similarly, the ears and nose tip are flexible because they are not made of bone, but of cartilage. In fact, the skeleton of a foetus is initially made of cartilage too, but bone cells start to appear in the seventh week after conception.

So much for the bones. But how do we move them? This is where the muscles come in—collections of strong fibres which can contract forcibly to manoeuvre the body into different positions. Muscles are tied to the bones by tendons. They account for just over one-third of the body's total weight. And they fall into three groups: skeletal or 'voluntary' muscles, which we use to move ourselves around; cardiac or 'heart' muscles, which keep our heartbeat going regularly; and smooth or 'involuntary' muscles, which operate automatically to run our internal systems, such as breathing and digesting food.

How efficient is the human muscular system?

At first sight, it doesn't appear very impressive: the average human body is only 25 per cent efficient, which means that three-quarters of the energy it generates is simply squandered. But then most machines are even less efficient. A finely-tuned car can achieve 30 per cent efficiency, but a human body in top physical condition can soar as high as 50 per cent.

Muscles work by contracting—suddenly tensing themselves to become much shorter than usual (some muscles will contract by as much as two-fifths). This means that every movement they introduce is a pull, not a push, even when the body itself is pushing something. You can easily see how this works by pushing your arms against a hard surface, such as a wall, and feeling how your arm muscles tense up. When muscles are repeatedly used, without being given enough chance to rest, they will eventually lose their power to contract at all. On the other hand, if muscles are not used enough, they will atrophy, and again lose their power.

There are some muscles over which we have complete control. Thirty muscles, for example, supply the amazing range of expressions and contortions a human face can achieve. But others aren't under our direct conscious command. What is it, for instance, that makes our heart muscles speed up, during strenuous exercise, from the steady rhythm of forty-five beats a minute to something maybe four or five times as fast? And what slows it down again afterwards?

The accelerator for all of our involuntary muscles is the 'sympathetic nervous system', and the brake is the 'parasympathetic nervous system'. By working regularly in opposing motion to one another, they produce strong waves of muscular contraction throughout the body that help to keep the body's processes going. It is this process, for instance, which pushes food along the twenty-five-foot channel of our digestive tract.

Is it ever possible for us to control these processes directly? Not much is known. But Dr Elmer Green of the Menninger Foundation, Topeka, Kansas, has carried out some tests which at least indicate a possibility. In 1970 he tested an Indian yogi, Swami Rama, who claimed to be able to stop his heartbeat altogether. Although this did not happen, the Swami did manage to achieve 'atrial flutter'—an amazingly high heart rate of 300 beats a minute, which should have left him unconscious, but didn't. Clearly concentrating the mind can have *some* effect on physical processes.

The workings of the body

So much for the body's framework. But what of the processes that go on within it? Here we have space to look at only two of the most important: breathing, and the role of our blood.

Breathing is something we do most of the time without thinking about it. But we do an enormous amount of it, getting through something like 3,300 gallons (15,000 litres) of air each day, which means anything between 10,000 and 20,000 breaths per week. The purpose of all this activity is to bring quantities of oxygen into the body, and get rid of the carbon dioxide and other substances left behind when the oxygen has been used. Human beings cannot cope with much carbon dioxide: if we breathe in air which contains more than 5 per cent of it, we will probably

faint. (We can, however, put up with a lot of impurities in the air we breathe: it has been estimated that the average city dweller breathes in 20,000 million particles of foreign matter every day.)

We draw breath in by expanding the lungs. This happens when we do two things simultaneously: the diaphragm pulls itself downwards and the rib muscles contract. This expands the chest wall and thus creates a slight vacuum, which air from the outside rushes in to fill up. Breathing out simply reverses the action, and as the lungs are forced inwards again, the pressure drives the air out. But not all of it. Only about one-sixth of the air which is already in the lungs will be changed over in any one breath. So it's possible that some molecules of the first breath you take as a baby will still be there in your lungs at the end of your life!

Once the air is in the lungs, the oxygen needs to be distributed throughout the body. For this purpose, the lungs have a vast surface area—somewhere between 800 and 1,000 square feet (90 square metres); books about the human body often compare this to the size of a tennis court. This colossal area is necessary so that the blood cells can be charged with oxygen regularly and quickly enough to keep the body surviving. We will examine this more closely in a moment.

Our breathing can sometimes produce strange side effects. Why do we yawn, for instance? Nobody really knows. Anthony Smith suggests that it 'may be a physiological attempt to get more blood to lungs and brain; but blood flow is frequently boosted on many other occasions without the bewildering grimace of a jaw-cracking, ear-popping yawn.

Hiccups are another mystery. Probably the nerves controlling the diaphragm are responsible for it, but why does it happen? And what is the best way of stopping it? There are hundreds of folk remedies, but sometimes they all fail, and a victim can be hiccuping for months or even years.

Laughing, crying, sighing—the ways in which we vary our breathing patterns are strange indeed. One of the strangest is called 'hyperventilation'. This is an extremely rapid breathing process which often occurs in unusual states of consciousness, and during mediumship. Perhaps the unusually fast arrival of oxygen in the brain alters perception in some way. Yoga meditation, too, uses a special breathing technique, pranayama, which reduces the body to stillness very quickly.

The blood system is the body's distribution network. Blood carries all sorts of things from one part of the body to another: oxygen and carbon dioxide, as we have already mentioned, but also hormones, various nutrients, antibodies which prevent infection, and water.

The average body contains 10.5 imperial pints (6 litres) of blood. It causes no harm to the system for a blood donor to give away a pint or so in blood transfusion and even as much as a third of the body's blood can be lost without serious trouble. But if more than half goes missing, life will no longer be possible.

Our blood supply is constantly engaged in an endless journey round and round the body. By the end of your life, your heart may have

A giraffe's is a prince among necks. A whale doesn't have one. Yet both have the same number of vertebrae — seven. And human beings have seven as well.

pumped the equivalent of 50 million gallons (227 million litres); at its maximum rate, it can push through 5.5 gallons (25 litres) a minute, which means sending the entire blood supply right round the body several times in sixty seconds!

What happens to all this blood on its journey?

The trip starts in the right side of the heart. From there the blood is pumped to the lungs, where it is squeezed through 'blood capillaries', tiny channels so narrow that only one red blood cell can pass through at a time. Each cell will have only three-quarters of a second in the capillary before it is pushed out by the next ones following it, but that is long enough for it to jettison the cargo of carbon dioxide it is carrying, and pick up fresh oxygen atoms instead.

From there the blood goes back into the left side of the heart, and is pumped on again—this time through a 60,000-mile system of arteries, capillaries and veins, giving up its load of oxygen where it is needed and taking on board carbon dioxide to dispose of as refuse.

Why do we feel dizzy sometimes when we leap out of bed? Because when we are lying down it is not so difficult for the heart to pump blood lengthways to the brain. When we stand up, the increased gravitational pull means that the heart has to work faster to get the oxygen up to the head; and so momentarily we have a reduced supply, which makes us feel faint.

But blood does other things, besides acting as the transport system. As well as red cells, the blood contains 3,000 million white cells which are the body's main line of defence against invading bacteria or viruses.

Once a germ has managed to slip into a vulnerable area of the body, the white blood cells start to multiply at the point of attack. Here they kill off the enemy by eating it and digesting it. (For this reason, they are also called 'phagocytes', literally, 'eating vessels'.) The germs release poisonous toxins in their own defence, and these wake into life another sort of white cell, an 'antibody', which produces defence chemicals to counteract the poison. After the germs have been destroyed, the antibodies stay around. They remain in the bloodstream for some time, ready to repel the invader should it come again. That is why you are unlikely to catch measles or chickenpox more than once!

The body's defence system is highly versatile. In a lifetime it may come up against 100,000 different poisonous forces—and produce antibodies to deal with every one. One of the few things to outwit it, unfortunately, is the common cold! So many different viruses can cause it that the body never has a chance to build up a resistance to them all. That's why cold cures make so much money for pharmacists. And why none of them can be guaranteed to work!

The body's information systems

How many kinds of signals do we receive from our senses? We know the difference between seeing a pretty girl, hearing a brass band, tasting a mouth-watering meal and touching wet paint. How many sensations does our body receive?

Earlier this century a distinguished American psychologist, Edward Titchener, started counting. Eventually he proclaimed that we have 46,709 elementary sensations, not counting an indeterminate number of smells. He counted 11,000 tones that our ears can recognize, but only four basic tastes.

Nobody would place much reliance on Titchener's work today, but it does show what an immensely complicated job the human senses do. Take the sense of sight, for example. The human eye is such a complex instrument that Charles Darwin, when first he formulated his theory of natural selection, was at a loss to explain how the eye could have developed simply by chance. 'When I think of the eye,' he wrote, 'I shudder.'

What happens when a light wave strikes your eye? First it passes through a layer known as the 'cornea', which begins to focus it; then it penetrates through the 'pupil' gap. (The pupils of our eyes dilate or contract depending on how much light they are receiving, but they are also affected by fear, interest in a subject which is being discussed, sexual excitement, and other emotional states.) Then the 'lens' of the eye picks up the partially-focused beam and sharpens the focus fully. The light travels on to the 'retina', the part of the eye which decodes the signals and sends the proper message about it to the brain.

The retina contains an enormous number of receptor cells to do the 'decoding' job. 125 million of them are called 'rods', and enable us to detect different shades of grey, thus making it possible to see at night. The other 7 million are 'cones' (the name comes from their shape); they help us distinguish colours, essential for day vision.

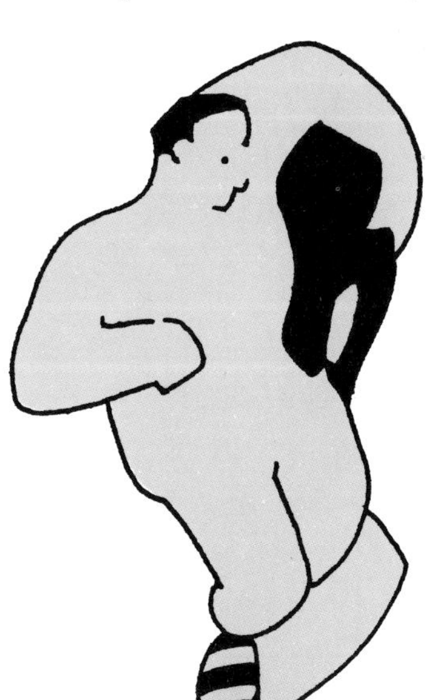

What do you see in this picture? Just one image, or more?

The combined messages of the receptor cells are put together in receiving stations known as 'ganglion cells'. This explains why one can actually see and distinguish objects whose image on the retina is narrower than a single cell across. A telegraph wire is visible against a bright sky at a distance of a quarter of a mile. Its image may cover no more than one twenty-fifth of the receptor, yet it is seen sharply.

From the ganglion cells, the optic nerve transfers the information to the brain, and recognition takes place.

What we 'see', however, does not simply depend on the information which the retina passes on to the brain. The information coming in is checked against our previous knowledge of patterns, shapes and appearances, and we classify the new experience in terms of what we already know. (For instance: I have hardly noticed what my wife is wearing today. I am so used to seeing her that I do not need to look at her very closely to identify the fact that she is there; and so I do not 'see' her directly; I 'see' my mental image of her instead. When psychologists ran a test in which various men were dressed up to look as if they had lost a limb, wives of the volunteers were less likely to notice anything wrong with their husbands than with strangers.)

And so our eyes can be deceived. But nevertheless they give us a vast fund of information about the world around. And they have tremendous adaptive ability: when we are thrown into a darkened prison cell, our eyes will rapidly grow accustomed to the light—in the first hour sensitivity increases by 75,000 times.

Eyes are never still. Apart from the fact that our head is always moving slightly the eyes also dart about, constantly changing the pattern of light which is being directed on to the retina. Otherwise fatigue, and perhaps blindness, would inevitably follow. And we need to blink: although we're rarely conscious of doing it, we take this automatic step of caring for our eyes from six times to thirty times a minute. Few people can last a full minute without needing to blink.

Our other senses are just as intricate.The

human **ear** can distinguish about 1,600 frequencies of sound, at 300 different intensities in volume, between twenty cycles per second and 20,000. This is a startlingly wide range, although dogs can hear higher frequencies and grasshoppers lower. (Just for comparison, a male voice is around 100 cycles per second, a female voice 150, and middle C on a piano 256.)

What is it in our **nose** that makes us able to smell? Tiny cells with long hair-like 'cilia', embedded in a layer of mucus. There aren't nearly so many sense receptors for the sense of smell as for sight (only fourteen), yet since they operate in different combinations in a flexible pattern, we can still, with a little practice, detect over 10,000 different odours. (All of which seems quite pathetic to a dog, whose nose is a million times more acute even than that!)

For the sense of **taste,** we have receptors located in our 3,000 taste buds, which can be found on the front, back and sides of the upper surface of our tongue. (There are some in our palate, pharynx and tonsils, too.) It used to be thought that there were different receptors for the four 'primary sensations'—sweet, bitter, sour and salt—but research has shown that the pattern is much more complicated. It is still true, however, that we sense most sweet and

IS THERE A BIOLOGICAL CLOCK INSIDE US?

Why is it that most normal births take place between midnight and eight in the morning? Why can you be fairly confident, if you are still alive at ten in the morning, that you will probably live through another day? Why do we so often set our alarm clock for a certain hour in the morning—and then wake up just before the alarm is due to sound?

All of these strange facts are explained by the discovery that there are a number of 'clocks' inside us, regulating our lives by different rhythms, ensuring that physical changes take place at the appropriate moment.

The most obviously recognizable rhythm is the daily one: every night, our life processes slow down, as we go to sleep. If we try to disrupt this rhythm, we are in trouble—like a nurse friend of mine who found when she was on night duty that she was waking up to go to the toilet at all the wrong times. 'Jet lag' happens when we cross quickly from one time zone into another. Our bodies keep on working according to the time schedule of the zone we have left, and the 'clock' will not be 'reset' for three or four days after our arrival. This is why long-distance jet pilots are less healthy than average, and have a shorter life expectancy, while pilots who operate within just one time zone have a normal expectation of life.

If we adjust our clocks permanently—for example, by staying on the night shift for several years—we suffer no ill effects: the body adjusts. Night workers actually tend to be slightly healthier than those on a day shift. All the same, there are some humans who operate best at night, and others who work best in the morning. This has a physiological basis: 'night birds' really do take longer to get going in the morning, with a slightly subnormal temperature and heart-rate for the first hour or two after waking up. This tendency seems to be inherited.

The daily rhythm is not the only one. There is a twice-daily one too: our heart-muscle rate slows at around 1 p.m. and 9 p.m., inducing less efficiency and alertness. Just before lunchtime is not a good time to be doing work which requires care. This seems to have something to do with the regeneration of cells in our bodies: just at the times when our active energy level is lowest, cell regeneration reaches its highest point.

Then there are rhythms which are longer-term. Patients in mental hospitals, for instance, can show behaviour which changes from day to day according to a certain cycle—altering from 'almost normal' to 'extremely disturbed'. And there are the once-for-all changes which take place when (for example) a boy who has shown no interest in the opposite sex suddenly starts to feel a desire for a girlfriend, or a married woman who has never really wanted children becomes desperately keen to have a baby. The clock's hands have moved on one more minute—and there is no reversing the process!

salt tastes with the tip of the tongue, sourness at the sides, and bitterness at the back.

Is **touch** one sense, or several? Again, the picture is complicated. There are some parts of the body where one set of nerve endings seems to have the job of reporting *all* the touch sensations to the brain, and other parts where there are specialized endings for touch, pressure, pain, heat and cold. We have four million receptors in all; pain receptors far outnumber the others. And it is a good thing that this should be so!

Pain is the body's early-warning system of impending danger; a woman without pain can break her ankle and not notice, or suffer severe internal injuries and not discover them until it is too late for her life to be saved.

We suffer two kinds of pain. There is the sharp, stabbing pain which warns you instantly that you have done something wrong (cut your hand with a knife, for instance); and there is the dull, settled, aching pain which will continue until you have treated your hand and healing has begun.

These two types of pain each have their own separate nerve system—A-Delta fibres and C fibres—because they have separate messages to deliver. One is saying, 'Quick! Get out of trouble *now*!'; the other is insisting, 'I'd just like to remind you of a matter which requires some attention. . .'

Pain messages are oddly unpredictable, however. Sometimes there is *no* warning when trouble is on the way (such as, for instance, a sudden heart attack or appendicitis); sometimes the message is too shrill (the raging pain of toothache when there is really very little wrong); and sometimes, curiously, we may feel no pain when we are shocked—after a road

WHAT IS PAIN FOR?

Anyone who has suffered appendicitis—or an ingrown toe-nail, or protracted dental treatment—knows about pain. It isn't a pleasant experience. Why do our bodies allow it to happen?

Confusingly, pain and pleasure sometimes com very close together. Sinking into a hot bath at the end of a busy day, experiencing the enjoyable aching of the limbs and the stinging heat of the water—this has an obvious link to pain, but it isn't like the dentist's chair. The *Kama Sutra*, a famous Oriental 'love manual', recommends scratching and biting to heighten sexual pleasure, and sexologist Alfred Kinsey noticed that the movements and facial expressions of people at the point of sexual climax are virtually identical to those of people suffering agonizing torture!

Approximately one child in 400,000 is born with a total inability to feel pain. This is caused by a rare genetic disease called 'familial dysautonomia'. In a short life this child may suffer deep cuts, severe burns, broken bones and internal injuries without knowing anything about it. Such children may not realize there is anything wrong with them until it is too late for medical care.

Pain is nature's early-warning system, telling us that something is wrong before we damage ourselves too severely. Without it, we are in serious trouble. It may at times be inconvenient, but it can prevent many worse things happening.

The body even grades the kind of pain messages it sends through, in order to tell us how bad the problem is. The three layers of the skin, for example, send out different pain messages: an itchy feeling from the top layer, when it is disturbed (for example, by something we are allergic to); a stabbing pain from the layer underneath, when a pin is stuck through it; and a deep settled ache from the lower layer when the trouble has gone further (such as when the pin has gone right through). The system is not foolproof, of course; Manchester City goalkeeper Bert Trautmann played right through a Wembley Cup Final without realizing his neck was broken, and excitement often blunts the edge of pain. But it is nonetheless a very useful system.

And, says Rabbi Harold Kushner, 'Only human beings can find meaning in their pain.' He points out that two of the most painful things we can suffer are giving birth and passing a kidney stone. From a purely physical point of view—the way in which animals experience pain—these events are equal. But the difference in purpose between the two—simple malfunction and creative, productive pain—can make them an entirely different experience. And so, Kushner says, 'When we understand that, our question will change from, "Why do we have to feel pain?" to "What do we do with our pain so that it becomes meaningful and not just pointless empty suffering?"'

Lepers feel no pain. As a result their feet and hands often get damaged by burns or cuts from which the rest of us, taught by pain, would instantly withdraw.

accident, say—or engrossed in what we are doing. Rugby players and warriors in battle can sustain fearsome wounds without really noticing until later.

Some years ago, at Harvard University Medical School, 162 people who were recovering from operations were given injections by doctors. Supposedly these were of a pain-killing drug, but in fact it was nothing but salt and water. Yet half of them reported relief from pain as a result of the injection.

Perhaps, as scientist Ronald Melzack has concluded, 'Pain is a function of the whole individual.' What we actually feel is a combination of what our senses tell us, *together with* the convictions our brain already has on the subject. But we will look more closely at the workings of the brain in another chapter.

Colour of skin has become the great symbol for humanity's racial variety.

The wrapper round it all

It has been said that if you asked a good tailor to create a close-fitting garment to cover the whole of your body, he would need six yards of material thirteen inches wide (or 5.5 metres, 30 centimetres wide). Yet every few weeks our own bodies supply us with a new covering of twenty square feet (two square metres) which completely replaces the old one and fits us perfectly.

The reason why our body needs to replace it so frequently is that we are always wearing it away. The friction involved in washing and normal movement grinds away the surface of the skin, and it needs to be constantly renewed. Skin does a lot of things for us (apart from preventing our insides from falling out!). It keeps moisture out of the body; it forms a barrier against germs and dirt; it keeps moisture *in*, too, so that we don't start drying out; and, together with the fatty layers underneath, it helps to cushion us against all the bumps and knocks we encounter.

Skin consists of two main layers. The upper layer is called the 'epidermis', and its surface is made up of dead cells (living cells cannot survive when exposed to air). Because these cells are soon flaked away, others are constantly pushing up from below to take their place in the front line. The epidermis is as thin as a sheet of paper.

The lower layer is the 'dermis', which contains fat cells, hair roots, sweat glands and capillaries to conduct blood (which is why even a small cut will always draw blood). The dermis is responsible for the pattern of our fingerprints. As almost everyone now knows, your fingerprints are one of the most distinctive features of your body; no two individuals seem to have an identical set, even though there are only four basic patterns (whorls, loops, arches and composites) producing the endless variations. It is humbling, though, to realize that the Chinese were using fingerprints as a means of identification in AD700, over a thousand years before Western police departments 'discovered' them!

The sweat glands in the skin (700 to the square inch; about 270 per square centimetre) release salty water which then evaporates and keeps the body cool. Even in a temperate climate, we sweat about half a pint a day; in the tropics, this can rise to about six pints.

The skin also contains oil-producing 'sebaceous glands' (the amount of oil they produce determines whether you need shampoo formulated for 'greasy hair' or 'dry hair'), and their product lubricates the skin, making it waterproof. Also found in the skin are bulb-like hair follicles. It is a fallacy that men have more than women. The hair is less obvious on the female body, but the quantity is exactly the same.

Sometimes our skin does funny things. What produces 'goose pimples', for example? The answer is the tiny muscles in the hair follicles; in cold conditions they contract, and this produces the unusual pimply, hair-standing-on-end condition. In some animals this manoeuvre is an effective device in warding off cold; humans have less hair, and so it does not work particularly efficiently. But it does remind us to put a coat on.

Skin also contains a pigment called 'melanin', which guards us from the heat of the sun. Melanin explains the difference in colour between races, and also why fair skins tan when exposed to sunlight. Sometimes the melanin in a body groups itself together in clumps and then we have what we call 'freckles'.

Eventually, later in life, our skin will start to wrinkle. It no longer fits the body quite so well. This is because in old age the fatty tissues which lie beneath the skin gradually disappear; the body shrinks in size, but the skin does not shrink with it. Young mothers have a similar problem when they try to get rid of stretch marks after pregnancy.

Skin, like many other features of the body, is something we take for granted most of the time. But in reality it is an indispensable marvel—just one of many in the amazing human body.

This Good Friday penitential procession in the Philipines shows people will go to great lengths to master their bodies. But does such humiliation reveal a wrong view of what our bodies are for?

The real value of the human body

In the week in which this chapter was written, a helicopter pilot lost his life when his craft crashed into a Scottish mountainside. He was trying to rescue the body of a woman climber who had died in an accident on that mountain.

Why take such risks for something which is inert and useless? Yet within the Christian tradition, the body has always been highly regarded—even after death. People spend vast sums to have the bodies of relatives flown home, after they have died abroad. Elaborate funerals treat corpses with great respect. In more warlike days, a way of inflicting the ultimate degradation on an enemy was to assault his body after death—hanging, drawing and quartering, perhaps, or cutting off the head and displaying it on a pike. Rotting bodies were left on gibbets as a warning to other criminals.

There is some evidence that traditions of respect for bodies go a long way back. Archaeologists working in Northern Iraq have uncovered the remains of a grave from thousands of years ago, where flowers had obviously been solemnly collected and arranged around the body. 'It is difficult to dismiss the conviction,' writes David Hay, 'that at that Neanderthal funeral 60,000 years ago there was a religious

ARE THERE STRANGE POWERS OF HEALING?

Oskar Estebany is a retired Hungarian Army colonel who claims the power to heal people by laying his hands on them. Just a bizarre claim—or the truth? In 1972 he was put to the test when researchers in Montreal took forty-eight female mice and removed an oval piece of skin from their backs. They kept them in groups in separate cages, then called in Estebany to see if he could heal one group.

For fifteen minutes at a time, twice a day, Estebany held the 'treatment cage' on his left hand and poised his right hand over it—without touching. He concentrated his mind on attempting to heal the wounds of the mice. After fourteen days, the treated mice had wounds which were only two-thirds as large as those of the untreated mice. Somehow, the 'radiation energy' of Estebany had helped. A second test confirmed the results.

Do some people have special healing abilities? The claim goes back to the earliest days of humanity. And today, there are thousands of unorthodox healers all over the world, using a colourful variety of techniques. In Britain the General Medical Council has now given permission to doctors to refer their patients to healers, provided they maintain overall control of each case. A Christian movement concerned for spiritual renewal, the 'charismatic movement', has since the 1960s brought a new interest in the 'gifts of healing' mentioned in the New Testament. Many baffling cures have been reported.

Doctors emphasize that we need to be exceptionally cautious. Many so-called healers are frauds. A number of the 'psychic surgeons' who plunge their hands into patients' bodies without even cutting them open, and somehow magically pull out diseased organs, cancerous growths, and the like, have been shown to be impostors. Also, it is possible for a disease to be wrongly diagnosed; in which case it may clear up with dramatic speed and surprise everyone into thinking that a 'miracle' has occurred. Or 'spontaneous remissions' can take place, when a patient suffering from an illness will suddenly, quite unaccountably, feel much better and stop showing signs of disease. This is not a cure, though, and the disease may later return in strength.

For all this, there seems to be plenty of evidence to suggest that some people do have a natural ability to bring health improvement to others. It is not always necessary for the person being treated to have much faith in the cure; often children and animals are cured, and sometimes total sceptics. Healing seems to be confined to certain kinds of problem. Some types of disability seem more amenable to such healing than others. Says Christian healer Canon Jim Glennon, 'I do not consider it reasonable to believe that an amputee can grow a new limb.'

Many Christians believe that there is a special gift of healing given by God. Non-Christian healers may therefore have a genuine ability, but until it is surrendered to God and brought under his control, it will not operate as it should. And none of this in any way replaces the work of doctors and hospitals; medicine is a vital gift from God as part of his care for humanity's needs.

New Age thinking believes the mind to be just as important as the body in illness and healing.

tenderness for the departed person which would be perfectly recognizable to modern man.'

Other traditions have had a different view of the body's importance. In some Greek philosophical thinking, the human body was just the prison house which incarcerated the really valuable part—the human spirit (we saw this in the last chapter). Plato's *Phaedrus* talks about four kinds of 'divine madness' (including inspired prophecy, divine love and artistic inspiration) which take us beyond the physical level into true 'spiritual' reality.

Influenced by these ideas, Christians have sometimes thought that it is extremely spiritual to think of the body as dirty, worthless and untrustworthy. When the third-century church leader Origen was an enthusiastic young extremist, he voluntarily castrated himself in an attempt to become more spiritual—an act which he later regretted. But this is not how the Bible approaches the subject. Old and New Testaments show a healthy respect for the body as part of God's creation. When the apostle Paul uses the word 'flesh', he does not imply distaste for the body and its functions; many modern translations render this word as 'sinful nature'.

The old Platonic view survives today in various psychic movements who try to explore out-of-the-body experiences, such as astral travel, or ecstatic experiences, such as the higher grades of Transcendental Meditation, as routes to spiritual power or awareness. We will say more about these attempts in chapter five. In the days of the early church, something quite similar was going on in the city of Colossae, and Paul wrote scathingly to Christians there about the 'hollow and deceptive philosophy', 'idle notions' and 'harsh treatment of the body' which was involved.

The great Eastern religious traditions, such as Hinduism and Buddhism, also have fairly dismissive views of the body. The real 'you', in Hindu thought, is not to be identified with your body, or even with what seems to be your personality, because these things will pass. When your body wears out, you will simply reincarnate in a different one, and so the more honour and attention we pay to our body, the more confused we will become about our real identity. This is why the spiritual tradition of Hinduism is such an ascetic one: denying the body's wishes, ignoring its demands and rising above physical processes, are ways of achieving spiritual understanding. Yogis who hold their breath for exceptionally long periods, or sit on beds of nails, or exist on a handful of food daily, are not just performing party tricks. They are trying to conquer their body, which is a hindrance to finding God.

This same view has been taken into many modern religious fringe groups. Scientology, for example, propounds an elaborate mythology according to which we are all several trillion years old, and have existed in this galaxy or others for lifetime after lifetime in a bewildering succession of different bodies—sometimes made of different substances. And so Ron Hubbard, founder of the group, talks contemptuously of our 'Meat Bodies'. 'In Scientology,' comments

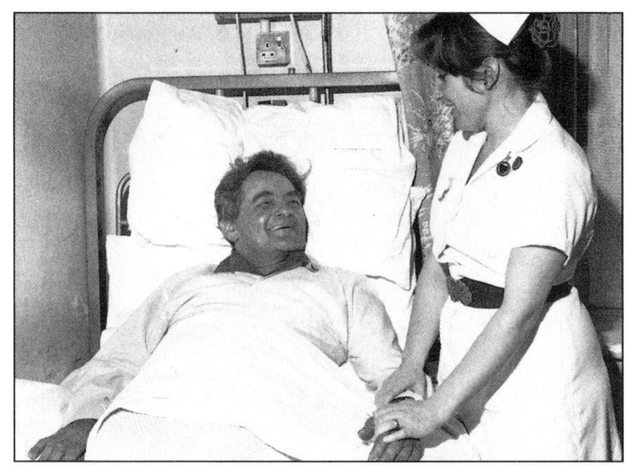

Modern hospitals are in direct line of descent from Christian foundations in previous centuries. Right from the days of Christ the healer, Christians have been concerned to cure people's illnesses.

ex-follower Cyril Vosper, 'there is a revulsion and contempt for bodies and indeed, all materiality.'

One indicator of how we think of our bodies is the way we try to heal them. Holistic medicine has become very important to 'New Age' thinkers (those who believe the world is starting to undergo a transformation of consciousness which will radically alter our view of life, society, politics, sex and spirituality). In her best-seller *The Aquarian Conspiracy* Marilyn Ferguson announces the death of 'the old paradigm of medicine', which treated the body as a 'machine in good or bad repair'; under the new paradigm, the body becomes a 'dynamic system, context, field of energy within other fields'. The body is important because it is inextricably linked with the mind and spirit (indeed, the mind is the 'primary or co-equal factor in *all* illness'). This isn't far from the Christian view, but it goes beyond Christian claims in assuming that the body and mind together can introduce us to the realm of spiritual reality. Christians would claim that a spiritual rebirth has to happen first, and that without it, explorations into 'natural' spirituality are an exotic wild goose chase. But more of this later.

Buddhist thought is close to Hindu ideas when it comes to the body. And so in Tibet funerals can be rather different, as one Western teacher discovered:

The sky burial is a part of Tibetan Buddhism. . . When a person dies, they chop the body to small pieces—or burn it, like that one over there. They chop the body ritualistically, starting with the feet and working up. They break the bones. They smash the skull in. Then they feed it to the vultures. So they commit the person to the sky.

When the Buddha died, say the sacred scriptures, it was 'with that utter passing away which leaves nothing behind'. The dead body is just a souvenir of a previous existence, a reminder of a life which is no more. It has no intrinsic importance in itself.

On the other hand, some writers who have no belief in a religious dimension see the body as very important indeed, because it is one of the few solid realities of life. Perhaps our bodies contain the real key to why we act as we do, what life is really for, even what the future holds? Transplant surgeon Christian Barnard has written, in a book with John Illman:

We live but to create a new machine of a little later model than our own, a new life machine that in some ineffable way can help along the great process of evolution of the species somehow more efficiently than we could do if we were immortal.

Later they add, 'It is as if the world is a laboratory and we are the experiments.'

Nobody has taken this kind of thinking further than Richard Dawkins, author of *The Selfish Gene*, whose book caused a sensation by advancing claims like these:

The argument of this book is that we, and all other animals, are machines created by our genes. Like successful Chicago gangsters, our genes have survived, in some cases for millions of years, in a highly competitive world. This entitles us to expect certain qualities in our genes. I shall argue that a predominant quality to be expected in our genes is a ruthless selfishness.

And so human bodies are just 'survival machines —robot vehicles blindly programmed to preserve the selfish molecules known as genes'. But if we amounted only to this, there wouldn't be much point in our knowing about it—as the philosopher Anthony Flew observed in a stinging retort to Dawkins:

If any of this were true, then it would not be a bit of use to go on, as Dawkins does, to preach: 'Let us try to teach generosity and altruism, because we are born selfish.' No eloquence could move programmed robots. But in fact it is none of it either true or even faintly sensible. Genes... do not and cannot necessitate our conduct. Nor are they capable of the calculation and understanding required to plot a course of either ruthless selfishness or sacrificial compassion.

According to a popular view of human nature, our behaviour is rooted in animal instincts; we are really 'naked apes'. But aren't the differences between people and animals more fundamental than this?

A more sophisticated writer of the same sort as Dawkins is Harvard biologist Edward O. Wilson. His book *Sociobiology* suggests that 'in a Darwinist sense the organism does not live for itself... the organism is only DNA's way of making more DNA'. All human behaviour therefore has a genetic base: 'Altruism is conceived as the mechanism by which DNA multiplies itself... spirituality becomes just one more Darwinian enabling device'. And 'beliefs are really enabling mechanisms for survival'; we behave in certain ways because these give our genes the best possible chances of survival into another generation.

But, as Flew points out, this does not say anything about whether or not the beliefs we hold are *true*. 'The questions whether and in what way it is rational to support the norms which we do support are... not biological questions.' And, Keith Ward objects, sociobiology is attempting to reconstruct our experience of the world according to an artificial scientific model—which means leaving out the things which are most immediate and most undeniable in our experience:

Genetic theories are, after all, abstract, generalized and mathematically specified models of the real world, using certain very precisely defined technical concepts. The aim of these abstract models is to help us to understand organic and human life better. Something has gone drastically and fundamentally wrong when we begin to talk about the model as though it was the reality, and about the real world it should be helping us to understand as though it did not even exist. Sociobiology... is one modern equivalent of those pure theoreticians who refused to look through Galileo's telescope to see the facts, in case the sight spoiled their theory.

An even more popular author (whose work has encouraged several imitators) is Desmond Morris, to whom the human being is just *The Naked Ape*. As we have already seen, that description is zoologically incorrect, but Morris uses the arresting phrase to sum up his view of humanity: as carrying round with us conditioning traits and ways of behaviour which we have inherited from our animal past. Morris believes that if we explore our biological links to the animal kingdom, we can discover the truth about why humans act as they do.

A human being is just 'a primitive tribal hunter, masquerading as a civilized, super-tribal citizen'. Our learned behaviour, which we pick up from society around us, ultimately doesn't count for nearly as much as the old, deeply-buried animal instincts which are still there inside us, and will not be denied. 'The fundamental patterns of behaviour laid down in our early days as hunting apes still shine through all our affairs, no matter how lofty they may be.'

But this is just to ignore the very real differences between human beings and other species—the chief one being, as we saw at the start of the chapter, the human discovery of ways of storing and passing on knowledge, so that each new member of the race no longer has to learn everything from scratch. The triumph of learning and education over inherited instincts has been the major factor in human dominance. To deny its importance is to turn everything we know about the world upside down.

It would be more plausible if Morris founded his theory on unassailable data. But in the estimation of scientific writer Denis Alexander, 'there is little real evidence for some of these speculative ideas... the attempt to extrapolate from theories about animals to theories about man... takes us far beyond the evidence that is in fact available'. In the final analysis, Morris is making a subjective, loosely documented statement of personal belief—not a scientific argument at all.

Not our own

The body as a loathsome prison house; the body as a temporary transit vehicle; the body as the undiscovered director of all our behaviour. Does Christian teaching follow any of these lines? What do Christians believe about the body? Does it tally with what we know about the complexity and wonder of our physical being—and yet not claim too much for the body's importance, as Morris, Dawkins and others seem to do?

The basic Christian claim about the body is that it is part of God's creation, in fact a crowning part. In the creation story of Genesis, human bodies are formed 'from the dust of the ground'—of the same basic stuff as every other living creature—but they are made on the climactic 'sixth' day of creation, as one of the most important things God put together.

And so Christians believe in treating the body with respect. 'You are not your own,' writes the apostle Paul to some early Christians. 'You were bought at a price. Therefore honour God with your body.' A Christian's body, Paul writes, is a 'temple of the Holy Spirit'—spiritual life and physical life are not opposed to one

Human bodies are wonderful mechanisms, of which robots are fumbling imitations. But people are more than machines.

another, but go hand in hand.

And so right down through the history of the church Christians have always been concerned about meeting the needs of people's bodies as well as doing something to their souls. It has been estimated that 85 per cent of all hospitals in the world have been founded by Christians. By contrast with other religions, which have often adopted a passive attitude to physical misfortunes, Christians have been in the forefront of attempts to feed the hungry, care for lepers, relieve the needs of prisoners, reform the medical system.

As we saw in the previous chapter, Christians do not see 'body' and 'soul' as two detachable components, but as inextricably bound up with one another. Consequently, the Christian vision of the future is that some day whole human beings—body as well as spirit—will be permanently in God's presence, enjoying the totality and fulness of his plan for human life.

Our bodies then will be somewhat different. Paul writes, for instance, about the difference between the 'natural body' which goes into the grave and the transformed 'spiritual body' which comes out. But it will be the same basic body. How can this work? C.S. Lewis pointed out that our bodies are a bit like waterfalls—constantly changing their contents. Any one droplet of water is part of the waterfall only for as long as it takes to shoot from the top to the bottom; it is immediately replaced by thousands of others. In the same way, the cells of our bodies are constantly being renewed; you do not consist of the same 'materials' that you did seven years ago! But there is continuity in the waterfall because of its overall shape and structure; and so, perhaps, it would be possible for the molecules of a human body to be arranged in a different way, with different abilities, while that body would still continue to be, recognizably and genuinely, the same entity as before.

Certainly the Bible emphasizes that our body will be part of us for ever. The marvellous machine which is the vehicle for your life is not just a disposable wrapping, but an integral part of God's purposes for you.

HOW THE BRAIN WORKS

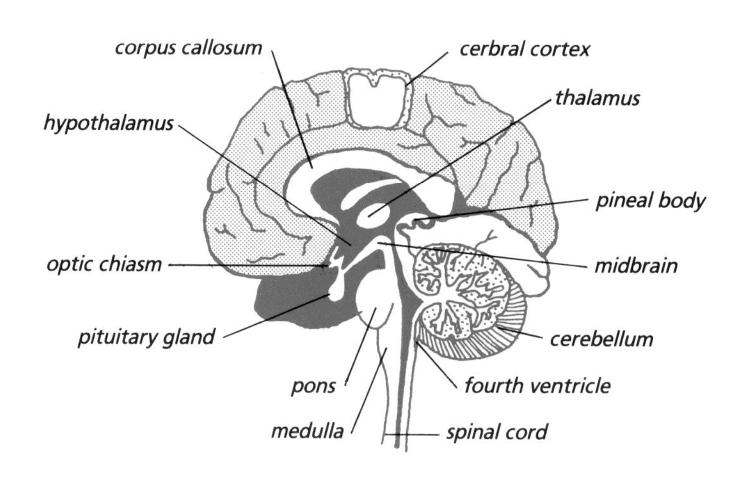

At first sight it looks rather unpromising. Two handfuls of pinkish-grey, crinkled tissue, looking a little like an elderly walnut and feeling as floppy as jelly. Yet the human brain has something like sixty times the informational complexity of the entire United States telephone system.

Our brains are not even as big as the brains of some animals. But in the average human life, the brain's owner will stow away 500 times as much information as there is in the *Encyclopaedia Britannica* (or 500,000 times as much, if you count items that are stored more than once). And some people have been able to do amazing things with their brains.

Take for example Karl Friedrich Gauss, a mathematician. When he was six years old his teacher asked the class to add up all the numbers from one to ten. Gauss raised his hand and gave the answer immediately. He had spotted right away that the ten numbers included five pairs each of which added up to eleven. Not surprisingly, when he reached the age of thirteen Gauss was told by his teacher not to come to school any more: there was nothing else he could learn there.

Or take Shereshevskii, a failed Russian musician and journalist. He was able to memorize poetry in languages he did not know, long strings of numbers, complicated mathematical formulae—and repeat them all without error several years later. Bruno Furst was just as unusual. He memorized the entire German Civil Code, comprising 2,385 paragraphs of tortuous legal statements, and could quote any paragraph on request. He also committed to memory hundreds of poems, dozens of plays, about twenty novels, and literally thousands of addresses and telephone numbers. One of his favourite tricks was to fan out a deck of cards after shuffling it, examine it for a few seconds, and then repeat the sequence of cards purely from memory. Two decks took him just over a minute. (And this man had still not learnt his multiplication tables by the age of ten. But then Albert Einstein, too, learnt to speak very late and was once refused a place at a polytechnic.)

People like this are quite obviously exceptional. Yet, says psychologist Morton Hunt, *every* human brain is special.

It is just because most of our thought processes are so ordinary that we rarely realize how remarkable, how unlike anything else in the known world, they are. When we watch a bird building a nest, we marvel at the skill and complexity of its performance. Yet we take for granted the vastly more skilled and complex mental acts we ourselves routinely perform every day, and even every waking hour.

For example, look at this sentence:
The brain is a wonderful thing.

What took place in your mind as you read it? You had to recognize the shapes of the letters, compare them with those in your memory, perceive the complete words they made up, identify the meanings of the words, and make sense of their relationship in the whole sentence. And how long did it take you? Less than a second?

Or try another example. Answer this question:
What is the best route from your house to the Post Office?

This time, you probably conjured up a picture in your mind, a sort of internal map; and then found words to express what you were viewing on your internal screen. Once again, the process was amazingly quick. How did you manage to select the correct picture so fast, from all the thousands of images stored in your head?

Just one more demonstration. Read these words:

The rear controls on this set have been factory adjusted and should need no further attention. If however your picture is moving upwards or downwards, adjust to the vertical hold control he is marked V. HOLD until the picture is correctly locked and steady position.

As soon as you begin to read this paragraph, your brain starts to work out what is happening, not just from the information contained in the words themselves but also from your mental reserves of knowledge and experience. You probably saw immediately that this was an excerpt from the instructions for some electrical equipment. After the second sentence you knew it was a television set, although nothing there says so. And you probably realized quickly that it was of foreign manufacture, because your brain instantly spotted something wrong with the English. Not a bad performance for a few seconds' work.

Hippocrates, a great Greek physician who lived centuries before Christ, wrote:

Men ought to know that from the brain and the brain only arise our pleasures, joys, laughter and jests as well as our sorrows, pains, griefs and tears. . . It is the same thing which makes us mad or delirious, inspires us with dread and fear, whether by night or by day, brings sleeplessness, inopportune mistakes, aimless anxieties, absent-mindedness and acts that are contrary to habit. . .

Nothing but. . .

What is the brain, and how does it work? And does the brain relate to the 'mind'? Is there such a thing as the mind, or are our thoughts, dreams and emotions simply the by-products of chemical reactions? Some scientists have thought so; psychologist B.A. Farrell announced bluntly, 'A human being is a modulator of pulse frequencies, and nothing more.' That makes us simply complex machines, relatively advanced computers. Is there anything more to human beings than this?

Earlier this century, a Russian experimenter, Ivan Pavlov, insisted that all our behaviour could be explained in terms of automatic reflexes. Pavlov proved that it was possible to 'condition' dogs to do things that they would not do naturally, to alter the pattern of their responses so that they behaved in certain predetermined ways; and he argued that the

Nobel Prize-winner Ivan Pavlov used his famous dog in experiments to demonstrate the 'conditioned reflex'. He showed that behaviour can be controlled by conditioning. But is this all there is to psychology?

same thing ought to be true of human behaviour. The machine could be tampered with.

Shortly afterwards, the influential psychologist J.B. Watson launched in America the new ideas of 'behaviourism'. This is a school of psychology which refuses to admit anything real about human consciousness. As Watson wrote:

The time has come when psychology must discard all reference to consciousness. . . its sole task is the prediction and control of behaviour; and introspection can play no part in its method.

Watson claimed that, given twelve healthy infants, he could pick any one at random and bring him up successfully to become 'any type of specialist I may select'. Human personality was unimportant; anybody could be conditioned into anything.

Are the behaviourists right? Today a growing amount of evidence suggests that they have got it wrong. For one thing, it makes the study of psychology very narrow and restricted; behaviourists are cut off, by their principles, from examining the kinds of experience which people find most interesting: dreams, moods, hallucinations, fears, desires. These mental events are the ones which we experience most acutely, and seem most real to us as individuals. Suddenly to declare them all insubstantial is to box oneself in to a very unnatural universe indeed.

And when behaviourist therapies were tried out on human beings, in an attempt to change their 'conditioning', they failed to work very well. Behavioural sex therapies and marriage therapies have to be combined with other approaches if they are to achieve lasting results. 'Aversive' therapies, which attempt to destroy alcoholism, gluttony or homosexual behaviour, tend to work for a while and then wear off. And the reason is not hard to work out: dogs or rats do not know that an electric shock is being deliberately given to them for a purpose; but human beings do. And they know that after the treatment they can go back to their former ways without fear that any further unpleasant shocks will be administered.

Even simpler animals than ourselves refused to behave in a 'behaviourist' way. Rats, for instance, were supposed (according to the theory) to learn a certain route through a maze towards food, and then for ever afterwards to choose that route automatically in order to arrive at the desired reward. They would memorize their way through the maze by learning a pattern of muscle movements to take them round all the right corners. But rats are curious; after learning the route, they would often wander round the rest of the maze, just to see what was there, rather than streaking straight to the reward. And even when a rat had been through a maze several times before, he would still often stop at a corner, look around himself, and perhaps even take a few steps backwards before going on. Clearly he was considering various alternative paths in his mind, and choosing between them.

The 'pattern of muscle movements' theory was torpedoed when someone had the rather cruel idea of cutting off the rats' back legs, or (less drastically) turning the maze upside down. The rats still managed to get to the food, whether or not they had legs, whether or not the right turns had suddenly become left turns.

Obviously, brains work in a rather more complicated fashion than the stimulus-and-response way envisaged by behaviourists. One problem is memory. The behaviourist theory stated that a series of trials and reinforcements would build up a conditioned response in us; in other words, the harder we worked at memorizing something, the more likely it would be to stick in our minds.

Now some memorizing does happen in that way (I spent three years learning French irregular verbs by constant repetition!). But not all. For instance, someone told me her telephone number yesterday, and I managed to hold it in my memory for five minutes until I could write it down, but now I have no clue what it was. Yet the most inconsequential things, which I have made no attempt to learn, will remain effortlessly in my mind: the

WHY DO WE DREAM?

Everybody has dreams. If you meet people who claim they don't, they are simply mistaken. Some of us cannot remember our dreams afterwards, but everybody dreams. And if we did not, the results would be catastrophic.

We know this because scientists have discovered that sometimes, when we are asleep, our eyes dart back and forth as if they were watching some action, even though our eyelids remain closed all the time. These movements are called REMs (Rapid Eye Movements), and they signal that a dream is going on. From observing them, we know that dreams can last quite a while: only two to ten minutes in the early part of the night, but up to an hour as morning draws near. The old idea that dreams last only a split second has no basis in fact.

What happens if we are not allowed to dream? Scientists explored this by monitoring people for evidence of REMs—then waking them up as soon as the REMs began. Before long, these hapless subjects were suffering hallucinations and daydreams. It became obvious that prolonging the experiment would put their mental health at risk. Now it has been calculated that the longest any human being can survive without REM sleep is about ten days. After that, mental breakdown is inevitable.

In the 1920s in America there was a craze for 'dance marathons'. This cruel type of contest (outlawed in 1933) offered cash prizes to the couple who could dance the longest—after everyone else had literally dropped down with exhaustion. The effort of staying awake for long periods led to all sorts of problems, and one young man fell down dead in 1932 after forty-eight days of dancing. Obviously, not much REM sleep was possible under these conditions, and contestants often suffered mentally. A similar victim was New York disc jockey Peter Tripp, who kept himself awake for eight days in aid of charity. Sitting in the window of a Times Square store, he went visibly to pieces before the end of the week, and suffered a three-month depression as a result.

Why is dreaming so vital to our health? Sigmund Freud, the father of psychoanalysis, was the first person to suggest a convincing answer. He believed that in the depths of our subconscious lie buried thoughts, wishes and emotions which are so unacceptable to our conscious minds that we never let them rise to the level of consciousness. But they must find expression somehow. And so a dream is 'a disguised fulfilment of repressed wishes'.

Experiences of the previous day form the starting-point of a dream, Freud taught, and these trigger off the 'latent dream thoughts' which cry out for expression. Because these thoughts are so unacceptable to us, we dress them up in symbols and pictures—a process called the 'dream-work'—and the true meaning of the dream becomes distorted into the strange jumble of fantasies which we remember when we wake up. But a skilled psychoanalyst can undo the 'dream-work' and give us a clue about what we have in our minds that triggers off a certain dream.

Freud's theories have undoubtedly helped us understand much better what goes on when we dream. It is a curious fact, though, that many of the symbols, ideas and situations which crop up in dreams are the same from person to person. And so other psychologists—notably Carl Gustav Jung—have suggested another explanation. The imagery of dreams may be related to ancient myths and symbols which control the human imagination—Jung called this the 'collective unconscious'. This provides us with a ready-made way of evoking the thoughts and wishes we want to express. Probably both ideas are partly true.

registration number of an old Bedford van my parents owned thirty years ago; the details of my seventh birthday party; the stray fact that since 1904 forty-nine dead mice have been found in unopened bottles of Coca Cola; and so on. Behaviourism has no explanation for this.

In his book *Battle for the Mind*, psychiatrist William Sergeant tried to show that religious conversion was based on behaviourist principles: when the correct stimulus is presented to our brain, we give the appropriate response and become 'converted'. Sergeant drew direct parallels between the work of evangelists such as Billy Graham and Pavlov's experiments with his dogs. Yet some of the cases he examines destroy his own argument: John Wesley was not converted in the heat of great excitement (which is how Sergeant says it should have happened), but in a quiet, unemotional Bible reading. The apostle Paul became a Christian despite having strong beliefs that should have 'inoculated' him against conversion.

It is not so much that behaviourism is wrong. Some of its tenets are true: we *do* sometimes learn things by mechanical stimulus -response means, especially when we are young (or mentally retarded); but there are other, more complex ways of learning, choosing and thinking. Behaviourism is incomplete; it describes a tiny part of the experience of being human.

And that is just as well. Brain researcher Steven Rose writes of the danger of so concentrating on what he calls 'lower-order', purely chemical explanations of behaviour, and ignoring 'higher-order' explanations such as our social experience. 'From here to social control by the use of chemicals and to an argument that one must change humans to fit reality rather than change reality to fit people, is but a step.'

Rose criticizes other kinds of thinkers who make the same mistake as the behaviourists—beginning their statements with the words 'Human beings are "nothing but. . ."' He calls one group 'machinomorphs'. These are the thinkers who claim that the human brain is 'nothing but' a computer, and that sooner or later we will develop computers which will be more powerful and intelligent than ourselves.

Is this a realistic idea? It has furnished the

THE POWER OF THE MIND?

The First Church of Satan may sound like something out of a Dennis Wheatley novel. But it exists, both in America and in Europe. Actually, it is less interested in worshipping Satan than in exploiting unusual sources of power. It holds 'hate rituals' in which people concentrate their minds on one person to whom they wish to do harm; and 'lust rituals' in which members focus on an individual whom one of the membership wishes to seduce. They say it works.

A group of researchers in Toronto once decided to 'invent' a ghost. Having created an imaginary historical figure and decided on the details of his life story, they tried to make contact with him by concentrating hard. 'Philip', their ghost, eventually obliged—producing strange rapping noises and making tables move. 'He' even did it for the television cameras.

In her book *The Autobiography of a Witch*, Lois Bourne tells how a coven of white witches trained her in supernatural abilities. 'They confirmed that what I felt inside me was the incipient witch power. They taught me how to release it, to utilize it and how to harness all the forces of nature which were all around me, and by the development of my mind and will, to project this power into a specific objective.'

All of these are examples of how the concentration of a human mind, or several minds together, can sometimes produce unusual effects. This is a major part of the technique of magic. Occultist Peter Underwood calls it 'the means whereby can be discovered unknown forces of nature, and the harnessing and employment of those forces'. Spells, rituals and elaborate equipment are all aids in focusing the mind in the desired way. 'To be an effective practitioner,' claims magician Gareth Knight, 'one needs to be skilled in the techniques of visualization, to be capable of long, sustained concentration, to possess controlled psychic sensitivity, and to have that depth of intuitional understanding that comes only from long practice of meditation.'

Are the results of magic purely imaginary, or are they genuine? Sometimes it is hard to tell. Certainly many of the great magicians of the last hundred years—Eliphas Levi, Sar Peladan, S.L. MacGregor Mathers, Aleister Crowley—have been unusually vain and self-important people with a colourful and inaccurate imagination. On the other hand, successes such as the 'Philip' story take some explanation. And it is likely that poltergeists (those strange 'spirits' who sometimes move tables and chairs at night, cause objects to fly around the room, induce malfunctions in electrical apparatus, and generally cause a lot of household mischief) are not really 'spirits' at all, but have their origin in the subconscious mental processes of someone living in the affected house, who is 'having a nervous breakdown outside his own head'.

If it is true that the mind can affect physical circumstances in this way, it seems possible that fierce concentration really can produce results. There are only two problems. First, the results are not always what was hoped for. The 'Philip' researchers wanted him to

120,000 soldiers form up before Hitler at Nuremberg during the 1930s. The Nazi propaganda machine cajoled millions of people into acting against conscience.

materialize, not make rapping noises; I have known people who have concentrated on a ouija board, hoping to receive messages, who have accidentally levitated chairs instead! Second, if the Bible is correct, God has not invited us to tamper with the inner workings of the universe this way. Real power is found, not in trying to 'play God' with nature, but in allowing the real living God to inform and empower our lives.

HOW DOES BRAINWASHING WORK?

The colourful term 'brain-washing' was coined by an American journalist, Edward Hunter, to describe techniques used in China after the Communist take-over. The same phrase—*hsi nao* ('wash brain')—was used by his Chinese sources to describe the methods which led to dramatic changes of political opinions, vivid confessions of unexpected crimes and odd personality changes in people who had experienced the treatment. Since then, 'brainwashing' has been associated with all kinds of repressive governments, anti-spy agencies and extreme religious cults. But what is it? And how does it operate?

Obviously, the idea of literally washing someone's brain clean of all past memories is quite impractical. The memories that cause our key beliefs are caused, not by a single impulse, but by experiences recorded over years, and it seems unlikely that any memory which was really important to our belief system could ever be totally eradicated—except by damaging the brain physically, and even that would not achieve reliable results. But it is possible to destroy people's sense of their own individuality so completely that they gratefully accept a new identity, ready-made, from the people who have removed their former personalities.

This, says psychiatrist Joel Kovel, is what goes on in 'est training': a very expensive form of mind-conditioning course popular among career people. 'From one side, haranguing and privation are battering resistance, while from the other the group experience leads a person to dissolve his or her individuality, and its stubborn resistance, and to psychologically merge with the others in the room. . . The result for the individual is a state of openness, receptivity: and weakened discrimination. Into the gap steps the 'est' philosophy. . .'

Robert Lifton analyzed the way in which brainwashing was practised on prisoners in the hands of the Chinese. The first stage, he said, was **the assault upon identity**: the prisoner was given a number, not a name, and continually surrounded by other prisoners exhorting him to confess. He began to become extremely disoriented, and the poor diet and sudden bursts of interrogation confused him further. The next stage was **the establishment of guilt**: all of us have guilt feelings, real or imaginary, which can be played on, and constant appeals for a confession make the prisoner start to feel he must really have done something wrong. Next comes **self-betrayal** when a confession is actually given, falsifying what the prisoner once knew to be reality; but the captors do not appear satisfied. They want more. At this point the prisoner reaches the stage of **total conflict and basic fear**, when his personality seems to be disintegrating completely, and he can no longer hold on to any sense of individuality at all. When they see that this is happening, his captors move to **leniency and opportunity**, suddenly becoming kindly and offering a new kind of hope for the future. There are five more stages after this, but they are just the mopping-up operation. The job has been done.

These principles have been adopted by some religious cults who specialize in intensive indoctrination courses in remote centres in the countryside. But the claim made by some psychologists (such as William Sergeant in his book *Battle for the Mind*), that such manipulation explains *all* conversions, is far too sweeping. Professor Donald Mackay, who has studied the subject, points out that the experience of God's forgiveness 'can be received only at the personal level by a man in full possession of all his faculties. There is no substitute for personal reconciliation in mechanical manipulation. The mass evangelist ought to know about brainwashing techniques for the same reason that a dietician ought to know about poisons—not in order to use them, but in order to avoid damaging those towards whom he has responsibility.'

plot for a thousand science-fiction stories. But will we ever have machines which rival human brains? It might not be worth our while to try to build one. For computers have far more parts than human brains (as we shall see later in this chapter). Assembling a hundred billion transistors might take rather a long time. . .

And there are more important differences. In a computer, the input goes through a central processor which carries out some operations on it and then reports the result. The whole process is a chain of events, in sequence, each one depending on the last in the line. If you feed in rubbish at the start, that's what emerges at the end.

By contrast, the operations of the brain are interdependent. Any one cell is in constant communication with thousands of others, and decisions are taken by a kind of 'majority vote' rather than in a blind sequence of events. And so even if we could build a computer with 100 billion mini-computers inside it, we would still have to link the mini-computers so that every one affected nearly every other one. Not a job for a Saturday afternoon.

Furthermore, thinking processes do not take place in just one part of the brain at a time. Studies of brain-damaged patients show that for normal thinking to take place, many different brain centres need to be working in harness with one another. This was confirmed by a Danish group of physiologists who injected radioisotopes into the bloodstream of volunteers in order to see how blood flowed through the brain. (The levels of radioactivity they could then detect at different points in the brain showed them where the work of the brain was being concentrated.) They concluded that the brain's thinking system involves a complex interplay of different 'sub-routines'.

All of this means that computers are much more predictable than human beings. The output can be foretold from the input (assuming the computer is working properly). But the interconnections in the brain make it virtually impossible to predict with any accuracy what conclusions it will produce. Human beings do not function like Mr Spock in *Star Trek*.

Steven Rose adds:

And this says nothing yet about the programme. In general, computers are doing one or a few specific jobs at any time, corresponding to individual programmes fed into them. The brain, by contrast, is performing a vast number of separate tasks at any one time. As I write this my brain is not only concerned in the organization of the thoughts which will enable me to compose coherent grammatical sentences and a (hopefully!) powerful argument, and the direction of my hand, holding the pen, across the page, but also continuously monitoring random visual input, the noise of someone whistling elsewhere in the house and the pressure of the chair on my back, while my hypothalamus, limbic and reticular systems are regulating drives, homeostasis and attention. . .

All of this means that computers have no 'real-world knowledge' which is anything like ours in complexity. We can understand what is going on behind a conversation like this:

Boy: You doing anything tonight? *Girl:* I'm washing my hair. *Boy:* How about Thursday? There's a good film on. *Girl:* Why don't you drop dead?

We understand all sorts of things about this exchange on the basis of just a few verbal clues, because we have a lifetime of experiences in the world to draw on. A computer's experiences are artificially given to it. And the array of equipment needed for it to harbour the same amount of information as we store is absolutely unthinkable.

That is why the most clever computers still have problems with human symbols and their meanings. Asked to translate a sentence into Russian—'The spirit is willing but the flesh is weak'—one computer came up with words which meant 'The vodka is fine, but the meat is tasteless'.

Finally (although there is much more that could be said), what is the real purpose of computer operations? A computer works towards a 'known-end state': a goal defined by its

Painter Salvador Dali, athlete Carl Lewis, Nobel Prize-winning medical scientist Sir James Black — the particular abilities of individual brains can bring excellence in totally different areas.

creator. A machine can learn to improve on its own programme, but not to alter it radically. Yet human beings change their minds about the most fundamental things all the time. They are much more creative than machines could ever be—because of the intuitive, non-logical processes that spark off ideas and discoveries, and the creative work of the 'unconscious'. A computer is bound by logic. It has no 'unconscious'.

And so 'machinomorphs' are wrong to say 'Human brains are nothing but computers'. And Steven Rose goes on to attack another group of thinkers whom he calls 'chimpomorphs'. They are the people who claim, 'Human beings are "nothing but" sophisticated animals.'

There are many similarities between the brains of some animals and our own. Many scientists believe that this is because our brains were once the same as theirs, but we have now evolved further. If so, the old animal brain is still there inside us. And some popular writers have claimed that this is the ultimate key to human behaviour.

Writers such as Desmond Morris (whom we mentioned in chapter three) and Konrad Lorenz and Robert Ardrey (whom we shall meet in chapter six) make detailed parallels between aspects of human behaviour—such as sexuality, aggression and competitiveness—and the social behaviour of animals, especially apes. And so marriage is just an example of the 'pair-bonding' practised by some species; war and territorial disputes are just an echo of the instinct animals have to defend their own private space. Robert Ardrey says that we will not be able to build a just society until we accept that we are animals, with certain undeniable, built-in drives and behaviours, and stop trying to pretend that we are anything more:

When we renounce our hubris; when we see ourselves as a portion of something far older, far larger than are we; when we discover nature as our partner, not our slave, and laws applying to us as applying to us all: then we shall find our faith returning. We have rational faculties of enormous order. We have powers granted never before to living beings. But we shall free those powers to effect human solutions of justice and permanence only when we renounce our arrogance over nature and accept the philosophy of the possible.

Is this truly what we are? Would we be fooling ourselves to claim that we are free, choosing beings—because we are actually puppets manipulated by the strings of our own evolution?

If so, we are condemned to hold a pessimistic, even reactionary view of human life: change is not to be expected; nothing will get any better; human beings are treacherous animals who need to be carefully watched and forcefully controlled. But human society has in fact made staggering advances over the last 5,000 years (chapter eight details the story), and this marks it off sharply from the unchanging, static world of apes and chimps. Human society is ever changing from century to century; it is transformed by humans themselves as they think great thoughts, try out temporary fashions, make technological advances, overthrow governments. To compare this with the rigid arrangements of the animal kingdom is to oversimplify dreadfully. Human beings are different.

One reason that we are so different is that we can talk to one another. Language (as we saw earlier) is something which no other species commands, and it creates a traffic of relationships between us which is entirely unknown in any other animal society. If we didn't communicate verbally, our social life would be terribly impoverished. It is foolish to ignore the tremendous difference between the rich culture of language-users and the monochrome interactions of less fortunate species.

In fact, our brains contain only a very small remnant of what may be 'animal brain', and an outstandingly large area of 'uncommitted cortex'. We will look at what the 'cortex' is in a moment, but the phrase means that a large area of our brains—larger than in any other species—is unassigned to any particular task or function. It is available for complicated processes of thought, rather than having all of its time taken up monitoring basic bodily functions. And as a result we can control whatever 'evolutionary remnant' of instincts we still have left, by bringing into play other parts of the brain which liberate us from having to follow the drives of our primitive instincts.

Mapping the brain

What is our brain, and how does it work? Even the first anatomists who took apart human brains realized quickly that to talk of 'the brain' is slightly inaccurate. There are several components in there—in fact, four separate brains, each with its own function.

As we travel up the human body from the neck to the top of the head, we find that the brain starts at the top of the spinal cord, with a couple of swellings known as the 'old brain'. At the back of these swellings is a wrinkled structure the size of a fist, the 'little brain' or 'cerebellum'. Further up, as the brain stem broadens out into the skull cavity, it blends into a number of odd-shaped structures which are linked to it by smaller stems; these structures make up the 'mid-brain'. Finally, wrapped over the whole structure is a crumpled sheet of tissue between three and four millimetres thick, called the 'cortex' or 'roof brain'. It is crumpled because of our level of intelligence; the rabbit's cortex fits quite smoothly into its skull, but ours is a tight fit. Strangely, the same wrinkles appear in almost exactly the same places in different human brains. And although the cortex is divided in the middle, producing two hemispheres, each side is virtually a mirror image of the other.

The 'old brain' is in charge of our automatic systems (heart-beat, respiration and the like). The central nervous system is organized from here, too, and it is the 'old brain' which gives the warning to the cortex when there is cause for alarm or attention. The cerebellum controls fine muscular movements and careful co-ordination; a snooker player's reputation depends heavily on the quality of his cerebellum. And it is the cerebellum which enables us to perform complicated tasks 'without thinking': driving a car, shooting a pistol, playing jazz chords on a guitar. At first, the effort of learning means that our cortex has to be involved. But as soon as a skill becomes 'second nature', the cerebellum takes charge.

These two brains are obviously important and basic, but it is the other two that are responsible for our conscious thought processes. The mid-brain is the centre of our emotional life, the cortex the analyzing and clarifying counterpart to it. A living animal without a cortex will still move around, see dimly, accept food and shun pain. But its sensations will be vague and imprecise: the mid-brain is collecting the necessary information, but the cortex is not there to explain it all.

The mid-brain is impulsive and impatient, prompting us to act suddenly and emotionally. The cortex tells us to wait, and calculates what the results of our actions will be. When we are in the grip of powerful emotions—fear, amazement, ecstasy—we often find it difficult to think clearly; and this is because the mid-brain is taking charge, refusing for a while to allow the cortex to tell us anything.

The cortex is made up of two kinds of substance. On the surface is a layer of 'grey matter' (actually white with a tinge of yellow), and underneath it is 'white matter' (which in fact looks pink). The 'grey matter' contains billions of minute specks with thin hairs sprouting from them. Each of these specks is a 'neuron' or nerve cell. There are about thirty-five thousand cells for each square millimetre of surface, and the whole brain contains something like a hundred thousand million of them. (Gordon Rattray Taylor observes, 'If your brain cells were people, they would populate twenty-five planets like the earth.')

Staggering enough. But it is the tiny hairs

that really explain the brain's complexity. They are called 'dendrites', and they ensure that each neuron is in contact with about six hundred other neurons. The inter-relationships are impossibly intricate: trillions of pathways constantly exchanging information. No wonder we can perform some functions with different parts of our brains, so that if one area is damaged, another will take over cheerfully and perform the same tasks; no wonder it doesn't matter that ageing people are said to lose 100,000 brain cells each day (they can spare them); no wonder we can recall information from memory much faster than any computer system could locate it.

The dendrites receive incoming signals, but outgoing messages travel from cell to dendrite via the 'axons'—long threads running from the neuron (in some cases for several feet), acting as channels along which electrical impulses can be sent to contact the dendrites of other cells.

The axons make up the white matter in an intricate interlacing network. They do not connect directly with the dendrites which receive their messages: at the end of the axon there is a tiny space called the 'synaptic gap', and when an electrical impulse is sent down the axon, it fires into the gap a volley of molecules (of norepinephrine, dopamine, or some other appropriate chemical). The molecules jump the gap, and try to influence the behaviour of a second neuron—either to persuade it to fire, or to deter it from doing so. But because similar messages will have arrived at exactly the same moment from hundreds of other neurons, our molecules will have only one vote among hundreds.

All of this is happening as you read these words, in billions of neurons in your brain simultaneously, and at a rate of several hundred cycles per second. Enough to make a computer manufacturer give up in despair.

If you were to stretch out the axons of your brain in a single straight line (which is not recommended), they would stretch three times as far as to the moon and back. Such is the length of inner cabling which you carry around in your head, and it is the secret of the power and flexibility of the human brain.

Sometimes it is suggested that, because we now know a lot about how the brain works, we should be able to find surgical techniques that will control human impulses, cure depression, remove a tendency to evil. But because of the complexity of the brain, things are not so simple. Psychosurgery certainly can achieve some results. But, as we have seen, particular jobs can be distributed in different parts of the brain: it isn't the case that one area produces aggression, another fear, another violence, and so on. It is not sufficient to find the offending bit of tissue and pull it out.

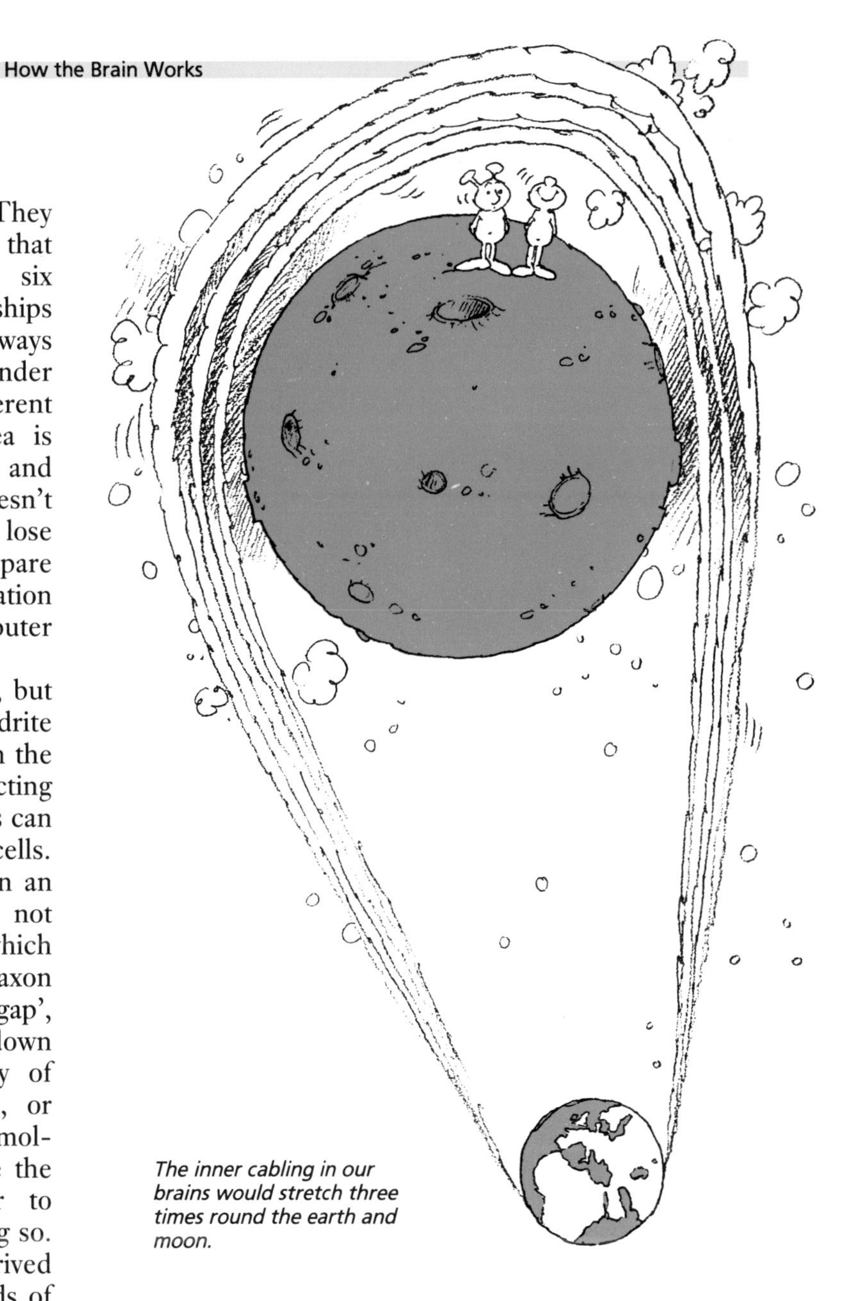

The inner cabling in our brains would stretch three times round the earth and moon.

Furthermore, there exists a sophisticated relationship between the brain and the world it lives in—a continuous, lifelong inflow of information and stimuli. So we cannot say that the origin of our impulses is purely within our heads. Our personalities are not dictated simply and entirely by our brain chemistry; the social factors which come into play when we contact the outside world also have an impact on our make-up. And if so, removing part of the brain of a criminal may not be addressing the real problem—the social circumstances which made him act as he did.

Unique and unrepeatable

It is just as well that our brains have this inbuilt unpredictability, since otherwise it might not be too difficult for an unscrupulous dictator with his team of neurosurgeons to dream of controlling his own world of mentally-doctored robots. But we are not so easily manipulated.

Nor are humans easy to duplicate. There has been a lot of talk about 'cloning': scientifically producing a replica of a human being by implanting the nucleus of one of his body cells in an unfertilized female egg. We could then, so it is said, produce hundreds of identical copies of Einstein, or Picasso, or Beethoven. There is no reason why such a technique should not one day be perfected. But would the replica really be a replica?

One writer has written: 'To produce another Mozart, we would need not only Wolfgang's genome but mother Mozart's uterus, father Mozart's music lessons, their friends and his, the state of music in eighteenth-century Austria, Haydn's patronage, and on and on, in ever-widening circles.' There can be no question that without Mozart's set of genes there would have been no Mozart. But, on the other hand, we have no right to assume the converse, that his genotype cultivated in another world at another time would have produced an equally creative musical genius. Cloning provides only part of a human being, and that quite drastically limits its alleged effectiveness.

Human beings are unique. The individual brain gives its owner a personal encounter with the world which cannot be copied by anyone else.

Nor can we make confident predictions about how someone else's thinking processes will work. Professor Keith Ward has remarked that the physicist Laplace (who taught that 'everything in the universe is completely predictable') could not in fact have predicted the very theory he came up with. And nor could anyone else:

Let us. . . pretend that we could predict the position and properties of all the quarks in Laplace's brain. Would we then know what he was thinking? We would obviously not—unless we knew a law stating that a certain state of his brain always correlates with, or causes the thought that, 'everything in the universe is completely predictable'. But how could we ever get such a law? We could not just magically intuit it out of the blue. We would have to get it, like all other laws of physics, from observation. But the plain fact is that we could never have observed the thought 'everything in the universe is completely predictable'. Because, until Laplace thought it, it had never occurred before, in the whole history of the universe.

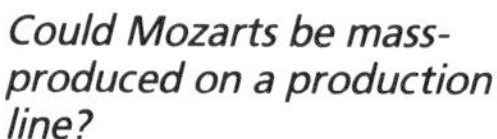
Could Mozarts be mass-produced on a production line?

There is no getting away from it. There is a freedom and unpredictability about the brain and its thoughts which is of vital importance for human life. It means that we are not merely automata, driven by inexorable laws of brain chemistry. Words like choice, dignity, responsibility, still have a meaning.

Some thinkers have suggested that, if we adjusted our use of our brains, we would become better human beings, and solve all our problems. Arthur Koestler, for example, felt that we ought to limit the use of the cold, inhuman cortex, and let the warm, emotional, intuitive mid-brain have more say. Robert Ornstein believes that the two hemispheres of the cortex have different functions, and that we are not developing sufficiently the mystical abilities of the 'right brain'. And 'New Age' thinkers such as Nona Coxhead and Marilyn Ferguson argue that a transformation of our consciousness—through meditation, biofeedback, or other mental therapies—will expand our consciousness and produce a better world.

But these patent remedies are all implausible. Koestler fails to realize that it is the impulsive wilfulness of the mid-brain that causes problems for human beings, and that the cortex is actually what holds us back from being too aggressive and selfish. Ornstein's theory is a long way from proven; when a human being has one hemisphere removed under brain surgery, it does not seem to change the intellectual style in any marked way. And as far as a 'transformation of consciousness' is concerned, Steven Rose comments, 'Over the last three hundred years the most effective utilization of the human brain has been brought about by. . . the application of precisely those rational techniques of inquiry and observation concerning the universe which the "mystic experience" relegates to a secondary or inferior place'. Would a consciousness transformation take us forward—or backwards?

The problem with the human being is not the way the brain is used. There are no miracle cures for evil, depravity and violence to be found by tinkering with the circuitry. Human beings are free, responsible individuals, and if their lives fail to match up to the highest moral level, it isn't because of anything wrong in their internal wiring. The problem is of a different order.

And that's a subject for another chapter.

HOW MUCH MORE DON'T WE KNOW?

Satya Sai Baba is a small, chubby Indian with a permanent beam and a shock of dark curly hair. He does not look at all extraordinary. Yet he claims to be able to produce objects from thin air—coins, crucifixes, flowers, even a mysterious 'holy ash' which is reputed to cure diseases when eaten. He is the most famous miracle-worker in India.

Rose Gladden is a mild-looking English lady from Hertfordshire. But her claims are extraordinary. She works as a healer, laying hands on sufferers and channelling energy by concentrating her mind to combat 'imbalances' and 'blockages' in the patient's body. (And not just the physical body, either. She claims to be able to see other dimensions of our existence in the shape of shadowy 'auras' surrounding the body, and to work on those.) 'We have dealt with most things over the years,' she remarks, 'arthritis, cancer, bad backs, epilepsy, multiple sclerosis, you name it and we've probably seen it.' There is no shortage of people who will testify that Rose Gladden has made them better.

Uri Geller rose to fame in the early 1970s as the man who could stop clocks and bend forks simply by using the strange powers of his mind. He is also reputed to have stopped a cable car in mid-journey, to have scored incredible results in dice-throwing ESP experiments, to have copied correctly drawings made by someone else out of sight. He was tested by American scientists at Stanford Research Institute, and the resulting report convinced many people that Geller was no trickster.

Uri Geller became famous in the 1970s as 'the spoon-bending man'. Was it genuine, or was it a trick?

What is the explanation for stories like these? Is there a whole range of undiscovered abilities waiting to be discovered within each of us? Do human beings have unexplored powers which go far beyond what we normally expect to achieve?

Unusual people like Sai Baba, Rose Gladden and Uri Geller have appeared in every age of history. And often more ordinary people have done or experienced surprising things. Mothers with no great physical strength have succeeded in lifting cars so that children who have been run over could be freed from underneath; in the panic and anguish of the moment, it has not occurred to them that they are attempting the impossible. The most unlikely people have seen ghosts and apparitions. Are there things we still have to discover about ourselves?

J.B. Rhine, experimenter into the paranormal, works with a subject at Duke University.

Researching the paranormal

It was to explore this question that a group of scholars and scientists formed the Society for Physical Research. The SPR, which began in England in 1882, had among its founders some of the most eminent minds of the day, and included sceptics as well as those who were convinced that there really was something special to explore.

At first the quest seemed quite promising. Some impressive results were obtained from mediums and psychics who were tested. But a number of hopeful results turned out to be fraudulent, or at least dubious; and in the end public interest declined. The First World War was the turning point. 'By the time peace returned,' observes Brian Inglis, 'all prospect of psychical research establishing itself as an academic discipline had vanished.'

That was to remain true until 1927, when modern parapsychological research began in earnest at Duke University in North Carolina. J.B. Rhine, a member of the psychology faculty, had already been involved in some testing of strange abilities, and knew how easy it was to be fooled. So he tried to set up a rigorously scientific style of experimenting, based on three principles:

- The people tested must not be famous professional psychics, who might be adept at cheating, but unknown volunteers, often students;
- Test procedures should be simple and easily controlled (no darkened rooms or complicated methods);
- Results should be evaluated statistically by the most exacting standards possible.

Despite these high aims, Rhine's first experiments were still open to many criticisms. But he refined his methods and continued to work with dogged integrity. His obvious honesty and his determination to get to the bottom of the problems started to capture the imagination of other young researchers, and gradually 'parapsychology'—the study of unknown powers in the human mind—became a serious field of study. (Yet still it was not until 1969 that the Parapsychological Association was admitted to the American Association for the Advancement of Science—the ultimate recognition that a scientific discipline really *is* science.)

In the first years of Rhine's research, he found some exceptional subjects who produced quite amazing results. But in time they left university, or tired of being tested, or else seemed somehow to lose their abilities; and it proved quite difficult to find others who could produce the same effects. Interest in the subject waned again, until by 1960 less and less work was being done.

Then, suddenly, a new wave of 'star performers' brought the subject back to popular attention: people such as Ted Serios, who claimed to produce photographs by staring into a camera lens; Nina Kulagina, who was said to move objects from one side of a tray to the other by the power of thought; Uri Geller and

Matthew Manning, whose strange energies interfered with electrical and mechanical equipment in dramatic ways. Television programmes and books fuelled popular interest, and an increasing number of colleges began to offer courses in parapsychology.

Much of this went outside the narrow field of interest to which Rhine's three principles had committed him. He had tested to find evidence of two abilities: 'ESP' (extra-sensory perception, the ability in a human being to perceive things which the normal senses could not perceive); and 'PK' (psychokinesis, the paranormal ability to affect the position and movement of objects). These terms were invented by Rhine, but parapsychologists now tend to use just one convenient word ('psi') to cover the field. 'Psi' simply stands for 'the unknown factor in psychic experiences'.

Today, parapsychology is regarded cautiously as a serious discipline by an increasing number of scientists, although many of them are reluctant to admit that anything definite has yet been proved. There are enthusiasts too; and there is a large, stubborn group of scientists (such as the members of the Committee for Scientific Investigation of Claims of the Paranormal) which resolutely refuses to believe there is anything real there at all.

And so the history of paranormal research has had three phases—the SPR period, the Rhine period, and the post-1960 period—each of which has had a curiously similar shape. At first there has been great excitement as a new crop of 'stars' have demonstrated unusual talents; this has been followed by a period of readjustment, in which testing has become more rigorous; then has come a tailing-off of results and a loss of interest. Supporters of 'psi' would say that this demonstrates what an elusive, unpredictable subject it is, and how much work we still need to do to be able to interpret what is going on. Opponents would argue that most of the impressive results were probably exaggerated or faked; especially since they seem to disappear when control procedures are tightened up. Who is right?

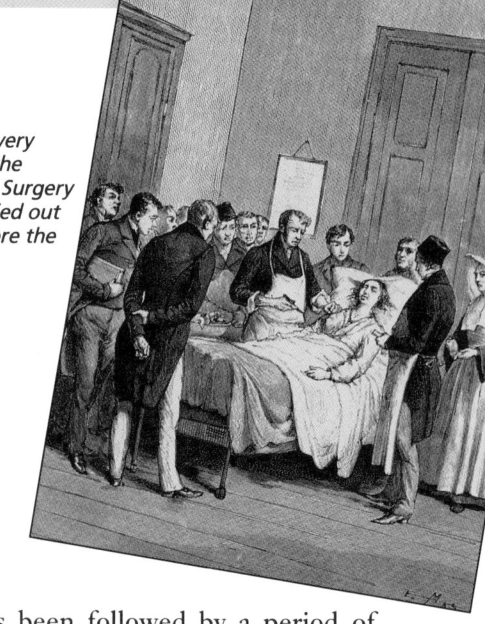

Hypnosis became a very popular pastime in the nineteenth century. Surgery was sometimes carried out under hypnosis before the days of anaesthetic.

There are certainly good reasons for scepticism. In a Lloyd Roberts Lecture to the Royal College of Physicians in 1985, Professor Lewis Wolpert said:

I am frankly hostile to the paranormal, partly because it deals with such apparently trivial phenomena, but mainly because it is antiscience in that it stops serious thinking about the world. One of my objections to pseudo-science and the paranormal is that it is a way of getting knowledge on the cheap. Whereas conventional scientific knowledge is obtained in a very tedious and painstaking way, with breakthroughs and flashes of insight being rare events, it is characteristic of the paranormal that major knowledge is as easily obtained without any special knowledge.

An early exponent of hypnosis gives a demonstration to scientific journalists.

Perhaps this is not fair to the painstaking work of J.B. Rhine, but it is a valid criticism of many of the inflated claims made for 'star' performers. And it is noticeable that would-be psychics are much keener to be tested by scientists (who may know a lot about their own field, but are no experts in trickery) than by conjurors and professional illusionists. One sceptical magician is James Randi, who has promised to give $10,000 to anyone who can demonstrate genuine paranormal abilities to his satisfaction. In over twenty years he has had applications from people who have turned out to be charlatans, or self-deluded; but no one who has come near to winning the money.

George du Maurier's creation Svengali, in his 1894 novel 'Trilby', picked up on public fascination with hypnotic power over others.

It has to be admitted on the other side that psychics may have good reason not to trust illusionists too far. Within the history of theatrical magic there has been a long tradition of hostility to psychic claims, and both fair means and foul have been employed to discredit the psychics. When Houdini, the escapologist, tested psychic
he triumphantly produced blatant evidence of her cheating. Sadly, Houdini seems to have 'planted' the evidence himself.

And so one of the biggest problems with this subject is in knowing whom to trust. There have been eminent fakes. None was more notorious, or shattering, than Walter J. Levy Jr., who directed Rhine's own laboratory and was Rhine's intended successor. In 1974 he was found tampering with equipment to produce improved results. He had to resign, and years of completed work came under suspicion.

Rhine's greatest British contemporary was Professor S.G. Soal, who achieved some exciting results in the early forties with a photographer called Basil Shackleton. But when subjected to statistical analysis his records clearly seemed to have been tampered with. And a young assistant of Soal's confessed that she had caught him altering figures.

This does not mean that parapsychologists are necessarily more crooked than other kinds of scientist. It seems that some of the greatest names in science—Ptolemy, Galileo, Newton, Dalton, Mendel—may well have 'improved' some of their results. It is an easy temptation to fall into when you want to believe.

And, of course, such an attitude of mind also makes it easy for others to fool you. In 1979 two teenagers approached the new para-psychology laboratory at Washington University and offered to be tested. Their ability to bend metal, cause objects to move across surfaces, and affect articles which had been sealed into jars, impressed the researchers for three years. The laboratory director announced that 'these two kids are the most reliable of the people that we've studied'. However, in 1983 the two held a press conference and revealed that the whole thing had been a stunt.

Experimenters and their subjects

The most important problem psi investigators face is that there has never been a psychic experiment which could be demonstrated re-

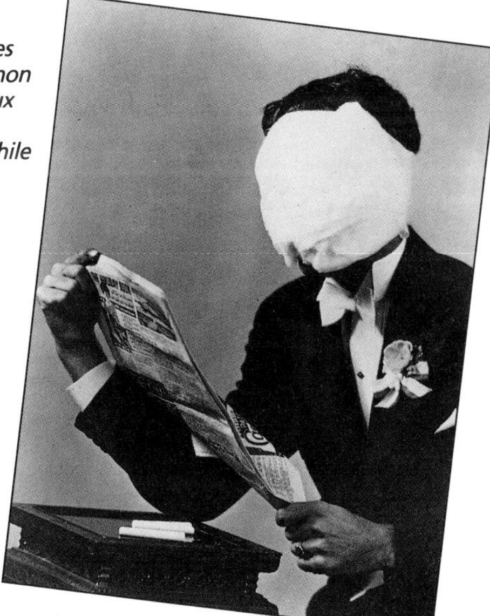

Many stage performances have used the phenomenon of 'psi', as when Kuda Bux purported to read an unfamiliar newspaper while blindfolded.

peatedly. We know that something is scientifically established when it works in the same way, time after time, in a cause-and-effect manner. With the paranormal, this is just not so. A psychic may manifest great abilities on Monday, Tuesday and Wednesday—then lose them all, bafflingly, on Thursday. These strange abilities cannot be produced to order.

This is why people who try to make a living from their super-powers frequently end up looking ridiculous. Jeane Dixon, an American clairvoyant, may well have predicted the assassination of President Kennedy—but before that she had predicted that he would not be elected. The night before Jacqueline Kennedy married Aristotle Onassis, Jeane was confidently claiming that Mrs Kennedy 'had no thoughts of marriage'. Those who keep score of Jeane Dixon's utterances claim that throughout the seventies her record of accuracy slipped to abysmally low levels.

Sometimes it may be that a psychic will begin with something which is a genuine gift, and then, because it cannot be produced on demand, start cheating just to save face. Perhaps that is what happened to medium Arthur Ford, who by the end of his career was keeping extensive files on major figures in American public life—so that he could 'super-

DO THE STARS INFLUENCE OUR DESTINY?

In 1939 a Swiss mathematician wrote to the German Intelligence Service, explaining that he was a student of 'astro-biology', and had determined from the stars that Adolf Hitler's life would be in danger between 7 and 10 November. The letter was dismissed as the work of a crank. That is, until Hitler narrowly escaped death from a bomb on 8 November.

Suddenly the Swiss mathematician found himself very sought after indeed! And once the Nazi hierarchy had satisfied themselves that he had nothing to do with the bomb conspiracy, he became an unofficial prophet for the Nazi leaders.

It was a demonstration of one of the most pervasive beliefs human beings have ever had: that what happens in the skies has some influence on human life. Astrology, the supposed science which studies this influence, has been with us for many centuries—arguably, claims Colin Wilson, for 100,000 years. And, he says, 'The labours of many serious investigators make it clear that it can no longer be dismissed as merely a manifestation of human gullibility.'

Certainly astrology is popular enough today. Most newspapers print horoscopes; the Faculty of Astrological Studies in London has no shortage of applicants for its diploma course; successful astrologers can become very wealthy people. But does it work?

R.B. Culver and P.A. Ianna spent several years collecting predictions from astrological magazines, well-known astrologers, and other similar sources. In the end they amassed 3,011, of which only 338 came true. One correct guess in ten is not impressive—especially since some of the correct guesses could have been caused by shrewd guesswork, vague wording, or 'inside' information. It suggests that people tend to believe in astrology because one occasional correct answer makes a much more striking impression than eight or nine that didn't work out.

The astronomical basis for astrology is quite spurious. The idea that the sun spends a roughly equal length of time in each 'house' of the Zodiac is just not true. Because of a phenomenon known as the 'precession of the equinoxes', the skies no longer look as they did when the dates were first worked out; and so if an astrologer tells you that your birth sign is Gemini or Scorpio or Libra, you may really be the next one along. And there is a thirteenth constellation (Ophiucus) which isn't taken into account by astrologers, since it was too faint to see with the naked eye when the original twelve were first discussed.

And yet it is true that many natural events do have an influence of some kind naturally' produce information about them when required.

So the obstinate fact remains: repeatable evidence of the paranormal is extremely hard to find. John Beloff, once President of the Parapsychological Association and a researcher noted for his painstaking honesty, has commented, 'No experiment showing the clear existence of the paranormal has been consistently repeated by other investigators in other laboratories.'

So must we conclude that psi does not exist at all? Not necessarily. Even if we have no rock-solid evidence, there are enough partial indications to make it likely that *something* genuinely exists. Philosopher Antony Flew confessed his puzzlement after twenty-two years of looking for confirmation: 'There is still no reliably repeatable phenomenon, no particular solid-rock positive cases. Yet there still is clearly too much there for us to dismiss the whole business.'

And perhaps there may be good reasons why evidence for psi is so unpredictable and elusive. An American psychologist, Professor Gardner Murphy, has pointed out how physicists have come to realize that we cannot understand the workings of things simply by looking at their constituent parts. Studying the behaviour of the individual particles in a field of energy does not necessarily tell us how the whole would behave: the whole is more than the sum of its parts. Perhaps we do not understand psi because we are studying individual human beings. Perhaps it has more to do with the relationships between human beings—and their minds—than with the single human considered alone. We may be talking about a 'psychic field' which links minds together, and in which—under unexpectedly favourable conditions—events may take place which are more than we would expect from studying the individual components who make up the field.

This is just one of many possible theories, and its development is hampered by the fact that no direct evidence supports it whatsoever. But it does show the possibility of conceiving plausible explanations for psi as a genuine phenomenon, yet one that behaves in strange ways.

Personally I am not convinced we will ever know for sure whether or not psi is real. There are just too many complicating factors which get in the way of research. One of these is the so-called 'sheep-goat effect'. This was first observed by a researcher called Gertrude Schmeidler. She carried out card-guessing tests on volunteers over a period of six years, and asked her subjects before testing them

on human life. It has been suggested that human blood is influenced by sunspot activity; that the human nervous system is affected by the earth's own magnetic field; that heart attacks and strokes are more likely at times of sunspot activity. So might there be influences from the planets—nearer to us than the sun—which affect human beings and help to make us the people we are?

Michel Gauquelin, a French psychologist and statistician, has produced some very carefully researched data which may well show that this is true. Those who excel in certain professions seem more likely to be born while certain planets are in clearly identified positions. Perhaps the personality trait that makes people rise to the top in athletics, for example, or military life, could have something to do with the precise moment of our birth?

It is too early to say. And Gauquelin emphasizes that this effect is one of character, not destiny. He has also studied athletes and soldiers whose careers were cut tragically short, and has found the same planetary positions for them; so the planets do not forecast our future. But they might just have a tiny part to play in determining the things we are good at in life.

whether they believed it was possible that they would demonstrate ESP in the test. If they said no, she classified them as 'goats'; if they thought ESP was possible, or if they were unsure, they were 'sheep'. The interesting thing was that 'sheep' scored consistently more correct guesses than they should have managed, simply by chance; and 'goats' scored many fewer. It was as if the beliefs of the subjects were affecting the phenomenon that was being tested. For the 'goats' were not simply scoring at a chance level; their score was well *under* what it should have been, as if something in their subconscious was deliberately guessing wrong!

As if this were not complicated enough, it was noticed that the doubters among the sheep (who were unsure whether or not it would work) scored better, not worse, than the totally convinced believers. Were the believers subconsciously trying too hard? There is no way of telling; all we can say is that if people's expectations can start fiddling with the results, it is going to be very hard to conduct valid tests.

Another problem for researchers is the 'experimenter effect'. It is well known that some researchers—especially those with a sympathetic attitude towards the possibility of psi—get consistently better results than others. Is this because they are cheating? Not necessarily; it could be that the attitude of the researcher as well as of the research-subject can affect the results of the experiment. If so, no wonder successful experiments tend to be unrepeatable; another researcher, with a slightly different attitude, could ruin the delicate balance necessary for success.

There are also other problems with the subjects who are tested. Some (as we have seen) will perform brilliantly for a while, and then their powers will seem to wane. They may guess correctly, time after time, which card is going to be turned up from the pack in the researcher's hand; and then twenty-four hours later get it all wrong. There is no ready explanation why powers vanish in this way. But it happens, and so another unpredictable element enters the situation. If I test a psychic who shows great abilities, say, in moving matches round a tray by the power of thought, and then hand her on to a colleague; and then all of a sudden the psychic can do nothing—what has happened? Have her powers somehow waned? Or is it the experimenter effect? Or have I just been easy to fool, while my colleague is more shrewd?

Then there are people who genuinely believe they have exceptional powers, when in fact they are fooling themselves. Randi comments that most of the applicants for his $10,000 fall into this category:

In the great majority of these cases, the persons involved have been convinced of their error, and

WHAT ARE BIORHYTHMS AND BIOFEEDBACK?

As the cells of our brain send out information to different parts of the body, by electrochemical impulses, they create wave patterns. Scientists have fitted electrodes to the scalps of volunteers and worked out what kinds of brain waves occur. Basically there are four types: alpha, which are produced when we are awake, but in a peaceful, relaxed frame of mind; beta, which occur at times of concentration and thought, and in normal daily alertness; theta, which are associated with the earliest stages of sleep, hallucination and creativity; and delta, characteristic during deep sleep.

In the late 1950s, an American psychophysiologist, Dr Joseph Kamiya, became fascinated with brain waves. He wondered whether people could be taught to discern their own brain rhythms, to sense what kind of waves they were producing at any given moment. And so he fitted electrodes to the scalps of some experimental subjects, monitored their brains, and asked them to guess at certain moments whether they were producing alpha waves or not.

At first guesses would be purely random. After an hour, the volunteer would be correct up to 60 per cent of the time. Two hours later, some people would be 80 per cent correct, and in the end a few volunteers would achieve 100 per cent results.

The next step was obvious. Could people be taught, not just to guess correctly, but to produce alpha waves on demand? Kamiya tested for this and, yes, it worked. Once people had learned to *recognize* their alpha waves, they could also *make them happen*.

When news of this dis-

covery filtered out into the mass media, there was a great deal of excitement. Enterprising firms started to market devices to enable people at home to do their own 'alpha-training', and a variety of 'pop alpha' groups sprang up to offer new improved ways of producing alpha waves. It was claimed that the more alpha we can produce, the more we develop the powers of the psyche. Alpha waves were touted as the key to Eastern mysticism, as well as a revolutionary means to better health, prosperity, peace of mind, better sleep, control of pain, and weight mastery.

Most of this is unproven and exaggerated, but 'biofeedback' has emerged from it all as a useful set of medical techniques. Biofeedback is the process of giving people 'feedback' about processes in their bodies of which they are not normally aware—brainwave activity, muscle tension and heart rate, in particular—and then getting them to use that information to begin controlling the processes. In effect, this is a means of changing consciousness, since the mind and body are so intimately linked. To quote biofeedback pioneer Dr Elmer Green, 'Every change in the physiological state is accompanied by an appropriate change in the mental-emotional state.'

Biofeedback certainly has a value in the treatment of hypertension, migraine, asthma and anxiety symptoms; it can help to retrain the muscles after serious injury. But how much more it enables us to do is still an open question. Research continues.

Biorhythms are not to be confused with biofeedback. They are supposedly rhythmic periods through which we all pass regularly. Dr Wilhelm Fliess, one of the pioneers, claimed that our bodies have a 'physical rhythm', a twenty-three-day cycle which determines how much strength, energy and physical confidence we will possess at any given time; and a 'sensitivity rhythm' a twenty-eight-day cycle which affects our creativity, mental co-ordination, and feelings of affection. It is also claimed that there is a thirty-three-day 'intellectual cycle' which controls our ability to think clearly and memorize.

Biorhythms had a brief phase of popularity in the early 1970s, but are now thought unproven and unlikely. 'In properly conducted studies,' says psychologist Hans Eysenck, '. . .none of the evidence supports the theory of biorhythms.'

have retired gracefully. A good example is a lady in Italy who had produced hundreds of supposedly 'spiritual' photos with a Polaroid camera. She demonstrated for me via RAI-TV in Rome that she was simply not able to use the camera properly. . . test prints were sent to the Polaroid Corporation in the USA for their opinion, which agreed in every respect. These were problems that the company was familiar with, and which crossed desks there every day.

This particular case was easy to sort out. But what about those where the subject unconsciously cheats, while believing that genuine phenomena are being produced? The medium Eusapia Palladino used to warn researchers, 'Watch me or I'll cheat; John King makes me cheat.' John King was the name she gave to the 'spirit' who directed her powers.

Is psi real?

All these factors mean that it can be genuinely impossible to tell what is really going on when someone claims a paranormal event has occurred. People who have strange experiences may be overwhelmed by them, and absolutely convinced that they are genuine; others may have different interpretations. For example, many hundreds of people have reported that, while they were undergoing major surgery, they 'died' for a few minutes and had the experience of tasting the afterlife. Typically, they report looking down on the operating room, and their own inert bodies, from a point near the ceiling; then they are drawn down a long, dark tunnel, and emerge at the other end into a place where they recognize figures whom they know to have died some time before. They receive interrogation from a 'being of light' who makes them re-evaluate their past life. Often people looking back on such an experience believe very strongly that they have crossed the barrier that separates this world from the next. But many scientists feel that they could simply be reliving the trauma of their own birth, in a confused way.

The interpretation is everything. Susan Blackmore was a student at Oxford when, under the influence of drugs, she had an 'out-of-the-body experience'—a sensation of leaving her physical body behind and travelling outside the room and building she was in. Now, after ten years' study of such experiences, she has come to believe that 'nothing leaves the body. . . Everything is seen from the person's own imagination.' The whole experience 'may be a process of exploring the contents of your own memory and imagination, brought to life by a new way of thinking in a special state of

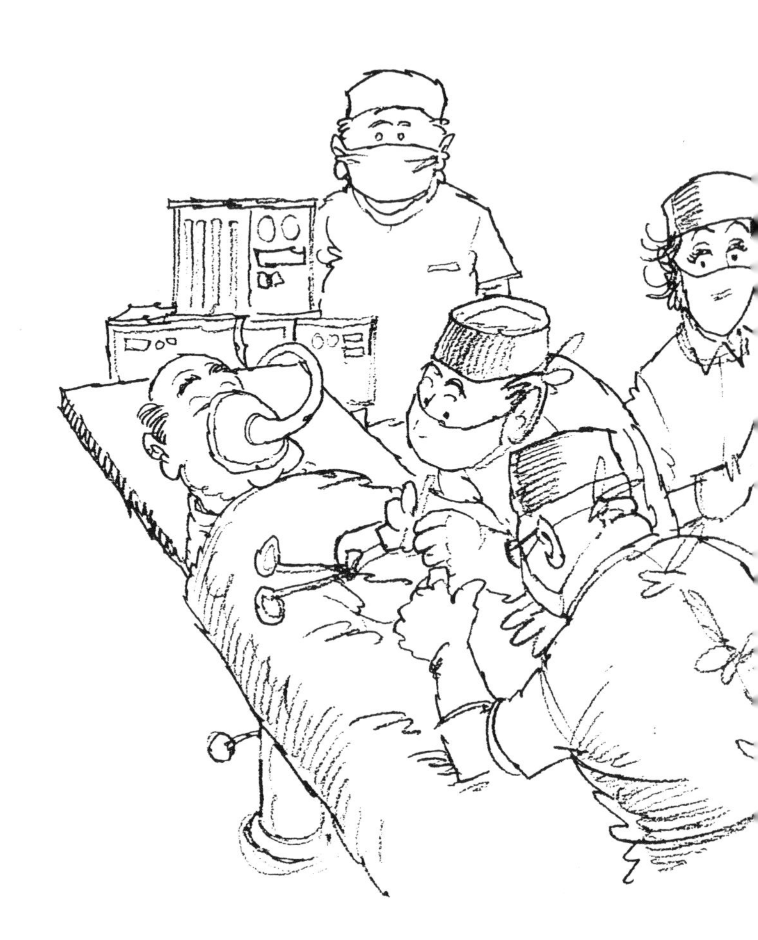

ARE THERE VAMPIRES AND WEREWOLVES?

Ever since Bram Stoker wrote his famous novel *Dracula* in 1897, people have been familiar with the idea of vampires. A creature that casts no shadow or reflection, with hypnotic powers and superhuman strength, rising from its grave each night to suck the blood of its victims with its pointed canine fangs. . . Surely nothing like this ever really happens? Wasn't it just a work of fiction?

Stoker's novel was certainly fiction. The real Dracula—a bloodthirsty tyrant known as Vlad the Impaler—was no vampire. But the tales about vampires come from many different cultures as far apart as China, Persia and Eastern Europe. And in the mid-eighteenth century there was an epidemic of vampire cases throughout Europe, which caused even the level-headed Jean-Jacques Rousseau to write, 'If ever there was in the world a warranted and proven history, it is that of vampires; nothing is lacking, official reports, testimonials of persons of standing, of surgeons, of clergymen, of judges; the judicial evidence is all-embracing.' Dom Augustine Calmet, a Benedictine scholar of repute who studied the cases, remarked, 'It seems

Some people who have been resuscitated after heart failure report that they became detached from themselves and looked down on their own bodies.

consciousness'. But for someone who has the experience, its reality seems quite undeniable.

Do human beings have unexpected powers? There seems to be no easy answer. Perhaps Uri Geller's abilities really are (as many people have alleged) nothing more than clever conjuring. Perhaps Rose Gladden heals people, not so much by psychic energy, as by implanting in them a strong belief that they will get better (though that idea raises many more questions again!). Perhaps Sai Baba, too, is a fake.

One thing seems clear. We know very little about the source and workings of psi; after a century of research none of the big questions have really been answered. Many researchers who have begun the study of parapsychology with great excitement have become quickly disillusioned with their lack of progress, and have dropped out to pursue a different branch of science. And if we know as little as this, it seems unlikely that we should pin our hopes on psi as a major prospect for human betterment. It seems unlikely that we shall become able to control and employ these odd abilities for any practical purpose. (And maybe it would not be good if we could; how would you like to live in a world where the man

impossible not to subscribe to the prevailing belief that these apparitions do actually come forth from their graves.'

One of these cases, in 1739, was that of Arnold Paul, who lived in Medreiga near the Turkish-Serbian border. It was reported that he had been sighted several times after his death and had done appalling damage. He was exhumed after forty days; his flesh was uncorrupted; the blood bubbled in his veins, and covered his whole body and shroud. When his heart was pierced with a stake, the vampire gave a horrible shriek.

What are we to make of this? Calmet pointed out that chemical substances in the soil could have conserved the corpse indefinitely, and nitre and sulphur in the earth can liquefy blood which has clotted. A stake through the heart forces air out of the body, and so can produce sounds like shrieks. Interestingly, none of the vampire stories mention that the earth was disturbed around the grave; which would surely have happened if the body really had come out.

And Calmet pointed out that there was no proof of nocturnal visits, or of bloodsucking. 'The allegation that they returned to haunt and destroy the living has never been sufficiently proved. . .'

It seems, then, that there is no factual basis for vampire stories. What about werewolves?

A werewolf (from *wer*, 'man', and *wulf*, 'wolf') is a living person who changes into animal form—usually a wolf, but in some cultures a jackal, tiger or leopard—and becomes a killer and eater of human flesh. Usually this is under cover of darkness, and the werewolf will change back to human form the next morning. Only a consecrated bullet, or a wound that draws blood, will cure a werewolf's strange disease.

Again, werewolves have been the subject of legends for centuries—from at least before the time of Christ. And two hundred years before the vampire 'epidemic', there was a period of the sixteenth century when werewolf stories abounded everywhere. But, as with vampires, there is no basis in fact. Insane people often *think* they are wild animals; but that is quite a different matter.

In this seventeenth-century woodcut, the devil marks a new disciple. Interest in personalized evil remains strong today.

DO HUMAN BEINGS LIVE MORE THAN O

Arnall Bloxham is a hypnotherapist who lives in Cardiff. He has made a speciality of hypnotizing people and taking them back to past lives. In other words, under hypnosis they will begin to come out with details of previous existences they have lived through. One person will speak as an eighteenth-century sailor, another as a twelfth-century Jewess, another a Victorian doctor. Does this prove that they really once were those people?

Eastern religions have taught 'reincarnation' (coming back from death to live another life) for many centuries. They have slightly different beliefs about it, but the central idea is clear. Something in us survives the death of the body; that something takes on a new bodily form, and then lives again. Reincarnation is now becoming a more-and-more popular belief in the West as well.

The problem is, as Don Cupitt comments, 'Reincarnation is unverifiable.' Just because some people can produce under hypnosis an incredibly detailed knowledge of certain historical facts, they have not necessarily gained the information by actually living through it. 'If the evidence exists by which you can verify the supposed memory, if, say, there is any means of checking. . . he could have got to know of it by telepathic or clairvoyant means.'

In fact, sometimes claims made under hypnosis have been checked out historically and found to be a mixture of fact, plausible untruth and total fantasy. The problem is that our brain has a facility for weaving stories together in a compelling way, as we discover whenever we dream. The information may be true, but that does not mean it has come from the dead. The manufactured ghost 'Philip', mentioned in a previous chapter, sometimes put his creators right about dates and historical facts. 'Philip' was always correct!

Professor Alan Gauld comments, 'I have strong

next door could read your thoughts?) Psi looks set to remain on the fringes of knowledge, as a curious, baffling enigma: never quite disproved, but resisting all attempts to prove it; never reliable enough to be used practically, but glamorous enough to provide a living for quacks and frauds of every description.

And there we could leave it—if the world were simply a closed system of cause-and-effect laws, natural properties, physical matter and nothing more. But Christians believe that there are other forces at work in the universe. The creating, sustaining activity of God, who holds the universe in being, and operates through the natural laws which scientists explore. But there is also, according to the Bible, an evil force at large in the world, which works for chaos and destruction, and can sometimes collide with the lives of human beings in a damaging, dangerous way.

Is it possible that this evil force is sometimes encountered in the search for paranormal abilities? The possibility has at least to be considered. Writing in the London *Times*, Clifford Longley commented that people still can become 'possessed' by evil in a way which science finds it impossible to explain:

Evil is now used as an emotive word to describe extremely inhumane or anti-social behaviour, not as a thing in itself. There is no conceptual language for talking about evil detached from personal behaviour, in the way that is implied by the term 'demon', or the idea of 'casting out'.

Yet the studies of the subject are all clear: what is being spoken about is not just changing behaviour. The 'possessed' condition is a radical change for the worse from normal, of which the best available analogy is of an invasion by something previously external, and which has to be made external again to restore normality. And the process of doing this invariably involves invoking another external image or entity, a supernatural God. . .

reservations about the hypnotic regression material. . . The hypnotic induction procedure seems to release powers of creative imagination that (the subjects) did not know they possessed.' It is not true that under hypnosis people will always tell the truth. They may lie or fabricate evidence without realizing it; they are certainly not helpless puppets who must inexorably do the will of their controller.

Another kind of evidence for reincarnation is sometimes called 'deja vu'. This is the experience of feeling that we have been in a certain place before, or done a certain thing, although we know that it was not in this lifetime. If this is so, it is argued, then we must have done it in some previous life.

The experience is very common, especially among children, epileptics, people who have undergone brain surgery and the semi-starved. That should make us suspect that perhaps it has more to do with the state of our body and mind than with our past lives; and indeed the most common explanation is that it is a functioning of the two halves of the brain out of rhythm with each other. This induces the feeling 'I've been here before', when really one side of the brain has simply perceived what we are seeing a split second before the other half has got there.

Peter Underwood has an alternative explanation. 'More likely it is the working of the subconscious mind triggered off on a particular course by an insignificant detail which escapes our conscious senses; and thus, reminding our unconscious mind of a similar incident or situation, persuading us that other details and happenings are also remembered.'

Either way, it makes little difference. There is no evidence to prove reincarnation.

Actress Shirley Maclaine has put forward a philosophy which claims to make sense of repeated incarnations.

IS ANYONE ELSE OUT THERE?

On 24 June 1947 a businessman called Kenneth Arnold was flying his private plane over the Rockies when he saw nine shining discs swerving in and out of the mountains with 'flipping, erratic movements'. He reported that they moved as a saucer might 'if you skipped it across the water'. The newspapers took it up, people started reporting similar sightings across America, and the term 'flying saucer' was born.

Interest grew. And it was fuelled enormously by the publication in 1953 of a sensational book, *Flying Saucers Have Landed*, by Desmond Leslie and George Adamski. Leslie's part of the book detailed historical records of flying- saucer sightings in previous ages; Adamski told the story of how he had actually met a Venusian in the Mohave Desert, and been allowed to photograph his spacecraft.

Unfortunately, Leslie's section was full of errors and mistaken claims, while Adamski's evidence—a picture of the spacecraft—failed to convince the experts that it was anything more than the top canister of a Hoover vacuum cleaner. But it made no difference: a new belief had been implanted into the public mind—that alien visitors have often visited earth.

What is the evidence? Certainly there have been some convincing claims of sightings, often made by people with no desire for publicity, who clearly believe they are telling the truth. On the other hand, the same is true of the 'giant airship' which was glimpsed by several hundred people above the United States in 1879 (its occupants\rather improbably singing 'Abide with me'). As far as we can tell, there was no such airship. And if so, honest eyewitnesses can be honestly wrong.

If there is any substance to the sighting claims, it could be, says Colin Wilson, 'a manifestation of the human unconscious. . . trying to prevent us from becoming jammed in a two-dimensional left-brain reality'. In other words, they are not objective reality, but the creation of our subconscious minds—a sort of 'super-poltergeist effect'.

It has been objected that if there are any beings out there, they are rather good at keeping quiet. Our planet is exceptionally noisy—our radio and TV transmissions must be capable of being picked up long distances away through space. But despite listening since 1948 we have never caught a snatch of an outer-space soap opera. And for all the thousands of sightings, no one item of outer-space origin has ever been found lying about afterwards. There have been claims; but nothing that could not have been explained away.

In fact we do not know whether there is anyone else there. Some scientists believe there probably is; more, it seems, believe there is not. The finely-balanced conditions which led to the miraculous emergence of life on earth may not have been duplicated anywhere else in the universe.

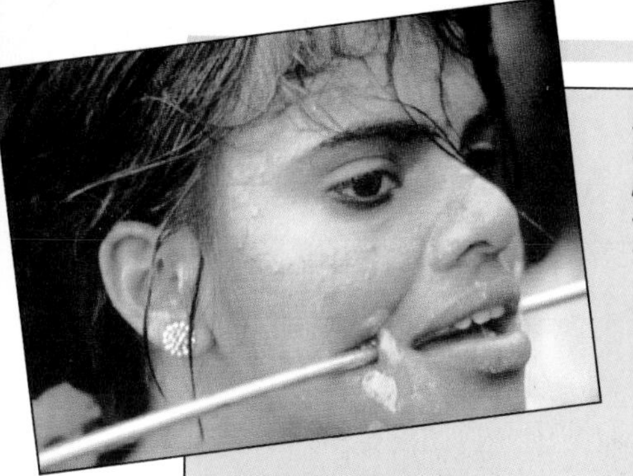

As well as walking on fire, some religious devotees push swords into themselves without apparent injury.

WALKING ON FIRE? RISING INTO THE AIR?

Some of the strange feats claimed for the human body sound quite impossible. Yet we find the same claims being made in culture after culture.

Take fire-walking, for instance. It was known before the time of Christ; Strabo, a Greek historian, wrote of priestesses in Cappadocia who could do it, and a tribe in Etruria were excused military service in the Roman legions if they could perform the feat. Fire-walking has also been part of religious festivals in India, Fiji, South Africa, Tahiti, Japan, the Philippines, and among American Indians. How is it done?

The answer is that nobody quite knows—although it indubitably happens, and even sceptical volunteers with no previous training have sometimes been able to walk across a bed of hot coals without any injury. One theory was put forward by psychic investigator Harry Price, who tested the ability of fire-walkers on beds of coals measured at up to 800 degrees Centigrade. He thought that the speed and confidence with which fire-walkers moved, and the low thermal conductivity of burning wood embers, protected the feet for just long enough.

Another theory is that perspiration on the feet of the fire-walkers forms a cushion of vapour which protects the sole of the foot from scorching. This was tested out by American scientist Mayne Reid Coe, who found he was able to stroke red-hot steel bars with the tip of his tongue without serious injury, dip his fingers into molten lead, and—as he had hoped—walk through a pit of burning embers.

Just in case anyone reading this should be inspired to try it out, we should note that many others who have tried to replicate these feats have been badly burned. Patience, caution and good fortune all seem to be required.

What about levitation—the ability to float in the air? It is reported that St Joseph of Copertino found himself frequently doing this, quite unwontedly, and on one occasion performed the feat in front of witnesses including the startled philosopher Leibniz. Last century a medium called Daniel Dunglas Home was famous for his ability to float in and out of windows; many theories have been advanced about how he might have faked it, but none yet sound convincing.

In our own day, graduates of the Transcendental Meditation 'siddhi' course claim the ability to levitate. Sceptics claim that their levitation is more like a series of short hops into the air and down again—and is probably caused by involuntary muscular action, propelling the meditator off the mat.

If poltergeist phenomena can make everyday objects float into the air, and even throw human beings out of bed, there may well be some sort of mechanism which we do not understand which would occasionally impel a human body to defy the force of gravity. All that we can say is that we do not know for certain.

Clergymen and others who have helped to deal with 'possessed' people have often found that they demonstrate involuntary paranormal powers—such as exceptional strength, flashes of precognition, or an ability to read thoughts. Is it possible, then, that occasionally the source of paranormal abilities may be evil from the supernatural realm? It is a possibility which must be taken seriously. Since we know so little about what psi actually is, it would be naive to laugh the idea out of court.

Tal Brooke, at least, has no doubts. He was one of the most intimate disciples of Sai Baba, with whom we opened this chapter. He saw at first hand the kind of supernatural feats which Baba was able to manifest. He was in no doubt about the reality of his guru's powers. But he came to believe that Sai Baba was more than a miracle-worker: he was tuned to a source of power which was ultimately destructive:

> *I will never forget my thoughts at that time. I had discovered an absolutely Satanic thing operating behind Sai Baba's veneer. . . Miracles, according to what I had just read in the Bible, were not infallible proof that one was divine, or in touch with God-consciousness. Or had transcended space. No. The powers of evil could work miracles. . .*

Was Brooke right? Certainly, many of those who have tried most deliberately to harness supernatural power have ended as broken people, alcoholics, sexually deviant, incapable of sustaining real relationships with others. There are dangers in the pursuit of paranormal abilities. And whatever we believe about psi, we would be foolish to forget them.

Part III

People Together

WHY PEOPLE DO WHAT THEY DO

One of our problems in examining human beings is that we know only one person really well: ourselves. We observe everybody else from the outside. And that can be deceptive; people can wear masks, tell lies, create misleading impressions. Sometimes they will not even be conscious that they are doing it themselves. Others are always capable of surprising us; the final core of mystery remains, even after years of friendship or indeed marriage.

And do we really know even ourselves? When Sigmund Freud first started to write about the unconscious, and the effect it has on our actions, many people were indignant and amazed. We do not like to think that we are not wholly rational, logical, self-controlled individuals. But Freud suggested that many of our motives are obscure and our actions fulfil needs that we don't consciously understand. One contemporary professor, when Freud's theories were being mentioned, banged his fist on the table and shouted: 'This is not a topic for discussion at a scientific meeting; it is a matter for the police.'

This was in 1910. No wonder there was so much panic abroad; several currents of thought at that time seemed to threaten established rational and religious ideas.

It was less than fifty years since Darwin's ideas had become well known, and Western thinkers had been forced to start regarding human beings as part of the animal creation, with clear links back to lower forms of life. In Bordeaux a rabbi's-son-turned-atheist, Emile Durkheim, was teaching a university course on religion which maintained that the faiths of

Karl Marx and Sigmund Freud both put forward highly influential explanations of why people act as they do.

WHAT MAKES PEOPLE CRIMINALS?

The soul-destroying life in prison can serve to reinforce people's anti-social behaviour.

When Richard Speck murdered eight nurses in Chicago, there was no question about his guilt. But his defence counsel hit on a brilliant idea. Speck, he claimed, had an extra Y-chromosome in his body, and since the Y-chromosome may be responsible for the aggression and combativeness which characterizes men rather than women, a double dose might turn a man into a murderer. Speck was not responsible for his actions; his body had made him a criminal.

In fact, Speck did not have the extra chromosome, and it is by no means certain that men who do will inevitably end up as criminals. But this was just the modern version of an old game: the attempt to link criminal behaviour to some physical characteristic. A hundred years ago, the most famous name associated with this kind of thinking was that of an Italian physician, Cesare Lombroso.

Lombroso believed that evolution held the key to criminality. Evil-doers were people who had been unfortunate enough to be born with ape-like characteristics—as throwbacks to a more primitive state of human life. They had long arms, narrow foreheads, large ears, thick skulls and hairy chests. 'They are true savages,' he wrote, 'in the midst of our brilliant European civilization.' He recommended that they should be carefully monitored from birth, and then exiled for life whenever their criminal nature asserted itself. (His admirers often wanted a more severe solution. One wrote, 'There is all the more reason for destroying them when it has been proved that they will always remain orang-utans.')

Lombroso was wildly wrong. But is it possible that the cause of criminality lies somewhere in our biological make-up? We do know that more women commit crimes when suffering from premenstrual tension. And sometimes brain surgery has removed deviant tendencies from men. Are criminals driven to their acts by their bodies?

The problem is that 'criminality' is not a scientific category. Criminal behaviour is criminal only because society says it is—and different societies have slightly different rules. And so some of the actions our society holds to be criminal may be committed because of some biological factor; but by no means all. Even Lombroso admitted that 60 per cent of criminal acts were nothing to do with evolution, but were the result of giving in to greed, jealousy and anger.

It is dangerous to try to impose biological answers. We need to look at all the factors which may be involved—social ones as well as physical. Soviet political dissenters have often been confined to mental hospitals because of their activities. Says Dr Gareth Jones, 'The use of psychiatry as a political weapon radically alters the nature both of political debate and of behaviour control: dissident behaviour becomes the product of an unbalanced mind—which is diagnosed solely on the basis of dissident behaviour.'

Human beings are people, and the motives behind their actions will be mixed. Some may be criminals because of their chemistry. Others will be criminals because of factors in their background, or because of the way society has treated them, or because they have been forced into criminal patterns of behaviour by the unjust structures of their society. For others, the only reason will be what the Bible calls 'sin'—an inbuilt bias all human beings have towards doing the wrong thing instead of the right, towards satisfying self rather than living for others.

And if we forget this final factor, we will never understand human nature.

humankind were important for reasons quite different from those officially claimed: the real ground of their strength and power was that they correspond to a hidden, unconscious need, deep within human beings. 'The reasons with which the faithful justify them may be, and generally are, erroneous,' he wrote. 'But the true reasons do not cease to exist, and it is the duty of science to discover them.'

It seemed as if the accepted picture of what a human being is—and how people arrive at their decisions and beliefs—was being turned completely upside-down.

As if all this were not enough, in 1910 the ideas of Karl Marx were gaining ground among intellectuals everywhere. In only seven years they would lead to the Russian Revolution. And Marx's claim was—once again—that human beings are not the free, responsible, rationally-choosing agents they fondly imagine themselves to be. Our actions and desires are dominated, according to Marx, by the economic circumstances of our lives; it is the sort of society we live in that makes us the people we are. Humans might feel themselves to be free, independent persons, but in reality we are shaped and conditioned by hidden factors over which we have no control, and to which we respond more or less blindly.

Over the last eighty years or so since 1910, we have grown more used to these ideas. We know that the deepest springs of a person's actions are often things that he knows nothing much about; and that human beings can be manipulated by forces outside themselves. We live in the century which has discovered subliminal advertising, political brainwashing, and even ways of selling religion by tapping the unconscious. Chris Elkins, who joined a religious cult as a result of the psychological techniques practised on him, reported afterwards that there is a '"process" that creates the "product" —that slow, almost imperceptible shifting of values, allegiances, and authority that transforms a person... into a member of a cult. This process is truly *subtle*,' he added, 'but rarely as *coercive* as some people would like to believe.'

All of this suggests another important dimension of human life which we need to investigate in this book. How do we know what makes people tick? Why do they do what they do?

ARE HUMAN BEINGS NATURALLY AGGRESSIVE?

In the 126 years between 1820 and 1945, it has been estimated that 59 million human beings died a violent death. This includes death through war, murder and fatal quarrels. And it is almost certainly an under-estimate.

Why are human beings so violent? It is calculated that in the last 2000 years we have enjoyed about 15 years of peace. Are we fated to be aggressive?

Some scientists blame it on the nature of our brain. Dr Paul MacLean points out that our brain can be divided into the two parts which come from reptilian or animal origins—and the part which is more developed in humans than any other species. He suggests that the older two parts have animal tendencies which conflict with our new powers of logical reasoning, and drag us back into warlike behaviour.

However, human behaviour is much more complex than this; the centres of 'reason' and 'emotion' in our brain cannot be so easily distinguished from one another. The brain does not operate in three competing bits, but as one functioning unit.

Violence can often seem totally futile and purposeless. What is it that makes people aggressive?

Other psychologists have held that human beings would lose their aggression if the frustrations were removed from the process of growing up. And so children should never be reprimanded or restrained. Unfortunately for a nice idea, children brought up under such a regime are often more aggressive and contentious than those who have been disciplined.

Certainly, aggression always seems to have been a part of human life. Even the most primitive societies show plenty of evidence of violent practices. And those who do not, usually live in the neighbourhood of much more violent neighbours, and seem to have developed a 'peace-at-any-price' strategy of survival by submission to their oppressors.

It is often claimed that men are more aggressive than women. This is borne out by studies of the games children play, and also by the crime statistics: men are several times more likely than women to be arrested for crimes of violence. What causes the difference?

Is it that the male is always more aggressive than the female, in any species? Not necessarily. This is often so, but there is a lot of variation, and anyway to make generalizations from animals to humans is a risky business.

Could it be caused by the hormone testosterone, secreted in boys at puberty in larger quantities than happens in girls? Could there be a link between this hormone and aggressive behaviour? Again, the evidence is not clear-cut. Even if a link could be established, it would not provide a complete explanation. Greater male aggressiveness is visible at three years of age—many years before testosterone is secreted.

It seems more likely that male aggression has its origins in the expectations we have of male behaviour, as a boy is growing up. Perhaps if feminists succeed in shattering some of the easy assumptions we make about 'typical' male or female behaviour, and which we pass on unconsciously to our children, the difference in aggression between men and women will disappear.

But aggression hardly looks like disappearing from human life for a long time to come. And perhaps this is as it should be. Our history has been shaped by controversy and competition, and without obstinate struggles we could never have come as far as we have. Perhaps aggression is not an undesirable evolutionary residue, but the wise gift of a loving Creator who intends us to keep our aggressive qualities, but control and shape them to useful, non-destructive ends.

W.M. Krogman, an expert on child growth, has written: 'Man has absolutely the most protracted period of infancy, childhood and juvenility of all forms of life. . . Nearly 30 per cent of his entire lifespan is devoted to growing.' This important difference between ourselves and other forms of life is what makes us a socially dependent animal, incapable of being fully human (as we saw in chapter three) unless there are others around with whom we can mix. Biologist Stephen Jay Gould explains it this way:

But what is the adaptive significance of retarded development itself? The answer to this question probably lies in our social evolution. We are pre-eminently a learning animal. . . To enhance our learning, we have lengthened our childhood by delaying sexual maturation with its adolescent yearning for independence. Our children are tied for longer periods to their parents, thus increasing their own time of learning and strengthening family ties as well.

This means that human beings have a much more flexible, shifting, complicated relationship to their environment than other animals do. Sociologists Berger and Luckman comment that 'man's relationship to his environment is characterized by world-openness', that human beings do not live their lives according to the dictates of a bundle of instincts which were already predetermined before the day of their birth, but that after birth, 'the process of becoming man takes place in an interrelationship with an environment'. Even some biological developments which in animals take place within the mother's womb are delayed until after birth in human beings. At birth, the brain of a rhesus monkey is already 65 per cent of its fully-grown size; but our brains are only 23 per cent of their final size when we make our first appearance. And so when we emerge into the world we are not so rigidly complete as other species. Berger and Luckman comment:

There is no man-world in the sense that one may speak of a dog-world or a horse-world. Despite an area of individual learning and accumulation, the individual dog or the individual horse has a largely fixed relationship to its environment, which it shares with all other members of its respective species. . . The developing human being not only interrelates with a particular natural environment, but with a specific cultural and social order, which is mediated to him by the significant others who have charge of him.

Human behaviour therefore depends very heavily on our relationships with other people. It is from others that we derive our original store of learning about the world: how we should cope with it, what we need to remember in order to survive, what society will and will not let us do. It is through others that we grow, receiving

ideas, mental stimulation, social pressure, examples to copy. It is with others that we encounter some of the major experiences of life—education, work, founding a family, belonging to a community. For most of us, solitary confinement is an unpleasant, even terrifying experience—it seems so unnatural. Human behaviour is social behaviour.

What brings people together?

What is it that encourages us to seek other people's company? Michael Argyle claims that there are at least seven basic drives, aimed at different goals, which spur us on to develop relationships with others. The simplest and most primitive kind is the drive which aims to satisfy biological or financial needs: sometimes people are drawn together in a common task in order to survive, or to live more successfully. That (as we shall see in chapter eight) was the origin of civilization: human beings in Mesopotamia clearly found that they coul organize the irrigation of their fields muc more effectively when they worked togethe rather than competing for strips of land. Fr there it was a short step to the emergence cities and more sophisticated forms of operation. And the same drive towards asso

tion continues today when, for ex form business partnerships w alongside, others to whom th naturally be drawn.

The second main impulse behaviour is something that beg life: dependency. Children n dependency on their parents, of life, and then have to be away from it as they grow up run along and play with t process which (in Western tends to be especially empnasi rather than girls. But the urge towards depend-ency can reassert itself, especially when we are in new and bewildering situations, or unsure of our acceptability. (This is why often a new student at college will link up with a more experienced one, and why a relatively plain girl will often make friends with a more attractive, assured and confident one.)

But why does the pretty girl want the plain one's company? Perhaps it is because of another of the drives: dominance. Many people have a need for power, or recognition, or ...ment: to make contact with others who ... messages about our ...f meeting these needs. ... most in groups, develop ... their ideas considered, ... hostility to others who ...t too. Not that everybody ... in the same way: someone ...ublic speaker, and derives ...rom the authority he can ...ence, may be ill at ease and ...us party.

...other of his seven drives 'the ...'. This means the hunger we ...mate relationships with close ... which propels us to strike up ... strangers. This urge probably ...dhood experiences of parental ...sychopaths who have no under-...ection often have a background ...aternal love). In Western culture ...d it easier to indulge this urge ...ut together in the same room to ...some simple engineering task, a ...ls achieved very little, but by the ...session knew all about one another; ...boys in the same situation were still ...ngers at the end of the session, but ...d much more effectively together.

...ree remaining drives are: sex (which ... the urge to flirt, to find romance, to ... the opposite sex, to reassure oneself ...e's self-worth by making casual 'con-...; aggression (which leads people to ...n relationships with each other very ... when, for instance, they crash into one ...r at traffic lights!); and self-esteem (the ... to find approval in the reactions of ...). All these factors draw human beings ...her.

...ut how do we behave when we actually meet?

When we first encounter another human being, both parties will have at least one of the motivations we have discussed, which will decide what they hope to gain from the encounter. Both will also possess a certain number of social skills: ways of acting towards

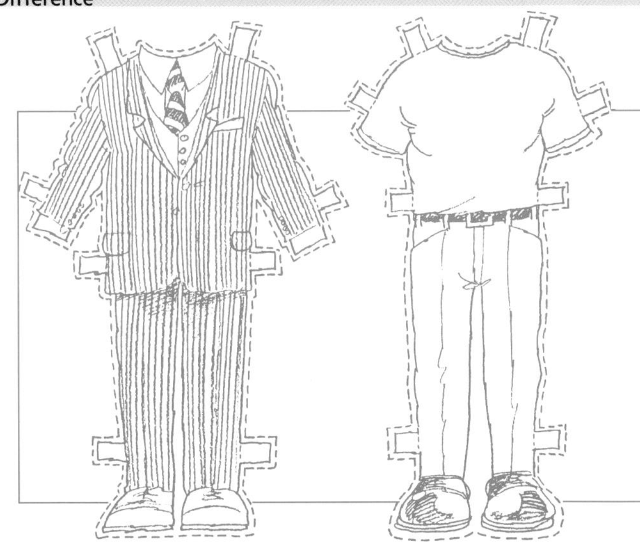

other people which they have gradually adapted, perfected and copied from others, through their years of growing up. Each will have learnt to perceive small cues in the other person's behaviour which give hints about how the relationship is developing; they will know how to use the right vocabulary and manner for the sort of relationship that is being built (you don't address your husband's employer as you would your hairdresser). Let's hope they understand how to talk in the right places, leave pauses of the right length, strike the right impression of interested attention without appearing too inquisitive. All these skills we naturally pick up as we go through life, without ever thinking too hard about them. What happens next is described by Michael Argyle:

A and B size each other up, in terms of their own private category systems, and select from their repertoire of social skills accordingly. It is almost certain that these two initial patterns of behaviour will not fit. . . it is very likely that one or both will find the other's behaviour not entirely satisfactory, in relation to his own need system. Both will be under some pressure to modify the state of affairs; they may change their own behaviour in order to synchronize better, or may attempt to change the other's behaviour. There is continual modification of behaviour until a state of equilibrium, more or less satisfactory to both parties, is arrived at.

What both A and B are doing here, as they chat with one another, is to think constantly: 'If I were him, what would I want me to say next? What would I expect?' George H. Mead has called this 'taking on the role of the other'. We say something which we think will elicit a certain response. If we get that response, we say something else along the same lines. If we don't, we swiftly change direction and try a different approach, until we find one which works. If everything we say brings a response we do not expect, we eventually retire baffled, and say to others, 'I really don't understand him.' We do not feel easy in our minds about our relationship with someone else until we can, at least partially, predict how that person is likely to react to what we say.

Mead points out that most human relationships are not simple two-way interactions. We do not take on the rest of the world one at a time. It is more like playing a game of football, where the man with the ball at his feet has to pay attention to the reactions of a whole number of different people at once—the opposing defenders, his own side, the goalkeeper ahead of him, the referee. And so our attitudes and actions become shaped, not by one person at one time, but by the normal, predictable reactions of all the people with whom we come into contact—what Mead calls the 'generalized other'. 'The attitude of the generalized other is the attitude of the whole community.'

So the behaviour of human beings is

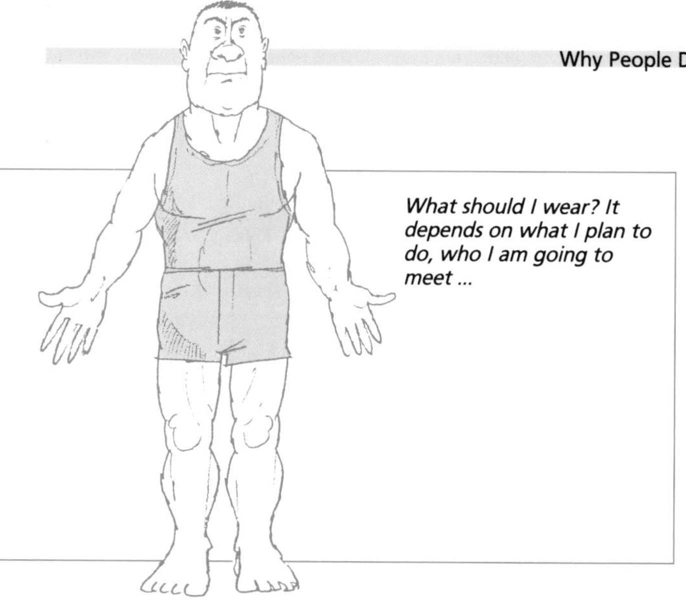

dominated, not just by their own free impulses, but by the reactions they expect to get from everyone else. This can affect even their deepest beliefs. Peter Berger has written of the 'plausibility structure' we all need to make our beliefs tenable. If there are others around me who believe as I do, I will not find it difficult to keep my views on life intact. But if suddenly I am plunged into a community that thinks differently and operates on different priorities (if, for instance, I am a Central African witchdoctor suddenly transplanted to New York, or a very young Christian in an army guardroom), I may suffer a tremendous shock to my whole mental system, and may in the end succumb to the ideas of those around me.

In 1830 four primitive South American Indians were brought back to England by the captain of the British exploring vessel *Beagle*. The aim was to 'civilize' them so that they could bring enlightened ways to their own people. Sure enough, with the exception of one who had died, the Indians returned completely altered, well dressed, proud of their immaculate appearance, and determined to settle in their former society with a new style.

A year later, when the *Beagle* returned to Tierra del Fuego, one of the 'civilized' Indians approached in his canoe. Charles Darwin, who was there, was amazed to see that he had become 'a thin haggard savage, with long disordered hair, and naked, except a bit of blanket around his waist... I never saw so complete and grievous a change'. None of the returned Indians had managed to retain their Europeanized ways. And some years later the 'savage' in the canoe was responsible for the massacre of six missionaries.

Putting on the style

If it is true that we act in ways which we think will please others, then obviously there is a certain amount of contrivance and pretence involved in our behaviour. Social anthropologist Erving Goffman has analyzed the 'personal front' which we all put forward to the world, in the hope that others will see what we want them to see, rather than what is really there.

The same woman who would die if anyone came to the door will look immaculate when she goes for a job interview.

We present quite differently, and feel different about ourselves, depending on our standing in comparison with the other person.

We want to manipulate their perception of us just a bit: to control the feelings that they will have about us. (And so the lady who has worked for hours to prepare a marvellous meal will strive to give the impression that it is 'just a few bits and pieces thrown together, really'; the boy who is quite capable of ironing his own shirts will pretend to be helpless in order to awaken his girlfriend's maternal instincts; and I will try to write this book in a smooth, flowing, effortless way that will totally conceal the sweat and agony that went into its construction.) Because we all know that others are playing the same game as ourselves, we accept the rules of the game. As Goffman puts it:

A tacit agreement is maintained between performers and audience to act as if a given degree of opposition and of accord existed between them. Typically, but not always, agreement is stressed and opposition is underplayed. . . Sometimes disruptions occur through unmeant gestures, faux pas, *and scenes, thus discrediting or contradicting the definition of the situation that is being maintained. . . We find that performers, audience, and outsiders all utilize techniques for saving the show, whether by avoiding likely disruptions or correcting for unavoided ones, or by making it possible for others to do so.*

This kind of 'performance' is not the same thing as the show put on by a confidence trickster, who is actually involved in a kind of double bluff—a performance of a performance. Goffman wryly comments, 'Perhaps the real crime of the confidence man is not that he takes money from his victims but that he robs all of us of the belief that middle-class manners and appearance can be sustained only by middle-class people.' Few of us are totally cynical about our 'performance', although this does happen occasionally, as when an obsequious waiter secretly despises his overbearing customers, or a *nouveau riche* rock star smashes up hotel rooms simply because that's what rock stars do. But then few of us are completely fooled by ourselves either; we know that we are presenting our 'best side'. And it is unsettling when we meet someone who 'believes his own publicity': the businessman, for example, who has surrounded himself with 'yes men' for so long that he now imagines he really is as dynamic, witty and brilliant as he pretends to be.

WHY DO WE WORK?

For most human beings in the Western world, work occupies nearly a third of our lives. Most of us need to work, to earn money to help us survive; but this is not the only reason we work. Unemployed people can feel a great emptiness in their lives as a result of having no work to do. Pools winners sometimes go back to their previous badly-paid jobs, even though they do not need the money any more, rather than exist without work. And management analysts who have explored ways of motivating people to work better tell us that more pay is not the answer. People do not work simply for money.

In his book *The Psychology of Work*, psychiatrist Donald Scott says that the true reasons are complex. 'Though man has the same basic drives as monkeys there are many other goals which are important. . . In addition his motives may often be mixed.' Scott distinguishes between conscious motives—such as achievement, self-assertiveness, mastery, gregariousness—and unconscious motives, fuelled by drives which we may not realize are there. For example, Freud saw the sex-drive as being extremely important in our functioning. Not all of it can be used up by 'love-objects'; in other words, the drive produces some spare energy which is left undirected. Scott explains that one way in which sexual energy can be used up is 'by sublimation, that is, it may be directed towards another end, so that states of high activity and high drive may appear'. Work is one way of using up the spare energy.

Some religious cults of the 1970s managed to extract astonishingly high work rates from some of their followers, by systematically focusing their attention on sex, and then frustrating their desires; so perhaps this theory is right. But whatever the psychological explanation, the Bible claims that work is something natural and necessary to humankind. In the Garden of Eden story, humans were involved in work activities before the Fall, that rebellion against God which brought disharmony into creation. Work is therefore part of God's good creation, not a 'necessary evil'. Christian psychologist Paul Tournier insists that 'the meaning of man's work is the satisfaction of the instinct for adventure that God has implanted in his heart'.

Work is not always like this for people today. Karl Marx complained that capitalist society has 'alienated' human beings from the true satisfaction they should feel in their work; he maintained that only revolution could alter this state of affairs. Work dehumanized people: 'The activity of the worker is not his own spontaneous activity. It belongs to another and is the loss of himself'. Communism, on the other hand, would be 'the re-integration or return of man into himself, the abolition of man's self-alienation'.

Christians would agree with much of Marx's critique of the modern industrial system. But they would raise three objections:

- Socialist countries do not appear to be having much greater success than capitalist ones in making workers fulfilled through their labour. There are just as dreary, pointless lives of labour to be lived in Eastern Europe as anywhere else.
- Although economic forces are important in determining the quality of human life, they are not the only things that matter. Work is important, but not ultimate.
- Work needs to have a meaning which goes beyond this present world. It finds value only in the context of a relationship with a God of purpose and creativity. Says Tournier, 'Man is seen to be a spiritual being in the very act of his desire to understand the meaning of things, the meaning of the world, of life, and to understand the meaning of his own work so as to be able to see the part played in the whole, in the destiny of the world, by his own personal contribution.'

In fact most of us tend to oscillate between cynicism and sincerity, not quite confusing our 'performance' with our real selves, yet tending to become more convinced by it as time passes. Robert Park observes:

Everyone is always and everywhere, more or less consciously, playing a role... It is in these roles that we know each other; it is in these roles that we know ourselves.

In a sense, and in so far as this mask represents the conception we have formed of ourselves—the role we are striving to live up to—this mask is our truer self, the self we would like to be. In the end our conception of our role becomes second nature and an integral part of our personality. We come into the world as individuals, achieve character, and become persons.

When we encounter somebody else's performance, we will either warm to them or dislike them. What is it that makes us like people?

Physical attractiveness undeniably has a lot to do with it. We have higher expectations of good-looking people than of the unattractive. Two American researchers in 1972 discovered that this principle even affects the way teachers

WHY DO WE PLAY GAMES?

Games are pointless. There is nothing to be gained by propelling a small white ball over miles of grass so as to lodge it in tiny holes in the ground. For thirty intelligent professional people to devote their Saturday afternoons to hurling themselves at one another, rolling in the mud, all to move a leather ball from one end of a field to the other, is a remarkable waste of time. So why do we do it? What are games for?

'They recreate the freedom, the remembered perfection of childhood,' says Christopher Lasch, 'and mark it off from ordinary life with artificial boundaries, within which the only constraints are the rules to which the players freely submit. Games enlist skill and intelligence, the utmost concentration of purpose, on behalf of activities utterly useless...'

Games give us a chance to withdraw from daily life into an imaginary conflict, in which there are defeats, triumphs, miracles, tragedies, frustrations and panics —just like reality—except that none of it matters. The game allows full expression to all the emotions we are capable of—but also the knowledge that at the end of the afternoon, when the whistle is blown, we will not have to live with those emotional states any longer. Games are a holiday from everyday worries.

They can also help to prepare us for situations we have not met yet, or give us a chance to try out roles we cannot normally try out in life (it is not unknown for mild-mannered little men to turn into aggressive tigers when let loose on the football field). These are uses that we have had for games since our earliest years, according to psychologist Gordon Lowe.

Children take play seriously, so seriously that it has been described as the work of children. In play, the child moves from the known to the untried and unknown. Play involves risk, mastery by repetition and practice, and problem-solving. The child may use it as a vehicle for other feelings, such as self-assertion, the expression of otherwise forbidden impulses, and as a way of revealing his own nature. So far from being an idle pastime, play trains the child in social relationships.

Games can be found in human civilizations right back to the earliest days of history. At one time many of them were unrestricted by too many rules—about the number of players per side, for example, or the area within which the game must be played. Then came the nineteenth century, that great age of rule-making, when bodies were formed to run individual sports, and codes of rules were drawn up. Now, some would say, games are becoming more individual and unbounded in their emphasis: instead of staying within the confines of a court or a pitch, pitting themselves against other humans, twentieth-century people have taken to hang-gliding, wind-surfing, abseiling; pitting themselves against the elements—and against themselves.

Are we taking games too seriously? Jan Huizinga's famous book *Homo Ludens* claims that we are. Work, he maintains, has become routine drudgery for many people. It is abstract and impersonal, and any element of 'play' has dropped out of it. And so people turn to games with unusual intensity, seeking sensation and controversy. This is why there is football violence, and why tennis players become heroes by swearing at umpires. Games have been given an artificial, inflated importance, because we all need to play.

treat their pupils. 'Evidence seems to indicate,' they reported, 'that academic grades given to students are influenced by the attractiveness of the child.' And also: 'When shown a set of children's pictures and asked to identify the child who probably created the classroom disturbance (or some similar act of misconduct), adults were likely to select an unattractive child as the offender.'

Another factor is the amount of time people spend together. When people are thrown together over a period of time, working in the same office, for example, they may well become friendly enough to set up further chances to meet outside their normal meetings (going out on the town together once a year). Familiarity through exposure increases people's attractiveness, which is why boys marry the girl next door, and bosses fall for their secretaries. A few years ago, lectures at Oregon State University were attended by an unknown student encased in a large black sack, with only his feet showing. It was part of an attempt to investigate student attitudes. The outcome was that the demeanour of the other students changed, from initial hostility, to growing curiosity, to eventual friendship with the man in the bag. When he became a familiar sight, he was no longer a threat.

But the main reason for liking others is that in some way they offer us a reward. Their company may stimulate us, or flatter us; their interest in us and care for us may bolster our self-confidence; their sharing our opinions may make us feel more intelligent, more secure in what we believe. And so it is not surprising that we tend to be attracted most to people like ourselves. They can talk to us most interestingly about the things that mutually absorb us, and provide social support for our attitudes and views.

What about 'opposite poles attract'? This holds true only in some kinds of relationship: a friendship based on dominance and submission, for example (such as the shy girl and pretty girl we mentioned earlier). And even when onlookers see two people as 'opposites', they may in fact be conscious of great undetected similarities between them, on which they base their friendship. But people who genuinely are opposites tend to stay apart.

Falling in love

So much for liking. What about love? Most of us know the earth-shattering sensation of being hopelessly besotted with one other human being. It is estimated (I have no idea how) that at any one moment there will be 1,680,466,201 human beings in love, and 424 million more recovering

from a past love affair. What is it based on? Why do we fall in love?

Clearly physical attraction has something to do with it, but different races and cultures look for different qualities. Fat calves, not a sign of beauty in Europe, are much prized among the Tiv of Nigeria. Kuwaitis like girls with a gap between their top front teeth. Black teeth attract the Trobriand Islanders, and extremely big hips are a distinct asset in Hawaii. There seems to be no one generally-agreed human definition of attractiveness.

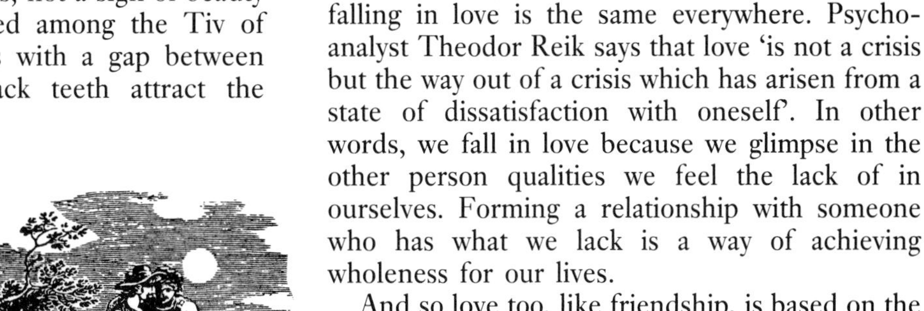

But the psychological mechanism involved in falling in love is the same everywhere. Psychoanalyst Theodor Reik says that love 'is not a crisis but the way out of a crisis which has arisen from a state of dissatisfaction with oneself'. In other words, we fall in love because we glimpse in the other person qualities we feel the lack of in ourselves. Forming a relationship with someone who has what we lack is a way of achieving wholeness for our lives.

And so love too, like friendship, is based on the idea of rewards. This also explains why people often fall out of love: the potential rewards in a love relationship are so great that it places a great strain on the couple's ability to relate their behaviour to one another. They need to synchronize their reactions very closely for the intimacy to continue, and of course few people get it right all the time. And so there are lovers' quarrels, episodes of kiss-and-make-up, cooling-off periods, and a general oscillation between intimacy and withdrawal as the relationship progresses. Engagement and marriage are useful social customs for one reason at least: they act as markers in an otherwise confusing, shifting situation, signalling to the couple concerned (and to everybody else) what stage the relationship has reached.

Something very like 'falling in love' happens in another major human behaviour upheaval: conversion. Why should someone's opinions suddenly go through a dramatic change of direction? No animal has ever had a Damascus Road experience, as the apostle Paul did; or left its settled background to live in a completely different way, like the Buddha. Yet human beings do have these sudden alterations of experience. A surprising number of people die as martyrs because of their Christian experience of conversion—something no other species will ever do. Why? Can we explain what is happening in conversion?

The answer is: yes and no. It is possible to see the human factors involved in a conversion to Hinduism, say, or Marxism or animal rights. But to explain such factors does nothing to invalidate the experience. We can examine the psychology of someone who has fallen in love, and find reasons to explain why it happened with that specific person at that precise time; but the data we collect will tell us nothing about whether the lover was *right* to attach himself to the object of his devotion. Whether or not he has made a mistake is something we will have to decide on other grounds.

In the same way, we can trace what human reasons were involved in a person's conversion to Islam, or fascism; but this does not tell us whether that person was right or wrong to embrace those beliefs. Christians claim (as we shall see in chapter nine) that when people become Christians, something supernatural takes place as God's power enters their lives. And even when we can see psychological reasons prompting a person's conversion to Christianity, there may still be another level of explanation: God revealing himself in that person's experience in an unmistakable way.

William Sergeant's famous book *Battle for the Mind* tried to link the mechanism of conversion with the kind of psychological conditioning to which Pavlov subjected his dogs. We saw in chapter four that this raises more questions than it answers; human brains are too complex to respond to simple stimuli in the same way as dogs. Although it is possible for dramatic, manipulative conversion techniques to 'condition' people for a while, by using such weapons as fear, excitement, exhaustion and repetitive indoctrination, no genuinely lasting results come in this way. (Chris Elkins, whom we quoted earlier, counsels the parents of cult members not to despair: 50 per cent of all members eventually leave the group, many walking away of their own free will. The 'harmony and blissful love is something that rarely lasts. Disillusionment is common. . .')

In fact, what happens in genuine conversion seems to be very close to the experience of falling in love. Social psychiatrist James Brown comments:

Religious conversion, considered from the psychological point of view, may take the form of filling a vacuum which has caused dissatisfaction with the existing personality in which case it supplies, as it were, the missing piece of the puzzle; or it may take the form of substitution of one piece for another which may have been lying dormant for years. . . The individual convert, in fact, is the man or woman in search of the system of beliefs which will integrate him more closely with what he regards as reality. They are not forced upon him by anybody, and the teacher is the occasion rather than the cause of his conversion.

Human beings are not robots who can easily be tinkered with. There is a genuine unpredictability about each individual we encounter. We can trace patterns in behaviour, as we have done in this chapter, and understand some of the mechanisms which make people act in society as they do. But however much we learn, there will always be the thrill of discovery and the anticipation of surprise whenever we meet a stranger. For every human being is different. And that is what makes social life so interesting.

WOMEN AND MEN

One of the most basic facts about human beings is sex. We come in two varieties. And in most cultures throughout history, the most important question deciding a baby's future destiny has been: is it a boy or a girl? Because we have very different roles in life for men and women to play.

Throughout history, it has usually been women who have had the worse of the arrangement. Men can be given so much power, so much attention, so much indulgence, that a woman starts to feel she has no real personality left. One has written:

When I am by myself, I am nothing. I only know that I exist because I am needed by someone who is real, my husband, and by my children. My husband goes out into the real world. Other people recognize him as real, and take him into account. He affects other people and events. He does things and changes things, which are different afterwards. I stay in this imaginary world in this house, doing jobs that I largely invent, and that no one cares about but myself. I do not change things. The work I do changes nothing; what I cook disappears, what I clean one day must be cleaned again the next. I seem to be involved in some sort of mysterious process rather than actions that have results.

And so one of the most important questions we must ask in this book is 'What are women *for*?' It is a question being asked with more and

Philippines' president Corrie Aquino has revealed an ability to touch the heart of a nation wounded by dictatorship. This spirituality, this sensitivity to emotion, is perhaps a gift women are particularly suited to bring to leadership.

Benazir Bhutto, Margaret Thatcher, Indira Gandhi — this generation has provided many national leaders who are women. Has this opened up greater opportunities for women in the nations they lead?

more urgency by women in Western society today.

The modern 'Women's Movement' owes a lot to a crusading book written in 1963 by Betty Friedan, a woman who had built her career out of writing for women and trying to interpret what they were really looking for. At first she had accepted the idea that women were most fulfilled when they followed the usual career path of marriage, motherhood, housewifery. Then she started to become aware of the existence of 'the problem that has no name'—the unspoken despair which existed among thousands of women who had done all the usual things and felt themselves losing touch with reality as a result. As one mother of four confessed to her:

I love the kids and Bob and my home. There's no problem you can even put a name to. But I'm desperate. I begin to feel I have no personality. I'm a server of food and a putter-on of pants and a bedmaker, somebody who can be called on when you want something. But who am I?

And so Betty Friedan wrote her book, *The Feminine Mystique*, to ask whether or not Western civilization had got it wrong. Since the Second World War it had been taught subtly by all the women's magazines, TV programmes and novels that a woman's real fulfilment lay in ministering to the needs of her husband and children; a glamorous 'mystique' had surrounded the role of housewife, which in fact was a boring, humdrum and often dehumanizing job, and it was time the 'mystique' was exposed for the lie it was. These kinds of societal arrangements were not the only way to carry on male-female relationships.

On that point at least, Betty Friedan was right. Anthropologists have shown that other human societies have sometimes had a different view of women, and would not accept the idea that women must be submissive, self-effacing, passive creatures. Margaret Mead, for example, studied three primitive societies which had very different notions. In one, the Arapesh, both men and women alike were 'feminine' and 'maternal' in personality; among the Mundugumor, both men and women were violent, aggressive, and 'masculine' in the way they behaved; and the Tchambuli expected the woman to be dominant and aggressive while the man was less responsible and emotionally dependent.

There are also societies in which the clear distinction of 'male' and 'female' is sometimes blurred. Among the Xaniths of Oman, for instance, there is almost a sense of being a 'third sex'. Xaniths are male homosexual prostitutes whose whole behaviour is female, and who are allowed by the rules of society to act in ways forbidden to other men—for example, talking freely to women in the street. Are they men or women? Biologically there is no doubt. Socially, it is not so easy to decide.

Telling them apart

Obviously we need to ask some very basic questions. Why are there sex differences anyway? What is a 'man', what is a 'woman', and precisely what differences are there between them?

When a baby is born, the first question people ask is about the child's sex. The way in which we tell is to examine the genitals. If a baby has a penis, it is a boy; if a vagina, it is a girl. Is this the way to distinguish 'male' and 'female'?

Not necessarily. There are plenty of species (birds, for example) in which the male has no penis. What is more, most of the time we cannot see one another's genitals—because clothes cover them up. Yet we have no difficulty in recognizing men from women. Clearly there is a complex set of signals and cues which allow us to work out the answer without inspecting each other's private parts.

In professional sporting events, men and women are sorted out by means of a 'sex test', which examines the sex chromosomes. All of us have forty-six chromosomes, of which all but two are organized into pairs. These two are called the sex chromosomes; in a woman they are identical, but in a man one is longer than the other.

Then are the chromosomes what finally distinguish male from female? Again, not always. Fish, amphibians and birds have the opposite arrangement: the male carries the identical chromosomes. And, confusingly, in some animals sex does not depend on chromosome differences at all, but on environment. A fish that would be female in some circumstances turns into a male when put somewhere else!

But there is one vital, general difference, which helps us to establish definitely what the difference is between male and female. It is a question of the 'germ cells' which an animal produces. If it produces a cell which contains food and is immobile, this is an 'egg cell' and the animal is female. If it produces a cell which is mobile, and contains no food resources, this is a 'sperm cell' and the animal is male.

The obvious question is: Why sex anyway? Plenty of living organisms reproduce by budding, or cloning, or hermaphroditical means (an individual creature producing both egg cells and sperm cells). Wouldn't this have been a better arrangement?

There are clearly lots of disadvantages in sexual reproduction. Budding or cloning produces a perfect copy of the parent; sex involves twice as much energy, from two individuals instead of one, and mixes up the genetic material contributed by both parents, creating a risk that the baby animal will suffer unexpected defects. And when we think about the time spent on courtship, the emotional and biological turmoil involved (for human beings at any rate), it all seems a complicated business.

Yet species that reproduce sexually have made much more progress and adapted to many more different conditions than others. So perhaps sex is actually an advantage to beings like us?

There are no definite answers. But many scientists point out that sex is a way of producing as much variation as possible in the next generation—and that means adaptability. If a species is to make itself at home in as many changing situations as possible, the more varied its offspring are the better. So sexual reproduction increases our chances of survival.

What is the difference?

It makes sense, then, that sex differences should exist. But are these differences just a matter of our role in reproduction? Or does

HOW DO I LOOK?

'I have this problem,' complains Professor Erica Abeel. 'Despite the consciousness revolution of the past five years, I still feel that I have to look beautiful. Men can look any old way.'

Why is this? Bertrand Russell once remarked that 'on the whole, women tend to love men for their character while men tend to love women for their appearance'. Men set a great deal of store by female beauty. (And they always have: psychologist Rita Freedman points out that even in the ancient ruins of Catal, in Asia Minor, we have found male burial sites full of weapons—and female burial sites full of jewellery and cosmetic devices.) This has created 'looksism'—'a form of social control that influences how people see themselves and how they are seen by others'. Women have to be pretty to make an impression on those around them. Otherwise, they have to be quite exceptional people.

This has been demonstrated in many ways. A 1966 survey of five hundred couples, who were asked the qualities they would look for in a 'date' and then paired up on that basis, showed that while women looked for a variety of qualities—good education, popularity, religious affinity—men insisted that their date must be good-looking.

Personnel interviewers tend subconsciously to grade women according to their looks, too. A number of them were shown the career details of a group of women, each with a photograph attached—in some cases before the woman concerned had undergone cosmetic treatment, and in some cases afterwards. It was found that the interviewer's

From Rubens nudes, through the covered Arab girl's face, to the fit young Western girl, the image of female attractiveness varies greatly from culture to culture.

being 'male' or 'female' affect our behaviour, so that we can expect boys and girls to show different traits and characteristics purely because of their sex?

Scientists are divided about this. Some claim that, yes, the biological differences do bring about inescapable personality differences along with them; boys are made differently from girls, and there is no way of escaping that. In

professional assessment of a woman's likely earning power would rise by as much as 12 per cent if the 'after' picture was studied rather than the 'before' one.

'Looksism' starts when we are children. Says Dr James Dobson, 'We adults respond very differently to an unusually beautiful child than to a particularly unattractive one, and that difference has a profound impact on a developing personality.' Thus appearance becomes desperately important even to a young girl. Clothes count for a lot; which is why a *New York Times* editorial asked in bewilderment, 'Why does a fourteen-year-old Brooklyn girl need to spend $40 on a manicure and $700 on pants, sweaters, headbands and make-up to complete her back-to-school wardrobe?'

The effects of 'looksism' can vary enormously. It is feared by educationalists that many bright teenage girls subconsciously decide to underachieve at school, simply because being good at science or maths is not very 'feminine'. On the other hand, some will try harder for academic success as a compensation for lack of beauty: a study of remarkably successful women, all with six-figure incomes, showed that most of them had been embarrassed about their unattractiveness when they were girls.

An extremely serious modern psychological problem is the 'slimmer's disease', *anorexia nervosa*, which has the highest mortality rate of any psychiatric illness, and is estimated to affect one female in a hundred between the ages of twelve and twenty-five. One psychologist explains what motivates anorexics in this way:

Their obsessive pursuit of thinness constitutes an acceptance of the feminine ideal, and an exaggerated striving to achieve it. Their attempts to control their physical appearance demonstrate a disproportionate concern with pleasing others, particularly men—a reliance on others to validate their sense of worth.

If our society cannot find ways of valuing people for what they are, rather than for the qualities they possess—whether beauty, brains or athletic ability—women will always be condemned to struggle against a stereotype which tries to shape their life. And for some of them, the struggle will end in death.

1972 John Money and A.A. Eerhardt claimed that sex hormones affect the brain before birth, and produce psychological differences which will show up in behaviour later. They claimed that a group of girls who had been exposed to the hormone testosterone before birth had become 'tomboys' with less maternal interests than other girls, and a streak of athletic competitiveness which made them enjoy playing with boys more than with girls.

But the way the researchers carried out these investigations has been criticized, and their results cannot be regarded as conclusive.

Other researchers would argue strongly that none of the differences between boys and girls are inbuilt and fundamental; the personality differences which emerge are merely a matter of the expectations of society. We all go through a variety of learning experiences—punishments and rewards, watching people whom we are encouraged to take as models, absorbing attitudes from our parents—which from our very earliest days give us a clear impression of the kind of behaviour society expects from a 'boy' or a 'girl'. It is because we live in such an environment that boys and girls turn out the way they do.

A third group of researchers would object that the first two both make the same mistake. They are treating the new human being as a totally passive object, simply driven by internal urges (in one version) or moulded by environment (in the other). But human beings come to understand their environment as they interact with it—trying out experiments, asking themselves questions, assessing messages that come from others. We arrive in the world with no set ideas about 'male' and 'female', but very quickly learn that there are two classifications of people. We use this fact as a way of making sense of the world, and deciding how we ourselves should act. And as we grow older, gradually the classification grows more and more elaborate, and we gain a more and more decided view of what it means to be 'a boy' or 'a girl'.

It all happens very quickly. When in 1978 some researchers gave 2–3-year-old children two paper dolls, one called Michael and the other Lisa, and asked them to imagine their activities and characteristics, they found that even at this early age the children had wide-

ranging ideas about which activities were 'right' for boys or girls, and how they would behave in a variety of situations.

There is no conclusive way of deciding between these three expert viewpoints. Perhaps each contains a part of the truth. There does seem to be some indication that at least some characteristics may be 'born into' the different sexes. An extra Y-chromosome can make men very aggressive, for instance, while an extra X-chromosome tends to undermine their masculinity. So it must be wrong to assume that all differences in attitudes and behaviour are the result of society imposing artificial sexual stereotypes.

Are girls and boys different by nature? Or are some of the differences caused by their parents' expectations?

Then what differences is it possible to trace between men and women? For one thing, men are 'less average' than women. In other words, it is in the male sex that extreme examples (of brilliance or idiocy, of tall or diminutive stature) are more likely to occur. And although males are generally bigger and stronger than females, women have a capacity for survival which men do not equal. Right throughout life—both in modern nations and developing countries, except where women have an extremely hard time—more males are dying than females of the same age. The United States census lists sixty-four specific causes of death. Of these, just two show a higher rate among females than among males, and five show about the same level; but for fifty-seven causes of death in the list, the toll of male deaths is greater than the female total.

Psychologically, there are only four traits where there seems to be a sex difference of some kind: girls have greater **verbal ability** than boys, although this does not show through until about the age of eleven; boys are better in **visual-spatial ability** than girls (for example, in seeing patterns in seemingly meaningless, unconnected lines on a piece of paper), and again this starts to appear in adolescence; teenage boys increase in **mathematical skills** faster than girls of the same age; and from the age of two onwards, males display more **aggression** and competitiveness than girls.

Women have a slightly different emotional make-up too, since the menstrual cycle each month can produce mood swings which men do not suffer. Too much can be made of this and it should never be used as an excuse to deny women jobs for which they are well qualified; it is not true that it impairs a woman's ability to think logically and make rational decisions. But 'pre-menstrual tension' is a reality. It is at this time in the monthly cycle that half of all females admitted to hospital will be taken there; that half of the females involved in serious accidents will have their mishap; and that most acts of suicide and violence committed by women will occur.

Are there other differences between men and women? Some would say that women are more responsive to sounds than men (mother will wake up when baby cries, father will snore peacefully through it all); and that men have a greater sexual *drive* (which makes them more impatient and hungry for gratification) while women have a greater sexual *capacity* (says Kate Millett, 'While the male's sexual potential is limited, the female's appears to be biologically almost inexhaustible'). But it has to be stressed that all these differences are relatively minor, and provide no excuse for the drastic judgments that have sometimes been made about the male-female divide. Socrates regarded a woman as an 'imperfect' man; St Thomas Aquinas said that a woman was 'defective and misbegotten', and that the birth of girl babies could sometimes be explained by the hostile influence of an adverse south wind!)

A woman executive has to work harder to maintain her position.

Why males dominate

It is noticeable, however, that throughout history men have tended to dominate women. There are plenty of examples of societies in which men have treated women as inferior menials; there are few examples of 'matriarchies', that is, societies in which the positions of leadership and authority are given to women rather than men. Even cases which seem to be exceptions turn out, on closer inspection, to prove the rule. Among the Iroquois Indians, it is true, the women played a central role in the selection of a chief; but the chief was always a man. In ancient Egypt, Queen Hatshepsut ruled the country just like a king; but in her sculptured portrait she is shown wearing a beard—as if to underline the fact that she was not acting as a woman but as an 'honorary man'. Mrs Thatcher has been one of the strongest British Prime Ministers of the twentieth century, but by far the majority of her cabinet have been males, and she has made it clear she prefers it that way.

Why do males dominate? Is it because they are bigger and stronger, and therefore capable of more strenuous, worthwhile activity? This may explain male dominance in ape societies, where there is a massive difference in size and weight between male and female, but among humans the difference is not so great, and anyway, in some male-dominated societies the women do much more arduous work. Another explanation which has been suggested is the economic one: primitive males were the hunters, and so controlled the food supply, which allowed them to assume authority over all the affairs of the tribe. But in many societies where women are treated as inferior, they—not the men—are the producers of most of the food.

There are lots of theories (Peter Farb speculates that men proved better than women at hand-to-hand combat, and so tribes in which men were dominant survived while others did not) but no certain answers. Yet the fact remains that throughout most of the history of Western society, women have been kept in a subordinate role, and have gradually

DO ALL HUMAN SOCIETIES PRACTISE MARRIAGE?

Human beings are unpredictable. Other animals may have a great variety of different mating arrangements—some coupling together just for the season, others staying together for life, others finding many mates, some even eating their mates after intercourse—but within the species we can usually expect to find absolutely uniform behaviour. Not with humans, however. We have evolved a startling variety of different customs.

In some societies one woman will have several husbands; in other societies the reverse will be true. Some cultures expect a liaison between a man and a woman to last for life; in others the arrangement will be much less permanent. Some couples are allowed to choose one another; elsewhere the family does the choosing, and the couple may not meet until the day they begin living together.

However, one thing remains true. Every single human society recognizes the need for some sort of established system to regulate relationships between men and women. There is no society in the world where promiscuity is the rule; that would threaten the proper care of the young, and gradually lead to the extermination of the society itself.

There is no culture in the world where the family does not exist, and all attempts to eliminate it have failed. In the early days of the Russian Revolution, an experiment in allowing people to form limited-term contracts with one another in place of marriage—for a few years, a few weeks, or even a single day—had to be abandoned when it was found that gangs of unwanted delinquent children were beginning to form. In an Israeli kibbutz, the children are cared for communally, and close family ties are discouraged; but even here natural family preferences keep on obstinately reasserting themselves.

Really only two forms of marriage—monogamy (one man, one woman) and polygamy (or more precisely 'polygyny': one man, several women) are common. It is sometimes claimed that polygyny has a lot of advantages: it takes care of any surplus of females in society; it provides a socially useful way of flaunting one's wealth (taking on an extra wife is better for society than buying a new Rolls Royce); and it allows socially superior males to father more children than the incompetent, who naturally cannot afford as many wives. But this theoretical picture does not work in practice. Most polygamous societies do not in fact have a 'surplus female' problem; polyamy simply causes jealousy and inequality among men, and unfair treatment for women; and the males who are likeliest to have most wives are the old, whose powers of reproduction are failing, but who have had time to amass enough money to afford more women.

The Unification Church (the 'Moonies') believe in arranged marriage, and sometimes huge numbers are wed in one ceremony. Can this take away from the truth that one man and one woman commit themselves to each other when they marry?

In fact, monogamy is by far the most widespread form of marriage, because it offers benefits no other system does. It allows social stability and protection of the young, unlike a casual 'living together' arrangement. It allows the maximum number of individuals to be involved in marriage—unlike polygyny or polyandry (one woman, several men). It minimizes sexual jealousy and allows an intensity of relationship between two people which cannot be found anywhere else; and it simplifies inheritance, property and kinship problems. That is probably why—even in an age of marriage stress and increasing divorce figures—so many people still instinctively feel it is the best solution.

The Bible's prescription for marriage is that a man should 'leave his father and mother and be united to his wife, and they will become one flesh'. It still makes sense.

been struggling towards equality. As far back as 1700, Mary Astel wrote:

If all Men are born free, how is it that all Women are born slaves? As they must be if the being subjected to the inconstant, uncertain, unknown, arbitrary Will of Men, be the perfect Condition of Slavery?

Even in a society where there is theoretically equality of opportunity for men and women, the unseen pressures of our social environment can condition us to behave in certain accepted, safe, unequal ways. As Betty Friedan has written:

When girls are invited to undertake domestic chores 'just like Mummy', the utensils on offer—half-sized irons, cookers, vacuum cleaners—supply no scope for the management, marshalling and manipulation which are implicit in the public character of the boys' equivalents: toy soldiers, model railways, garages and race tracks. While boys explore an expanding range of possibilities, girls serve a brief, narrow, private apprenticeship.

Often the literature provided for children reinforces the stereotyped ideas of male dominance and female submission with which we have lived for so many centuries:

Peter has a red ball. He plays with the boys with the red ball. Jane looks on. That was good, Peter, says Jane.

Jim quite enjoyed balancing on the metal rail. Susy stood and watched him with her hand to her mouth. Susy rarely did anything else when she was with him.

'Sex stereotyping' has a profound impact on the working careers of men and women. In Britain in the late 1970s, men outnumbered women in the professions at every level. Women made up 27 per cent of practising doctors, 8 per cent of all barristers (but only 4 per cent of solicitors), 2 per cent of engineers and 1 per cent of scientists and technicians. In America the figures were even lower. In the mid-eighties Diane Souhami reported:

'Seventy-five of the seventy-eight High Court judges are men, and the Civil Service is remarkable for its concentration of women in the lowest grades. In 1984 the gross weekly earnings of women in the Civil Service averaged 66 per cent of men's. No Permanent Secretaries are women, only 4 per cent

WHERE DOES HOMOSEXUALITY COME FROM?

Until Dr A.C. Kinsey, nobody realized just how many homosexuals there were. Kinsey was an American researcher who produced two reports, *Sexual Behaviour in the Human Male* (1948) and *Sexual Behaviour in the Human Female* (1952), based on over 18,000 interviews in which he questioned people about their sexual practices. He showed conclusively that homosexuality—harbouring a sexual preference for people of the same sex as oneself—was remarkably widespread. Only 4 per cent of men were exclusively homosexual, but many men carried on homosexual and heterosexual relationships at the same time, and in all, 37 per cent of the men surveyed had had at least one homosexual experience in their adult lives.

Kinsey's findings helped to change public perceptions of homosexuality. Previously it had been dismissed as a fairly minor problem; now it came to be realized that a large proportion of the human race has homosexual inclinations. Not surprisingly, since Kinsey there have been great changes in the laws regulating homosexuality in many Western countries.

In fact not all cultures have traditionally condemned homosexual activity; in many it has been an accepted part of life. C.S. Ford and F.A. Beach surveyed anthropological literature and discovered that out of seventy-six primitive societies which were described, forty-nine condoned some form of homosexual activity. The Siwan tribe in North Africa even thought a man peculiar if he did not sleep with both males and females; and the Aranda of Australia had a custom of homosexual 'marriage' which lasted for a few years until the older partner went off and found a female instead.

What makes someone homosexual? Many homosexuals claim that they have always felt that way, that their sexuality has been with them since birth. This could mean that those who are exclusively homosexual are **born** that way, perhaps through some genetic factor; or that hormonal imbalances in their body make them **grow up** that way; or that early experiences in life **predisposed** them to become homosexuals, before they were aware of sex at all.

The search for a genetic factor has been unsuccessful. Homosexuals rarely suffer from abnormalities in their sex chromosomes, and it has not been possible to detect any linking factor in the thousands of different homosexuals who have been studied. As for hormonal imbalances, experiments have been tried in which sex offenders in prison have been dosed with androgens (male hormones) in an attempt to change their *of Deputy Secretaries, 5 per cent of Under Secretaries and 10 per cent of Principals. Unsurprisingly, however, women make up 77 per cent of clerical assistants.'*

The story of feminism

It is facts such as these that have given birth to the movement known as 'feminism'—an attempt to achieve genuine equality of opportunity and status for women. Feminism has risen to prominence twice in recent history. The first time was the late nineteenth century when on both sides of the Atlantic women campaigned for the right to vote, equality of educational opportunity, and equal status before the law. It was a long, hard fight, on both sides of the Atlantic. In America, in 1872, a group of Rochester women went to register and vote, believing that the Fifteenth Amendment to the Constitution allowed them to do so. They were promptly arrested.

Anger and resentment grew, and by the early years of the twentieth century parades, picket signs, automobile rallies and speech burnings were attracting wide attention to the cause. In Britain, the Women's Social and Political Union was formed in 1905 by Mrs Emmeline Pankhurst and her two daughters. The movement became notorious for its dramatic and even violent methods: smashing windows, pouring acid into post boxes, setting fire to empty houses, women chaining themselves to railings. When imprisoned, they refused to eat. One 'suffragette', Emily Davison, made her way to the Derby race meeting in 1913 and flung herself to her death in front of the King's horse. Christabel Pankhurst wrote in a WSPU pamphlet:

It is only simple justice that women demand. . . For fifty years they have been striving and have met with nothing but trickery and betrayal at the hands of politicians. Cabinet Ministers have taunted them with their reluctance to use the violent methods that were being used by men before they won the extension of the franchise in 1829, in 1832 and in 1867. They have used women's dislike of violence as a reason for withholding from them the rights of citizenship. . . The message of the broken pane is that women are determined that the lives of their sisters shall no longer be broken, and that in future those who have to obey the law shall have a voice in saying what the law shall be.

By the end of the First World War, the valuable part played by women in roles which had never been open to them in peacetime had convinced many people that their cause was right. Votes for women (over the age of thirty, at least) arrived in Britain in 1918, and the United States followed suit in 1920 when finally thirty-six states passed the proposed legislation.

The next wave of feminism did not arrive until the 1960s, and it was provoked by Betty Friedan's book, which we have already mentioned. (An earlier book— *The Second Sex* by Simone de Beauvoir—had helped to prepare the ground a decade before.) Betty Friedan put into words what many thousands of women had been feeling: that despite the supposed equality which now existed, society was silently coercing women into accepting a narrow, reduced view of their potential in life, by squeezing them into the mould of 'housewife and mother'. The depression and emptiness they felt was 'the

sexual orientation. The effect was certainly to increase their desire for sex—but sex of the same kind to which they were already accustomed! There was no change to heterosexuality.

It looks at the moment, then, as if the most likely cause of homosexuality is psychological. Perhaps certain home circumstances and life-shaping events conspire together to produce in some of us a desire for our own sex. Developmental psychologist Elizabeth Moberly describes the process as 'an intrapsychic wound, borne repressed within the personality since early childhood, which has checked a vital aspect of the normal process of psychological growth since that point of time'. Whatever the cause, homosexual feelings cannot easily be removed.

Different religions have different stances towards homosexuality. The Christian tradition has always rejected homosexual *conduct*, but the Bible does not condemn the homosexual *nature* —which is something that the individual can't help. Most Christians (apart from a small and vocal minority in the Gay Christian Movement) believe that God's plan for sexual life is heterosexuality, the complementarity of male and female, and therefore homosexual acts are a distortion of the sexuality God intended.

problem that had no name'. She suggested it was a direct result of the Second World War:

A pent-up hunger for marriage, home and children was felt simultaneously by several different generations; a hunger which, in the prosperity of post-war America, everyone could suddenly satisfy. . .

For the girls, these lonely (wartime) years added an extra urgency to their search for love. Those who married in the thirties saw their husbands off to war; those who grew up in the forties were afraid, with reason, that they might never have the love, the homes, and children which few women would willingly miss. When the men came back there was a headlong rush into marriage.

Was Friedan right? Her ideas have been much criticized since. Marxist feminists complain, justly, that 'she excludes working-class women from the terms of reference and never penetrates the manifestations of women's oppression through the material structure of society'. Jonathan Gathorne-Hardy points out that her analysis of what happened after the war fits America much more convincingly than other countries; there had to be more factors at work than she claims. His idea is that Betty Friedan's popularity came because society was now intensely concerned with personal fulfilment and success in living as it never had been before:

The developments of the 1950s should be viewed as the expression of a generation—the Privilege Bulge Generation—brought up under the ever-growing influence of psychoanalytic ideas and in search, therefore, of personal happiness and fulfilment. . .

What, in a general way, has happened is that, for all ages, growth has joined sex and much else as the point of any relationship, including the most important relationship—marriage.

Be that as it may, Betty Friedan's work led very rapidly to the growth of a new network of women's organizations, including consciousness-raising groups, women's publishing companies, theatre companies, counselling services for rape victims, and refuges for battered wives. Much faster than the early feminists, today's activists have made an impact on the law: the US Congress passed an Equal Rights Amendment in 1972, and the British Sex Discrimination Act of 1975 set up an Equal Opportunities Commission to ensure fairness in employment.

Broadly speaking, there are now three main groups of feminist thinkers. One is the **liberal** feminists, of whom Friedan is one. These feminists want equality, but believe they can achieve it without any fundamental changes to the status quo in society. Elaine Storkey says about them:

Liberal feminists today would still argue that emancipation can be fully achieved without any major alteration to the economic structures of contemporary capitalist democracies. Nor would we expect to find any major challenge to the patriarchal system from 'mainstream' liberal feminism. For the problem is not with systems per se*—class or patriarchal. It remains at a deep level as one of individual freedom. . .*

Marxist feminists see the problem of female equality as being deeply embedded in the repressive structures of capitalism. Women will not be equal until we achieve socialism. But many of them point out that male Marxists have often failed to take female concerns into their thinking: Sheila Rowbotham argues:

In order for Marxism to prove useful as a revolutionary weapon for women, we have at once to encounter it in its existing form and fashion it to fit our particular oppression. This means extending it into areas in which men have been unable to take it by distilling it through the particularities of our own experience.

Finally, there are **radical** feminists, for whom the problem lies deeper than the economic argument between capitalism and socialism. Even supposing we had a revolution, they argue, we would just replace a male-dominated capitalist regime with a male-dominated socialist one. The real problem is patriarchy—the oppressive attitude to women which has permeated all society's arrangements throughout history. How is patriarchy to be eradicated? Some feminists see the answer as biological (women's bodies must be freed from the responsibility of giving birth, by artificial means of reproduction); others see it as legal (increasing the protection of women against rape, the massive potential threat which has always allowed men to keep women in fear and submission); others claim it is cultural (unpicking the threads of male-dominated educational systems, and rewriting history, sociology and

Women protesting about missiles at England's Greenham Common, mothers demanding the return of their vanished children in the then military dictatorship of Argentina — a leading role in modern peacemaking and human rights is played by women.

psychology from a female perspective).

Feminists disagree with one another about a great deal, but on one topic many of them are united. They see the Bible as anti-feminist, and Christianity as a system of reaction and oppression. Are they right?

Women and the Bible

Certainly it cannot be denied that some Christian leaders have been strongly convinced of the inferiority of women. 'The woman herself alone is not the image of God,' taught Saint Augustine, 'whereas the man alone is the image of God as fully and completely as when the woman is joined with him.' 'You are the devil's gateway,' growled Tertullian, to women in general; 'you are she who first violated the forbidden tree and broke the law of God.' But statements like this are not found in the Bible itself. Indeed the Old Testament contains a memorable picture of a fulfilled, successful, creative woman (in Proverbs chapter 31), and holds her up as an example of God's ideal. And in the New Testament, Jesus gave women a place of importance among his followers which was frankly scandalous to the orthodox teachers of his day.

Some feminists have charged the Bible with anti-feminism because it presents a God who is a Father. This is patriarchal, they argue. Why not a Mother Goddess? Plenty of the nations surrounding Israel worshipped female deities. But that was the problem, argues Mary Hayter: the idea of a goddess was tied up with ecstatic fertility religions of a kind which trivialized and cheapened the Israelite understanding of God:

To them, it seemed that the only way to purge the nation of the obsessive fertility cult was to remove all notions of a Goddess from Yahwistic religion, for in the ancient Near Eastern milieu any form of Goddess worship meant opening the door to the unequivocally sensual character of the vegetation

deities... Veneration of a Goddess alongside Yahweh involved ideas and actions which thoughtful Hebrews no longer found compatible with the nature of their faith in a unique and transcendent God... Therefore, the objective of Old Testament writers was... to avoid, as far as possible, any projection of human sexuality on to their God. They believed Yahweh to be neither male nor female but supra-sexual.

It is clear from a passage in one of the apostle Paul's letters that women were allowed to pray aloud and prophesy in public in the early Christian church—an astounding liberty which would not have been allowed in the Jewish synagogues from which some of them had come. And in his letter to the Galatians, Paul recites a formula which was probably repeated at baptismal services, when a new Christian was welcomed into the Christian church:

There is neither Jew nor Greek, slave nor free, male nor female, for you are all one in Christ Jesus.

Each morning an orthodox Jew would say the *beraka*—a special prayer in which he thanked God for not making him a Gentile, a slave, or a woman. Now the Christians were saying that these kinds of distinctions—racial, economic *and sexual*—had no meaning any longer. Women and men are equals. No wonder many Christians were involved with the early feminist movements; Betty Friedan quotes a black feminist named Sojourner Truth:

Look at my arm! I have ploughed and planted and gathered into barns... and ain't I a woman? I could work as much and eat as much as a man—when I could get it—and bear the lash as well... I have borne thirteen children and seen most of 'em sold into slavery, and when I cried out with my mother's grief, none but Jesus helped me... and ain't I a woman?

Christians are not anti-feminist—or they should not be. But they would want to say to liberal feminists like Betty Friedan: are you so sure that true fulfilment comes with equal opportunity, or is it possible that the emptiness you discern in women's lives needs a deeper fulfilment yet? And to Marxists they would want to say: where is the evidence that revolution will bring female equality? Aren't the radicals right in alleging that Marxist movements so far have shown no signs of an end to male chauvinism? And to the radicals, in the words of Elaine Storkey: 'Crucial to a woman-centred utopia must be love. Self-giving, sharing and caring, patience and joy are the very building blocks of the new future... But radical feminism can provide no basis for these qualities. If gender characteristics are all socially constructed, how can any such qualities be inherent in womanhood?'

In short, equality of men and women is important, desperately important. But it will not solve all the problems of the human race in one fell swoop; nor will it be achieved by the natural goodness and altruism of human beings. It will take a transformation of human character to make it possible.

And there, Christians feel, they have some unique solutions to suggest.

THE HUMAN RECORD

If an alien in a UFO had been skimming over the surface of Planet Earth 5,000 years ago, looking for signs of civilization, he might not have been very impressed by what he found. There would have been signs of life in several places, and evidence that human beings were learning to control their environment: dogs, pigs and cattle were being domesticated, crops were being grown. Our alien would have noted groups of people on the move in search of better agricultural land and living conditions. He would have noted flat-roofed mud houses in Bulgaria, and thatched villages in Holland. Stone-built tombs were scattered across the face of Europe. But civilization in any real sense had still to arrive.

If he had come back two thousand years later, the alien would have found a lot of changes. He would see evidence of extensive city building around Egypt, the Mediterranean, India and China. The 'Fertile Crescent' in the Middle East would have presented a hive of activity—with thousands of people building, travelling, fighting, trading. Altogether, he'd be much more impressed, and slightly amazed that so much was now happening in so many places unconnected with one another.

Two thousand years after that, the contrast would be even more startling. Now human civilization could be found, not just in a few important areas, but almost everywhere on the earth's surface. The Great Wall of China would already have been straggling across the map for three centuries. Great civilizations would have risen and fallen in Africa, and even in South America—quite uninfluenced by what humans were doing anywhere else. Roman and Greek architecture could be spotted in countries whole continents apart from one another. Persia, Ethiopia, Japan, Northern Europe—

wherever he looked, our alien observer would find human beings leaving their mark on the environment. Few parts of the world would have been left undisturbed by progress.

Let's imagine that our alien was overcome with curiosity and timed his next visit for only a thousand years thereafter. What would he find today? That a revolution in agriculture, science and technology has transformed the face of this planet even more. He would see more change in this last thousand years than on any of his previous trips. And he'd note that the buildings and human artefacts on different continents showed much more similarity than ever before: that the whole of human culture has become much more unified. He would see evidence, too, that we are preparing for another major change in our control of the environment: launching pads on at least two continents, showing that human beings have developed the ability to leave their home planet and travel into space. As he flew past drifting clouds of acid rain, and glimpsed polluted lakes thick with industrial effluent, the alien would also realize that another change has taken place. Human beings have now achieved so much control of their environment that they can destroy it, too. . .

The human race has come a long way in just over five thousand years. And the story has been one of gradual acceleration; at first the changes came slowly and steadily, but bit by bit the pace of change has quickened until now it is so rapid that human beings find it hard to adjust to. Alvin Toffler has written:

Take an individual out of his own culture and set him down suddenly in an environment sharply different from his own, with a different set of cues to react to—different conceptions of time, space, work, love, religion, sex, and everything else—then cut him off from any hope of retreat to a more familiar landscape, and the dislocation he suffers is doubly severe. Moreover, if this new culture is itself in constant turmoil, and if—worse yet—its values are incessantly changing, the sense of disorientation will be still further intensified. . .

Now imagine not merely an individual but an entire society, an entire generation—including its weakest, least intelligent, and most irrational members—suddenly transported into this new world. The result is mass disorientation, future shock on a grand scale.

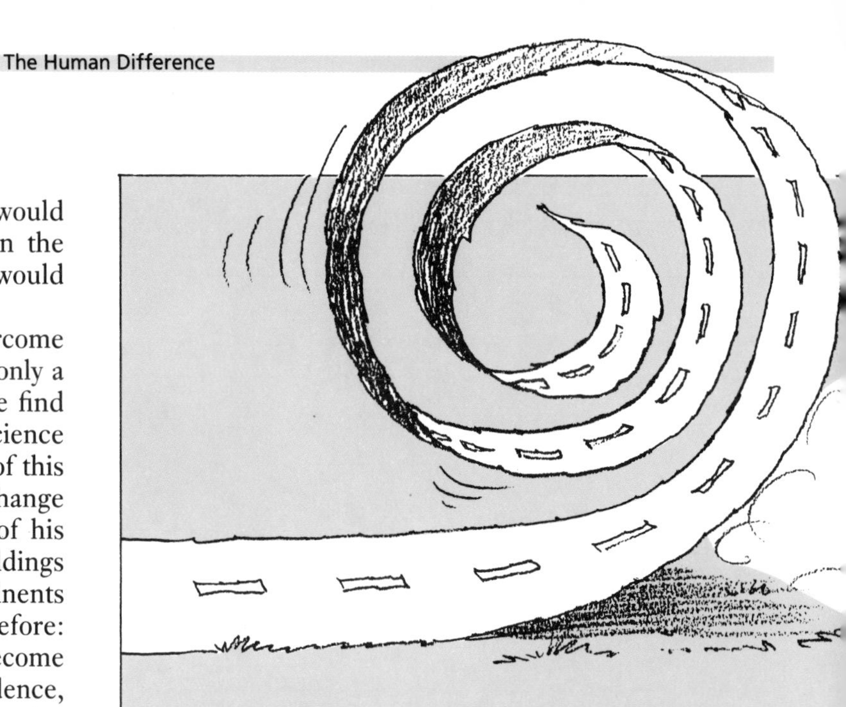

FROM AGRICULTURE TO INDUSTRY

According to an ancient Sumerian text, 'When the human species appeared, it did not know bread or cloth. Man walked on hands and feet. He ate grass with the mouth as animals do, and he drank the water of the stream.'

Just a mythical story, of course, but reminding us of something important: life has not always been this way. Human beings have gradually taken more and more command of the planet, and altered their own lives significantly in the process.

It has been claimed that 'for all but one per cent of our known existence' humanity lived by primitive hunting and gathering—relying for our survival on whatever we could find lying about. This all began to change some time after the tenth millennium BC, when human beings began living in villages, domesticating animals, and actively trying to make plants grow instead of just picking berries. This was the Agricultural Revolution, which started in the Near East and spread all over the world. Farming became the style of life of most human beings, and hunting decreased in popularity, until in the eighteenth century something new happened which made both hunting and farming secondary occupations.

This time it was the Industrial Revolution, which began in England, but in the twentieth century has affected most parts of the world. More than 80 per cent of the world's active population was engaged in agriculture in 1750. Two hundred years later it was around 60 per cent —and falling steadily.

The Industrial Revolution drew people into large towns and cities, and gave them jobs centred round machinery which increased human power over the environment to a staggering new degree. Not that everyone was involved directly in industry: unlike an agricultural society, an industrial society involves far less of its members in actual 'industry'. Instead, the industrialization allows the growth of a 'tertiary sector' of service activities—banking, insurance, government, the liberal professions.

These Revolutions were

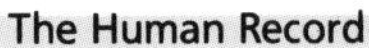

more than just twists and turns in history. They marked significant jumps ahead in the way people lived. Life changed almost overnight in the most bewildering fashion.

For one thing, the total amount of energy under human control increased enormously. Agriculture meant human control of 'chemical energy from edible plants and animals, heat from plants, power from draught animals. . . Populations expanded in size beyond any former "ceiling". . . Certain groups and classes at least became free of the continuous search for food. Specialization became possible and also higher forms of activity and leisurely speculation.' Industrialization meant completely new sources of energy—not just plants, animals and human labour—and expanded the possibilities for human life to an unimagined degree. In 1800 the world produced about 15 million tons of coal each year; by 1950 it was producing about 1,454 million tons.

All of this meant that life expectancy changed dramatically too. From what we know of pre-agricultural life, we can deduce that there was a very low density of population, with infanticide, war, headhunting and starvation frequent causes of death. In the 'agricultural' period, things were a little better, although life expectancy at birth was no more than twenty to thirty-five years, and the growth of population was slowed by recurrent waves of epidemics—clear evidence that humans had not yet completely gained control of their environment. In industrial society, famine and epidemic diseases have been successfully combatted, and the population of the world has risen dramatically. It took until 1830 for world population to reach one billion. By 1930 it had reached two billion. Now there are five billion of us, and more arriving every minute.

This is the prospect that man now faces. Change is avalanching upon our heads and most people are grotesquely unprepared to cope with it.

The story of human progress becomes even more startling if we look at the age of the earth we live on. We have really appeared very recently within history. Francis Crick has remarked that if we equate the age of the earth with a single week, 'Modern man would have appeared in the last ten seconds and agriculture in the last one or two. Odysseus would have lived only half a second before the present time.'

How have we reached our present position? Where did human civilization come from—and how has it grown? The story is almost impossible to condense into a short chapter such as this one. But perhaps we can have a look at some of its main outlines.

The first human civilizations

Around 3300BC southern Mesopotamia was a very wet place to live. Its fertile plain was bounded by two great rivers which often overflowed their banks, and the drainage from annual flooding made the soil more productive than anywhere else in the Near East. Not that life was easy; the constant peril of flooding, and the need to keep crops well irrigated when rain was infrequent, meant that systems of banking and channelling water had to be worked out with ever-increasing complexity. The land was fertile: it produced enough food to free some of the population from the necessity of working in agriculture. And irrigation channels were needed, and this forced people to work together on a large scale. Perhaps it was these two factors which led to the growth of cities, and a sophisticated pattern of life, earlier here than anywhere else.

For about a thousand years, the history of Sumer (an ancient name for the region) was a confused story of internal battles between city states led by warrior kings. But eventually—between 2400 and 2350BC—one great leader, Sargon I, conquered all the cities one by one and welded them into a unified empire. Sargon had trading links with countries as distant as the Levant and Syria, was rumoured to have sent his soldiers as far as Egypt and Ethiopia, and is said to have had 5,400 soldiers eating in his palace. The empire he built lasted for two centuries, until his great-grandson was overthrown. But Sumerian civilization continued until about 2000BC, when the central city of Ur was overthrown by invading Elamites.

The Sumerians achieved a great deal: an increasingly sophisticated system of writing; massive temples, palaces, and ziggurats; a remarkably well-thought-out legal system; and the first organized educational system in the world. But just as important was the effect they had on their neighbours. Sumerian civilization sparked off change in nations round about. One immediate result was the neighbouring empire of Babylon, which around 1792BC produced one of the greatest law-givers of ancient times, Hammurabi.

But things were stirring further west as well. Only a century or so after the rise of Sumer, a king called Menes succeeded in unifying the whole of Egypt—carving out for himself a kingdom six hundred miles long. This was the beginning of a civilization which was to last for two thousand years and span twenty dynasties of rulers.

Egyptian civilization was centred on the importance of the king. He was the supreme landowner, the source of all law, and also a divine figure. 'He is a god by whose dealings one lives, the father and mother of all men, alone by himself, without an equal,' wrote an Egyptian civil servant around 1500BC. But the king could not have kept his position without the civil service. Another Egyptian achievement was the building of an impressive bureaucracy to keep the state running, involving thousands of scribes, trained in history, writing, law, surveying and accountancy.

Writing (which took the form of hieroglyphics, much harder to learn than Sumerian cuneiform) was a skill jealously kept for the initiated few, like a trade secret. The Egyptians can take the credit for inventing papyrus, which took writing into new realms of flexibility that clay or stone tablets would not allow; without it we might never have had the modern book. But what most people remember the Egyptians for is their massive public buildings—the palaces and pyramids of the Pharaohs.

The pyramids are not actually remarkable for the technical skill employed in their construction. The Egyptians did not use winches or pulleys, just levers, and their feats were achieved by employing thousands of slaves to manhandle the gigantic blocks physically into place. The Great Pyramid of Cheops, for instance—which contains 2.5 million stones weighing from 2.5 to 15 tons—employed around 100,000 unskilled labourers as well as craftsmen and quarrymen. It took twenty years to complete.

About two centuries after Egypt became a nation, other civilizations burst into flower further north. On the small Mediterranean island of Crete, the Minoans were establishing a rich culture based on craftsmanship and trade—tin from Spain, gold and pearls from Egypt, ivory from Syria and North Africa. The Minoans produced complex metalwork, glazed faience earthenware, and gold jewellery. The sense of colour, the appreciation of nature and the exuberant joy of living which emerges from Minoan records is unlike anything else in the world of their day.

Just as Minoan civilization was ending (probably through the devastation caused by violent volcanic eruptions in 1400BC), another style of life was evolving in China. A tribe called the Shang became the rulers of about 40,000 square miles of territory, and built there a sophisticated culture with a common currency, ambitious building projects and a complex system of government. Eventually they were deposed by another tribe, the Chou; but the structure they had built remained, and helped to form the shape of later Chinese civilization. Order in society, the importance of the family, specified social roles for every citizen—these ideas were taken up later in the sixth century by China's great thinker, Confucius, whose influential teaching was to dominate the thinking of the Chinese for the next two thousand years.

Shortly after this came the first real African civilization south of Egypt—the kingdom of Kush (which in fact conquered Egypt and ruled it for some years)—and the beginnings of Indian culture with its caste system and elaborate religious philosophy. So far, civilization had sprung up on almost every continent, but little had happened in Europe. But that was about to change.

The great age of Greece and Rome

Somewhere around 1200BC, the country we now call Greece was invaded by a people from the north, who drove the original inhabitants out of their lands to take refuge in a few key cities and in islands around the Aegean. Four hundred years later, both the invaders and the original inhabitants were starting to think of themselves as one nation—and Greece was born.

Greek civilization was formed around the city-state—a small area of country ruled and administered by a city set within it. The cities were not large (few had over 20,000 inhabitants) but were self-contained centres with their own distinctive character. It is not surprising that the idea of democracy began in Greece, where every citizen could readily feel he had a vital part to play in the development of his own tiny state.

The first three hundred years of Greek life, the 'Archaic period', laid the foundations of Greek art. Lyric poetry started to be written, and intricate, beautifully decorated ceramic art was produced. Sculpture, too: and the Greeks specialized in realistic portrayal of the human body, in a quite unprecedented, startlingly lifelike way. The perfectly formed human body was thought to be the ultimate in beauty, and Greek fascination with it led to some amazing artistic achievements.

The Greeks also began the attempt to understand the workings of life and the universe by rational means. Philosophy, the 'love of wisdom', was another Greek innovation —and the foundations were laid in the Archaic period.

But it was in the following century—the fifth century BC—that Greece reached its golden age of poetry, drama, art and history. Herodotus, the writer who began historical analysis of an objective kind, was born in 480BC. Just ten years later appeared Socrates, most famous of philosophers—and close behind him came Plato and Aristotle. There seemed no end to the talent and genius emerging from the cities of fifth-century Greece. Medicine and science flourished alongside philosophy. Astronomy and geology made advances.

In the north of Greece, a warrior statesman called Philip of Macedon began to dream of

unifying the whole of Greece under one central government. If he could do this, he reasoned, he could lead a Greek army into Asia and take over new lands on which to settle Greek people. And despite Athenian opposition he succeeded in bringing Greece together, but then died unexpectedly before he could lead the army to Asia. Undeterred, Philip's son Alexander took over, and by his series of victories, all achieved before his early death at thirty-two, he managed to spread Greek culture widely over the ancient world.

Alexandria, a city established in Egypt by the Greeks, became the centre of this cultural diffusion: its massive port attracted ships from many countries, and its great library brought together the key literature of the ancient world. Alexandria was the place where Euclid worked out the foundational principles of geometry, and where Aristarchus of Samos calculated (centuries before Copernicus) that the earth goes round the sun.

Just as the Archaic period was beginning in Greece, a neighbouring civilization was establishing itself in Northern Italy. The Etruscans were spread over an area from the valley of the river Po down to the south beyond Rome—a fertile area with extensive reserves of iron, copper and wood. We know little for certain about Etruscan civilization (they left no history behind, although we know that they kept records). We have to guess about their life from the detail in their colourful paintings. They seem to have been keen on trying to foretell the future, using elaborate means of divination from the entrails of animals; a practice the Romans later copied. And they speculated a great deal about what happens after death. They also prized excellent craftsmanship, especially in bronze.

Then Rome itself broke free from the Etruscan grip, and started annexing more and more Etruscan territory. By 200BC Etruscan civilization was more or less over. Now it was the turn of the Romans to found an empire which would dominate the ancient world for half a millennium, and leave an indelible impression on the languages and even the landscape of Western Europe.

After breaking away from their previous Etruscan rulers, the Romans started to attract the loyalty of other small states in Italy. Eventually they became strong enough to challenge the might of another ambitious Mediterranean city—Carthage, in North Africa—and decisively win the contest. After that, they turned their attention to Greece: 150 years after Alexander the Great, Macedonia itself fell to Roman dominance.

The Romans continued to spread their influence further and further, and by the second century AD were holding together an awesome collection of nations and subject peoples in one vast empire. The *Pax Romana*, or 'Roman Peace', which linked together countries who would otherwise have fought unproductive wars against one another, enabled trade and the arts to flourish, and an increased standard of living.

What were the Romans' main achievements? They developed a new building material, concrete, which allowed them to construct durable architecture on an awesome scale. They built straight roads and aqueducts with a sure grasp of complicated engineering principles. The need to hold together an empire of very different peoples brought about the foundations of international law. Their literature and art may not have quite the disarming beauty of Greek culture, but it built on the achievements of the Greeks, and added some memorable works of genius.

Health care, sanitation, military thinking, town planning, the calendar—to list all the achievements of the Romans would take the rest of this chapter. One very important but quite unexpected (and at first unwanted) benefit of the *Pax Romana* was the growth of the religious faith which was to influence more people than any other in the world's history: Christianity.

Jesus Christ was born in a small province ruled by the Roman empire. The Jewish nation to which he belonged was small, but possessed

an impressive cultural history of its own. The Jews had a startlingly sophisticated religious tradition of faith in one Creator God, and the writings of their prophets and poets had developed their picture of the God they worshipped to a subtlety unmatched in any of the comparatively crude myths of their neighbours. Their belief in this one God had matured and deepened during traumatic periods of national disaster and years of captivity and exile.

Jews and Christians today would claim that the unusual religious grasp of this small tribe was no accident, but came from God's choice of Israel as his chosen people, to whom he planned to reveal himself gradually through the centuries. Christians would go on to say that his revelation reached completion when the time came for the arrival within that nation of God's own son. Jesus Christ was the fulfilment of that plan.

The early Christians, convinced that their leader had risen from the dead, spread the message about him throughout the ancient world. And here the *Pax Romana* proved extremely useful. Christian missionaries were able to travel with comparative ease from one country to another, and spread their ideas through the trading routes and cultural centres of the empire. They were so successful that despite fierce opposition the Roman empire itself eventually surrendered to them; Christianity became the state religion of the empire from AD329.

Greece and Rome were in many ways the most impressive civilizations of this period of history; but they were not the only ones. Two hundred years before Greece became a nation, settlers had moved into the area of Persia and set up two rival kingdoms—Media and Parsa. Four hundred years later they were one nation, united by Cyrus the Great, king of Parsa. And by 546BC his empire included Assyria, Babylonia, part of central Asia and lands in India. Twenty years later, Egypt too was part of this empire.

Cyrus planned carefully to hold his empire together. He was unusually tolerant of the religious faiths of his subject peoples (the Jews, for example, were given permission to rebuild the city of Jerusalem and re-establish temple worship—something their previous conquerors had not permitted). The legal system which operated throughout the empire was famous. Administratively, the whole territory was divided into twenty provinces, and a taxation system set up; the Persians invented the first internationally-used monetary system so that taxes could be paid in money rather than goods. A long 'Royal Road' ran right across the empire for 1,600 miles, up to the royal palace at Susa.

The Persian empire did not remain strong. It was conquered by Alexander the Great in 334–31BC; then the Parthians took it over in AD261; then Bedouins captured it in the seventh century and the Persian city of Baghdad became the centre of an Islamic empire. But Persia showed a peculiar capacity for winning over her invaders. Alexander married a Persian, and alarmed his advisors by proposing to restructure Greece along Persian lines; Islamic culture was to owe most of its shape to Persian cultural achievements, and its administrative arrangements to Persian ways of doing things.

India; the Pacific rim

While all this was going on, very different civilizations were taking shape further away. At the same time as Greek society was emerging, the foundations of Indian culture were being laid too. As Greece reached its 'golden age', India already had a system of kings ruling small areas, a caste system which divided people into sharply defined social groups, and an elaborate religious system, in which priests wielded enormous power over everyone else. Around 500BC their position was attacked by a series of reformers—of whom the greatest was Gautama Buddha, the founder of a new philosophy which sent its missionaries all over the East at the same time that Christian missionaries were evangelizing the West.

Most of north and central India was united in the third century BC, and the impact of Buddhism was soon felt when the third emperor Ashoka became converted (after a military campaign which sickened him because of the loss of life involved). As a Buddhist, Ashoka renounced war as a means of conquering his enemies, instituted medical services and social support systems, banned the killing of animals for sacrifice, and insisted that justice must be even-handed, treating the poor identically with the rich. Ashoka taught that kings were responsible to their people, as well as vice versa—a revolutionary thought for his day, and one that was to have no influence elsewhere for many centuries to come.

Under Ashoka, Buddhist teachers spread their message southwards, and won a growing following. Hinduism was not to take the initiative again until the emergence of the Gupta dynasty, around AD319. Their cultural influence (which included developments in painting, pottery, dance, and an appreciation of sexual skills—the *Kama Sutra* comes from this period) re-established traditional Indian ways of looking at life. Their policy of building new villages threatened the supremacy of the Buddhist monasteries, which by now were wealthy and confined to major centres.

In the end Buddhism was to lose the battle for India, but make its most important impact on other Asian cultures. One of those was China. After the Shang dynasty, which we have already mentioned, and the Chou who followed them, China splintered into a collection of warring states, and was not brought together again until the Qin dynasty imposed their authority in 221BC. They were harsh rulers, who lost popularity among the intellectuals by trying to stamp out all literature which was privately owned, and lost the favour of ordinary people by the suffering they exposed them to during the building of the Great Wall. Not surprisingly, there was a revolt, and the Han dynasty took over. Their four hundred years of rule, roughly parallel in time to the emergence of Rome, saw the beginnings of history writing; the invention of paper; an understanding of magnetism and the compass; and widespread use of cast iron (eighteen hundred years before Europe discovered it). But they proved incapable of holding their territory together, and from AD220 onwards China went through some very unsettled years.

But this was just the time when Japanese culture began to spring into life. A chieftain called Jimmu succeeded in conquering most of the country around AD300, and his victory made it possible for a Japanese society to emerge, closely copying Chinese culture, thinking, sculpture and architecture. (Even today the Japanese system of writing is unwieldy, involving 1,800 separate characters—which is because it did not emerge naturally within Japan, but was simply adopted from the Chinese system.) Buddhism, which had penetrated China during the Han period, arrived in Japan in the sixth century AD, and was adopted alongside the traditional Shinto religion.

Other things were beginning to stir. Across the Pacific ocean, in South America, the great city of Teotihuacan flourished from the time of Christ until six hundred years or so later. It was a major trading centre with a massive complex of religious and public buildings attached, and had a population of more than 100,000 people. It bestowed an enormous legacy on later South American civilizations, even after it had been mysteriously besieged and burnt in 750BC by unknown attackers.

One of the great civilizations to follow Teotihuacan was that of the Maya, who centred themselves on what is now Guatemala and south-east Mexico. The Maya built great architectural monuments in elaborate complexes, but did not actually live in them. These places were only for the priests and the leaders; the rest of the people lived in temporary forest huts, and moved to a new home every second year or so. This was because their fairly primitive agricultural methods exhausted the soil's capacity quickly, and they had to move on to new fields.

Despite these and other limitations (they never discovered the wheel, for example), the Maya achieved some startling things. Their elaborate calendar, based on careful astronomical work, gave them a grasp of the immensity of time which was superior to that of any other ancient people. The Mayans were able to imagine a prehistory of hundreds of thousands of years. Their greatest period was between AD600 and 900; but the last Mayan city did not fall to the Spaniards until 1699.

Mayan civilization was just beginning, and Jimmu was just conquering Japan, when the Roman empire underwent a dramatic shift. Constantine, the emperor who had embraced Christianity, decided that Rome was not a suitable place for the capital of a new Christian empire. It had too many traditional associations with the old gods. And so he moved his capital to Byzantium, an old Greek trading town on the Bosphorus, creating within six years a major city which came to be called (after him) Constantinople. He chose the site with care—it stood strategically on some of the most important trade routes in the world—and planned the city ambitiously. Byzantium became the focus of a fabulous amount of wealth and artistic enterprise.

The Byzantine empire lasted until 1453, when Mehmet II, a young Ottoman Sultan, conquered the city of Constantinople and turned it into an Islamic centre. But for all its long life it enjoyed scarcely a single year of peace. It was constantly under attack from envious neighbours; and within Byzantium itself there was an atmosphere of intrigue and suspicion. No less than twenty-nine of its eighty-eight emperors died violent deaths.

Byzantium was the centre of world Christianity for a while, and hosted some of the great councils in which disputed matters of Christian faith were resolved and creeds formulated. The Byzantine emperor was regarded as the earthly head of the Christian church, until AD800, when Pope Leo III crowned Charles, King of the Franks, as Emperor of the Holy Roman Empire. This split between two versions of Christianity—the Western and the Eastern—later had ruinous consequences, when in 1204 an army of Western Crusaders attacked Constantinople.

However it was excused, the primary motive for this sudden devastation was simple greed: the Crusaders wanted the wealth of the city for themselves. They had little appreciation of Byzantium's unique culture. The city was stripped bare of every kind of item of value, even ancient Christian relics. The shock to Byzantium's system was one from which she never completely managed to rally; and two centuries later Mehmet II ended eleven hundred years of illustrious empire.

But where had the Ottomans come from? And the Crusaders? To trace the story of their civilizations, we need to move back to a period five hundred years before.

This Hindu holy man has taken a vow never again to lie down. He sleeps supported by ropes. The holy men of India stand in one of the longest religious traditions in the world.

The barbarians and afterwards

Between the years AD300 and 500, it might have seemed to our alien observer that human civilization was going into reverse. For waves of nomads began to sweep through the most significant civilizations of the world, looting and ravaging as they went. Rome was raided and sacked in 410 by the Visigoths; the Gupta empire in India was destroyed by Huns in 465; the Ostrogoths terrorized Italy, and the Vandals roamed over Spain and North Africa (also descending on Rome, in 455). Not just to aliens in spacecraft, but also to ordinary people in the frightened West, these events seemed inexplicable and bewildering; and one of the greatest books in the history of the Christian church—Augustine's *City of God*—was written to try to explain from a Christian perspective what was happening to the old civilization.

In less troubled areas, however, good things were still happening. The Maya in South America were steadily building towards their greatest years. The Sasanid empire in Persia was bringing Persian art and learning to one of its most notable periods of greatness. And even the barbarians soon settled down—adopting Roman law and even Christianity. A new, independent, Germanic culture began to take shape.

But the biggest surprise was to come from the Arabian deserts—a strip of unpromising land significant for nothing but a few warring tribes and grazing herds. This was where the prophet Muhammad began at the beginning of the seventh century to preach a new faith—an urgent appeal to human beings to put away evil, submit to God's rules for living, and live in a brotherhood with other believers. The new faith was simple, compelling and authoritative; it rapidly won a following, and eager Arab converts began to overrun neighbouring countries. Less than a century after the death of Muhammad, their empire stretched from Spain almost to India; a hundred years later they were established in India itself, and two hundred years after that the great African kingdom of Ghana was conquered by Muslim warriors. It was an astonishing achievement—based, for once, not on an outstanding military leader but on the power of religious conviction.

The Islamic empire used the different skills of its subject peoples, and the commercial links it could establish with other areas, to build a rich, colourful and distinctive culture. Works of science and philosophy—all the scholarly achievements of the ancient world—were translated into Arabic, and Arab scholars made important discoveries in medicine, mathematics and science. Poetry, weaving, metalworking—in the arts as well as the sciences Arab culture advanced.

Meanwhile in China the Han dynasty had collapsed within the third century, and the country was plunged once again into a confused period of short-lived governments. But just as the Arabs were beginning to listen to the voice of Muhammad, another great dynasty—the Tang—arrived on the scene. Their achievement was to link China much more closely with the cultural achievements of other nations: through trade and travel, the Chinese of the Tang dynasty developed an appreciation for the best of what was happening abroad, and it created a new cosmopolitan style in art and literature. Pottery and landscape painting reached new standards of attainment. Alien visitors would not have noticed a wealthier (or indeed larger) city anywhere on the earth's surface than the Tang capital Ch'ang-an.

After the Tang began to lose their power, the country was re-united by a new dynasty, the Song. During their three hundred years of power, artistic masterpieces continued to be produced, but learning also began to be much more widespread. This had something to do with the fact that the Song had discovered the art of printing, which allowed them to diffuse ideas much more rapidly. In addition, they put the administration of the nation into the hands of civil servants who qualified for their jobs by passing examinations based on the Confucian classics. (This examination system continued until 1905.)

Human civilization had now reached the point where most different civilizations were at least aware of some of the others. Few were totally isolated any more. Civilization in Russia, for example, started around this time when Vladimir, Grand Prince of Kiev, sent envoys to look at various other countries to decide which religion the Russians should embrace. They investigated Jews, Muslims, Catholic and Orthodox Christians before selecting the brand they preferred—something that could not have happened a few centuries before!

But there were still some isolated spots on earth. And there, too, the human cultural enterprise was continuing.

Africa and America

Mali today is one of the poorest countries in the world. This certainly was not the case in the thirteenth century, when it absorbed the ancient kingdom of Ghana and spread to cover an area of West Africa measuring a thousand miles across. The ruler of Mali is said to have had ten thousand horses in his stables. Europeans who later came into contact with Mali's capital Timbuktu expressed shocked astonishment that a nation so far removed from the rest of the world should have produced such wealth and splendour.

Not that Mali was totally remote. Its rulers adopted Islam (although most of their subjects seem to have clung on to tribal religions) and in 1307 one of them caused a sensation when

ARE WE DESTROYING OUR PLANET?

'Human beings now have to live on a planet whose carrying capacity for all practical purposes is irreversibly less now than it was previously. Unless concerted action is taken immediately, there will be a further decline in the planet's capacity to support its population. Subsequent generations will be left a sorry heritage: less productive land; less diversity; less room for manoeuvre; fewer options; more people.'

These claims are made by Robert Allen, senior policy advisor at the Swiss-based International Union for Conservation of Nature and Natural Resources. He produces some arresting figures to back his argument. The world's deserts are expanding at a rate of 23,000 square miles per year—twice the area of Belgium. India loses 6,000 million tonnes of fertile soil annually. In North America, 4,800 square kilometres of excellent farming land disappear under concrete and tarmac every year.

Tropical rain forests are the richest land environments on this planet. Yet their trees are toppling at a rate of fifty acres *every minute*. By the end of this century, we will have just half the amount of unlogged productive tropical rain forest which exists at the moment. What are we doing to ourselves?

Then there are pesticides. When Professor Ralph Dougherty took semen samples from a test group of healthy students, he was startled to find that in every cubic centimetre there were only two-thirds as many sperm cells as in samples taken in 1929. He tested further, and found that the students' genitals contained chemicals that should not have been there. Particularly DDT—which has been banned since 1972, but is almost indestructible and clearly has not gone away.

At the time of writing, concern is rising about what we may be doing to the ozone layer of the upper atmosphere. Some types of aerosol spray have been shown to damage it. And that could be disastrous for human life—the ozone layer protects us from deadly solar ultra-violet rays, which produce (among other things) skin cancers.

It all sounds very gloomy! Yet Robert Allen's book is entitled *How to Save the World*. He believes that there is still time, provided we make the right kind of efforts quickly, to preserve a planet fit for our children and grandchildren to live on. Dr Ian Blair, of the Atomic Energy Research Establishment at Harwell, England, comments, 'The reality of the ecological crisis is becoming more visible with every passing day, and one therefore has reason to hope that necessity, together with that other human characteristic, self-preservation, may impose general acceptance of what Christians have been proclaiming for many centuries—that man is the custodian and steward of the earth and not its outright owner.'

The accident at the Chernobyl nuclear reactor in the Ukraine alerted humanity to the fearsome dangers inherent in modern technology. Are such technologies justified when the damage could be so great?

he made a pilgrimage to Mecca. In a much more remote part of the world, two civilizations were beginning their independent rise to greatness at this same time—and they would remain completely unknown until the first Spanish explorers landed in their part of South America.

In the twelfth century, the Inca tribe of Peru began to carve out a small empire for themselves by taking over neighbouring peoples. The Incas had little cultural originality of their own, but they knew how to adapt the skills of the people they conquered, and use them for their own ends. And between 1400 and 1530—a period tragically cut short by the depredations of the European invaders—the Inca empire reached heights of unexpected greatness.

The Incas lived in an area which combined, in a most unpromising way, deserts and snow-capped peaks, fertile valleys and bare crags, hot arid zones and wet tropical regions. Only a people with an extraordinary degree of engineering skill could have built an empire there; and the Incas met the challenge. They built 10,000 miles of roads, as well as suspension bridges, terraces on hillsides to increase land available for cultivation, and a royal palace with its blocks of stone joined so perfectly that no mortar was necessary to knit them together.

The Incas' craftsmanship in gold, silver and precious metals reached an extraordinary degree of perfection. This was made easier by the fact that all produce legally belonged to the state, and commerce did not exist. The highly-organized civil service kept a tight control on the lives of the people—restricting population movements, organizing marriages, and administering compulsory labour schemes. Individual freedom was a foreign idea; the good of the state was all that mattered.

The Incas rarely practised human sacrifice (although it did happen at times of crisis), but the other great South American civilization—that of the Aztecs—was built on it. One of the first Europeans to visit the Aztec capital, Tenochtitlan, reported seeing a massive rack standing beside the city's temple which contained 136,000 skulls. Aztec civilization was profligate of human life (the annual ceremony in honour of the maize goddess involved beheading young women as they danced; 20,000 captives were sacrificed to celebrate the dedication of a temple). But for all that it was a tremendous achievement.

The Aztecs (who inhabited central Mexico) were highly skilled in agriculture and in craftsmanship involving precious metals. Tenochtitlan covered an area of almost five square miles; it was built as an island, intersected by a network of canals, served with fresh water through a system of ramps. Inside a walled precinct at the heart of the city were massive temples and soaring terraces. The first Europeans to reach it had never seen anything like it in their lives.

While these civilizations had been growing, much had happened elsewhere. Hinduism had reasserted itself over Buddhism in India, and great temple cities had been built before Muslim invaders arrived in the thirteenth century. Their conquests had the effect of pushing Hindu peoples into new areas, where fresh centres of art and culture developed. The conflict between Islam and Hinduism produced several new religious developments. Guru Nanak (1469–1530) began a new religious philosophy—Sikhism—when he proclaimed, 'There is no Hindu, there is no Muslim.' It was just the message that many people, weary of conflict, wanted to hear; and the fact that Sikhism abolished caste distinctions gave it an immediate appeal to the poorer classes.

This was to lead to the establishment of a new empire in India: the Mogul empire, dating from 1556. The Moguls set out to be neither Hindu nor Muslim, but simply Indian. They produced art and buildings of great beauty—notably the Taj Mahal, which incorporates Hindu and Muslim styles with breathtaking elegance.

While Sikhism was gathering force in India, Western civilization was adjusting to several bewildering changes. Byzantium disappeared in 1453. Russia began to be unified in 1480. Around the same time, the invention of movable type made printing easy and quick, and allowed books to spread knowledge quickly and widely. And then in 1492 the Arabs were finally expelled from Spain; the long association of Muslim culture with Europe was over.

But something else happened in 1492—Columbus landed in America. And that heralded the real start of a new world. European sea

The Taj Mahal, legacy of sixteenth-century India, points to the serenity of a world beyond.

explorers were pushing back the frontiers of the unknown further and further, and drawing world history together.

European thinkers were beginning to rediscover the riches of classical Greek writers such as Aristotle and Hippocrates. The rise of universities had helped the new ideas to spread: now there were learned communities in all the major countries of the West (fifty-six universities were flourishing by 1400) which could store, teach and develop important thinking.

The name given to this gradual rebirth of classical learning—which actually spread over three centuries or so—is the Renaissance. It led to a new view of human beings and their relationship to the universe. Scientific discoveries were part of this: Copernicus, a Polish monk, shocked the church by suggesting in 1543 that the earth was not the centre of the universe; within a century Galileo and Kepler had proved him right. Artists started to develop a new realistic style. Literature began to be written in modern languages as well as classical. The Renaissance encouraged human beings to examine the whole world afresh and see what was really there.

One important outcome of the Renaissance was the Reformation. All the new learning was beginning to challenge the authority of the church, and to emphasize the importance of individuals forming their own opinions carefully by scrutinizing the facts. The Reformation started with a realization that the church had grown corrupt, tradition-bound and unbiblical in its teaching. Martin Luther challenged the authority of the church by preaching that a person's relationship with God depends on faith alone—and not on any other conditions invented by church authority. The Reformation spread quickly from Germany to Scandinavia, Switzerland, Holland, France and Scotland. The Church of England broke away from the authority of the Pope.

The following century saw the rise of modern science and philosophy. Newton discovered gravity, Harvey the circulation of the blood. Descartes revolutionized philosophy by insisting that serious thinking about the world must start with no hidden assumptions: a philosopher must systematically question each of his premises. The method of examining the world carefully, taking nothing for granted, was yielding exciting new areas of knowledge. Human beings had never understood their environment so well.

Meanwhile, elsewhere

The growth of European culture was to prove the most important force determining future world history. But there were other things happening, too. In Japan, as far back as the eleventh century, an aristocratic court society with few duties had had the time to produce sophisticated novels and poetry. By the fourteenth century, Japan's own form of drama—the *no* play—was fully developed. And when in 1603 Tokugawa Ieyasu became *shogun* (the officer given authority by the emperor to rule the country), a period of stable government started which allowed all the arts to flourish.

But the Tokugawa family became convinced that contact with Westerners could only be harmful to Japanese culture. And so they expelled the Portuguese and Spanish missionaries who had been in Japan since 1542, and condemned Japan to centuries of cultural isolation, which ended only in 1853 when America sent four warships to demand the

For all its faults, the United Nations is a historically unique attempt to bring all nations into co-operation for the benefit of all humanity.

opening of the country and the signing of a commercial agreement.

Christian missionaries had also arrived in China in the sixteenth century. They found there a well-developed culture, producing a fantastic array of luxury goods and priceless art works, under the rulership of the Ming dynasty. The missionaries were able to advise the emperors about such subjects as mathematics and astronomy; but the Chinese had very little interest in what they could gain from outsiders. Chinese society was self-sufficient and culturally superior to every other. What could they learn from Europe?

That remained the Chinese attitude right through to the end of the nineteenth century, when it became painfully obvious that the West was outstripping China in technological progress. Many of the political problems which have beset China this century can be traced back to the crisis of confidence which Chinese society underwent when it suddenly realized that it was not, after all, leading the world.

At the same time as the European Renaissance and the rise of the Incas, another great civilization arose mysteriously in southern Africa. The mystery stems from the fact that this civilization, Zimbabwe, never developed the ability to read and write, and so records are scanty. But we do know that Zimbabwe was an important city and royal capital from about 1400, until in 1830 it was destroyed by another African people. Ruins of a palace, a temple, and the great wall which encircled the city can still be seen today.

Two thousand miles away, the kingdom of Benin (in what is now Nigeria) had taken bronze sculpture to a high degree of refinement. Benin's heyday lasted from the fifteenth to the seventeenth centuries.

But by the seventeenth century the future lay very definitely with Western Europe. And so we must go back there to conclude the story.

The enlightenment and beyond

Seventeenth-century science had led to some amazing advances. And consequently many people in the following century felt a tremendous optimism about the future of the human enterprise. Reason and careful examination were the only keys needed to unlock the secrets of the universe; at last we were discovering the regular principles by which everything fitted together. Human happiness could be arrived at by applying reason to life; the unprovable dogmas of religion were no longer necessary. Paul Hazard has crystallized the intellectual mood:

Religion; revealed religion, that was what stood in the way; that was the major adversary. Once

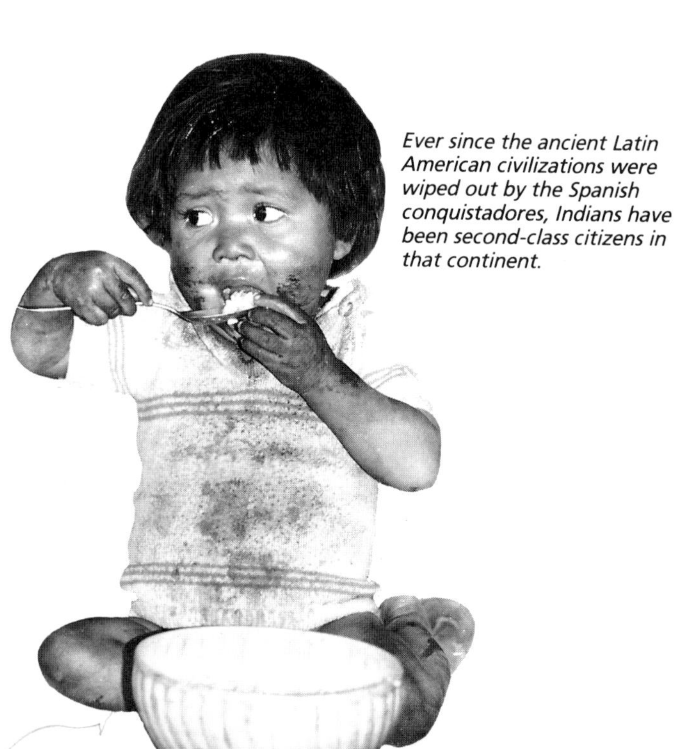

Ever since the ancient Latin American civilizations were wiped out by the Spanish conquistadores, Indians have been second-class citizens in that continent.

make it clear that, from the nature of the case, there could be no such thing... then the philosophers could go ahead... Every belief must be based on reason; to reason, even the Supreme Being himself is compelled to defer.

The Enlightenment, as this period of thought was called, produced a great deal of valuable philosophy, literature and political thinking; but its easy certainties were soon rendered obsolete by bewildering changes which transformed the face of the world.

The most obvious was the Industrial Revolution, which altered the economic relationships of human beings more dramatically (and more rapidly) than any previous change in history. Industrialization meant the growth of cities (London's population shot up from 875,000 to 5 million between 1800 and 1900), a new wealth and power concentrated in the hands of factory owners rather than the old aristocrats, and the emergence of a working class which (Karl Marx pointed out) was poorer than anyone in history before. For, he said, even the poorest weaver or peasant of the eighteenth century owned the tools he worked with; but the industrial labourer, working on somebody else's machine in somebody else's factory, owned nothing—not even his labour.

Industrialization also meant an increased quality of life for those who gained from it. More goods were available, at cheaper prices, and of more reliable quality. It also meant that Europe dominated the world — more successful in producing wealth and dominating world affairs than any previous culture.

Here we reach our own century, in which the Western style of thinking and technological development has left its impact on one society after another, all over the world; in which the 'super-powers', the Soviet Union and the United States, have emerged in place of Europe to dominate the international scene; in which our alien observer would have noticed the gunsmoke of two greater wars than the world has ever seen, and the mushroom clouds rising from the explosion of the first nuclear weapons.

What conclusions can we reach after surveying the human achievement so far?

SHOULD WE STOP BUILDING BOMBS?

When the first atomic bomb dropped on the Japanese city of Hiroshima in 1945, it was the biggest explosion the world had ever seen. Today it is estimated that both the United States and the Soviet Union have armaments capable of producing 500,000 explosions the size of the Hiroshima blast. And even Britain, not the world's greatest nuclear power, has enough for 11,600.

One frightening aspect of nuclear weapons is simply how much they cost. It has been calculated that to feed, educate and house the underprivileged of the world would cost $14 billion per year. An enormous sum—but no more than the world spends on armaments *every two weeks*. In other words, if we could stop the arms race for a fortnight, we could conquer world hunger.

Then there is the effect of nuclear weapons. In a one-megaton attack on Leningrad, 890,000 people would die 'promptly' (which means within thirty days), and 1,260,000 would be injured. A majority of them would die young as a result. A counter-attack on American military bases would produce between two and twenty-two million 'prompt' deaths. But if the Russians decided on an all-out attack, between 35 and 77 per cent of the American population would die 'promptly'. This is the terror we are building for ourselves. Why do we do it?

Small wonder that Christian pacifist Alan Kreider argues, 'Because of their tremendous explosive power, because of their radiation and fallout, because of the improbability of arresting escalation, because of the incredible problems of communication, command and control, nuclear weapons are a new phenomenon in the history of warfare. They are intrinsically indiscriminate, and thus intrinsically unjust.'

But not all Christians agree. Dr Delmar Bergen is a leading scientist at Los Alamos National Laboratory in the United States, actively designing and testing nuclear weapons. He says, 'People tend to focus on the nuclear wars aspect of nuclear weapons, but I am more interested in how science can create a situation where war cannot be considered as the solution to any problem. I believe nuclear weapons have done this by preventing wars. They have prevented major conflicts, I think, for the last forty years.'

There are no easy answers. Nuclear weapons are here, and they cannot be dis-invented; they give us an opportunity to do more spectacular harm to the human race than any generation before us. The real problem was analyzed accurately right at the start of the nuclear arms race, in 1948, when Dr Albert Einstein remarked: 'The true problem lies in the hearts and thoughts of men. It is not a physical problem, but an ethical one... What terrifies us is not the explosive force of the atomic bomb, but the power of the wickedness of the human heart, its explosive power for evil.'

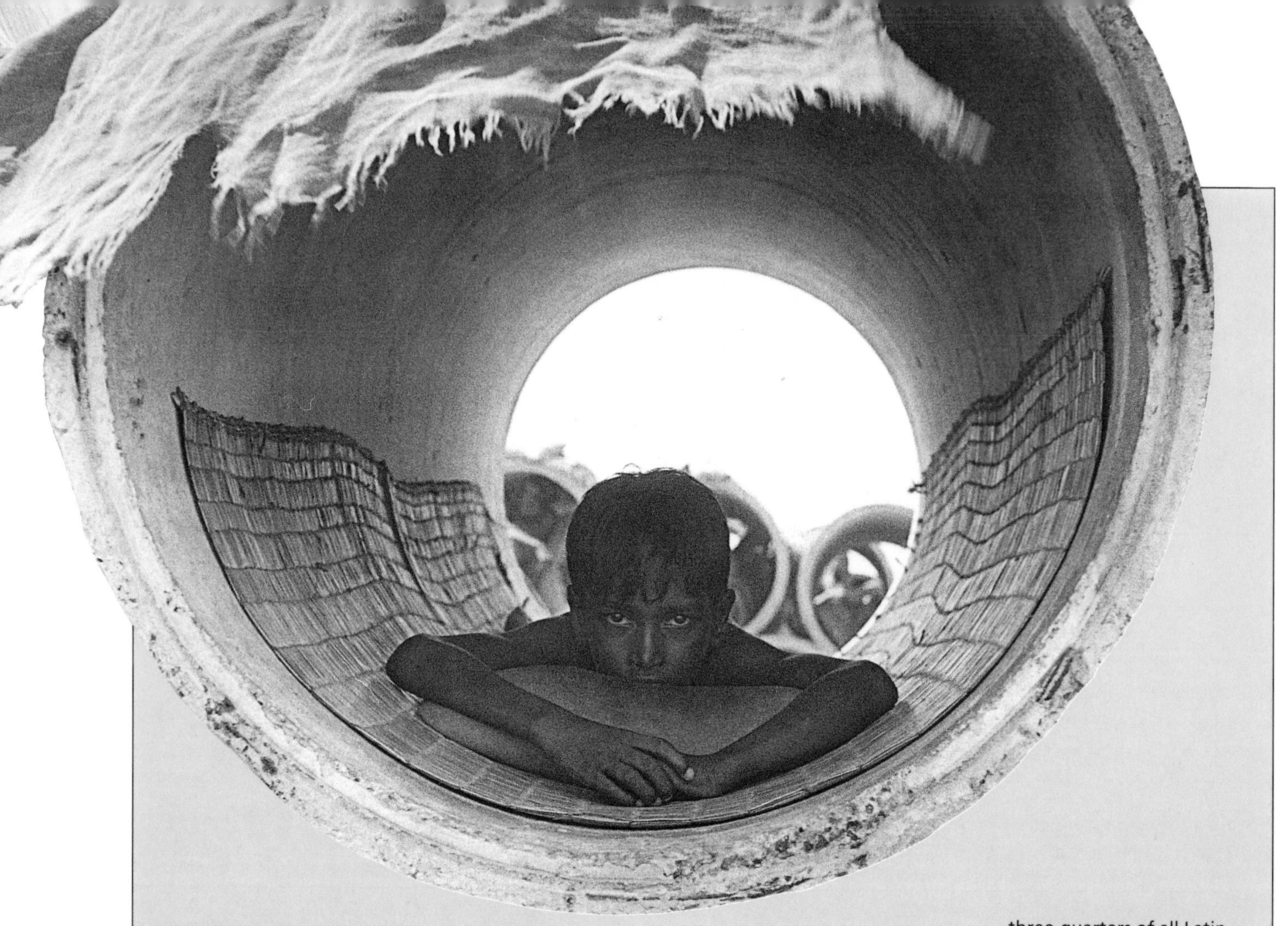

IS THIS PLANET OVERCROWDED?

Someone has estimated that more than half the people who have ever lived are alive today. Only a century and a half ago, the world's total population was one-fifth of what it is now. How many more can we take? Is this planet overcrowded?

Scientists have made mind-boggling projections for the future. Physicist J.H. Fremlin, calculating that the world's population is doubling once every thirty-five years, worked out that if things were to continue at that rate for about 900 years, there would be a hundred people standing on every square yard of the earth's surface (including the oceans!)—a total of 60,000,000,000,000,000 people in all. He commented that if they were all housed in a continuous 2,000-storey building, covering the entire planet, it might be possible to give them all three or four yards of floor space each.

Could we send them all off to the stars instead? Not unless things change dramatically. Professor Garrett Hardin estimates that if Americans were to cut down their standard of living to 18 per cent of its present level, they would save enough in a year to finance the sending of *one day's* population increase to the stars.

'An equilibrium must be reached,' says Professor Carlo Cipolla. 'But when will it be reached? And how?' We have no answers to this question. What we can say confidently is that at the moment we are a long way from such a frightening situation. There is more than enough food and space for everyone on earth; in 1984, for example, the world produced four times as much grain as it needed to feed its population. Yet over half the world's population is malnourished. Why?

The problem is not one of population, but exploitation. Those of us who live in Western countries make up only 5 per cent of the world's population; yet we consume over 40 per cent of the world's resources. It doesn't leave a lot for others.

And the truly poor are being concentrated in the wrong places. By the end of the century, we are told, three-quarters of all Latin Americans and one-third of all Asians and Africans will be living in cities. Today there are six hundred million landless poor in Africa, Asia and Latin America; by the turn of the century there will be a thousand million. Their first reaction will be to head for the city. How can stretched urban resources cope with this sort of influx?

Planet earth is not overcrowded—yet. But unless something is done, it soon will be. And even now we have a problem of distribution, as the poorest humans flock to places where they are least likely to receive help. If we are ever going to feed the world, we need to try a little harder.

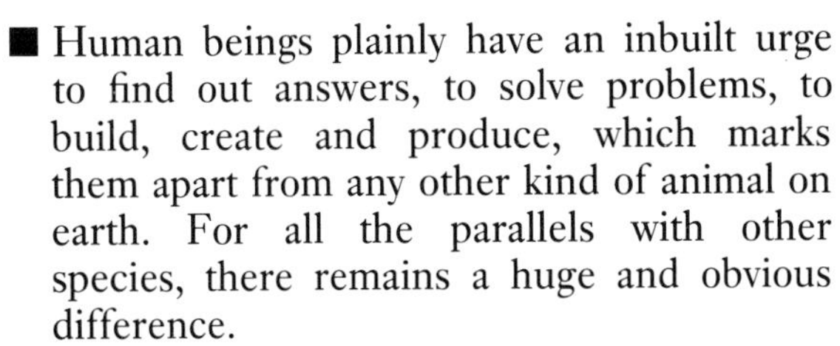

- Human beings plainly have an inbuilt urge to find out answers, to solve problems, to build, create and produce, which marks them apart from any other kind of animal on earth. For all the parallels with other species, there remains a huge and obvious difference.
- But there are some problems which human beings have never solved—because they are problems inside human beings themselves. The same 'inhumanity' which led to the Aztecs torturing children in their rain ceremonies, or to the total extinction of Carthage by the Romans, has produced in our own time the awful massacre of Kampuchea, the ghastly experiments Mengele carried out at Auschwitz, the bloody purges of Stalin. The idea that human beings can perfect themselves, and produce a trouble-free planet, seems more and more of an illusion with every newspaper we read.
- Today's world presents us with more urgent problems than ever before. We now have the technology to devastate the whole world if we choose. International trade and massive third-world debt can produce inequalities which result in mass starvation—on a planet well capable of feeding its entire population, three or four times over. The over-consumption of the world's resources by a tiny minority in the rich countries is leaving a large proportion of the world's population destitute. But there seems no way to change the situation.

Modernity itself is a threatening thing. It gives us more options than we have ever had before—as to what foods we will eat, how we will spend our time, what career we will

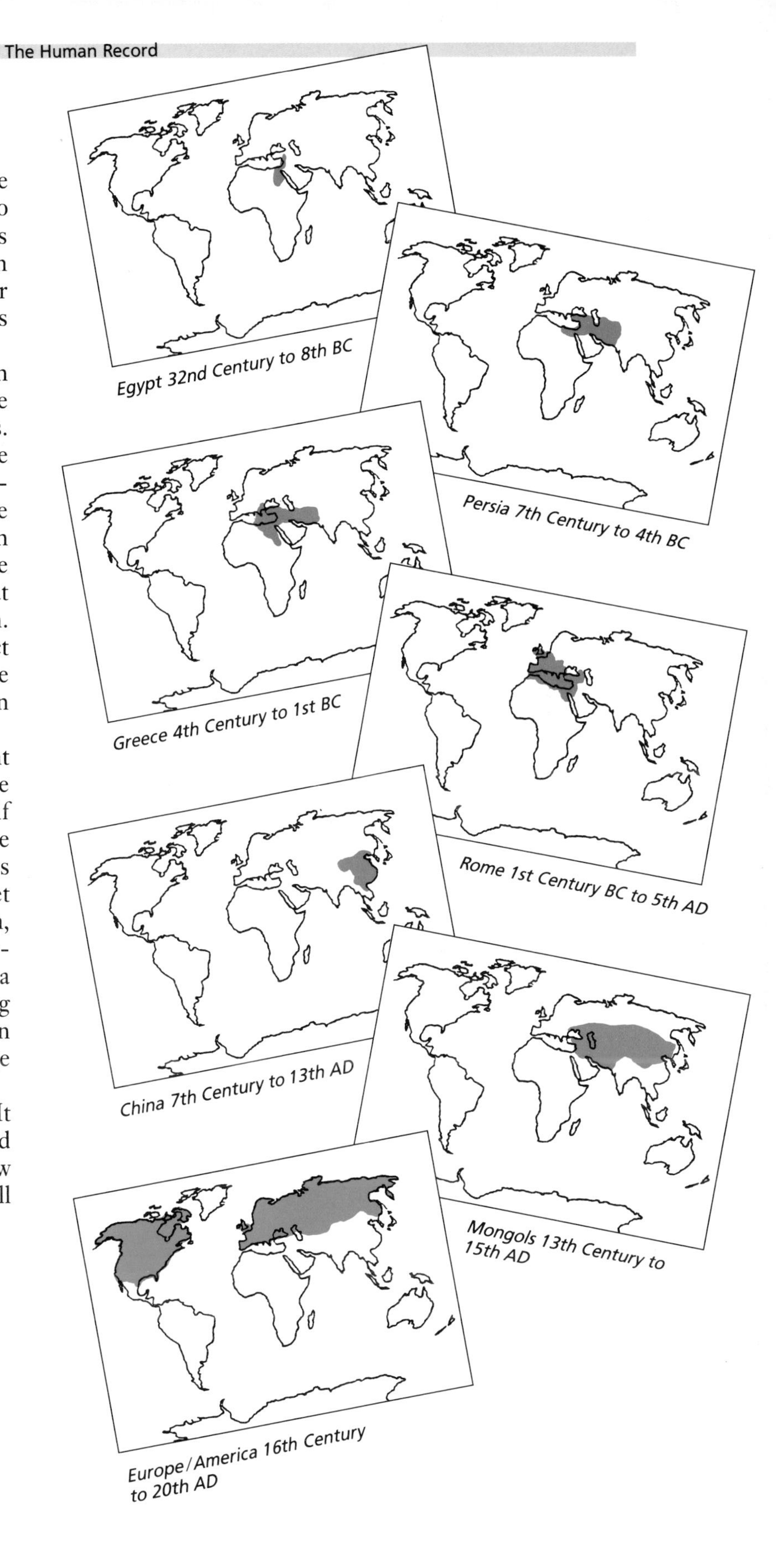

Egypt 32nd Century to 8th BC

Persia 7th Century to 4th BC

Greece 4th Century to 1st BC

Rome 1st Century BC to 5th AD

China 7th Century to 13th AD

Mongols 13th Century to 15th AD

Europe/America 16th Century to 20th AD

follow, what our beliefs will be. And so, says sociologist Peter Berger, we have the anxious task of making all the important decisions for ourselves:

Put simply, the individual is faced with a number of alternative careers, especially in his younger years, and therefore must make decisions about these available options. It is possible for the individual to imagine himself as having different biographies. . . it increases the likelihood of frustration regarding specific careers. . . This frustration will be linked with feelings of regret or even guilt if the individual believes that he has missed some options or made some wrong decisions in the past. The frustration will be linked to anxiety regarding present or future decisions.

And so Berger concludes that 'modern man has suffered from a deepening condition of "homelessness"'. We understand our world better than any previous civilization has done; but we feel less settled within it. We are painfully conscious of the imperfections in ourselves (and the discoveries of Darwin and Freud have served to underline how humble we need to be about our own potential). As we look to the future, we see mounting problems to which there are no immediate answers.

One wonders about the alien visitor, as he speeds away in his flying saucer and marks down 2100 in his diary for the date of his next visit.

Would he fly away feeling optimistic about our future—or the opposite?

Part IV

The Meaning of a Person

WHAT HAVE THE GREAT FAITHS TO SAY?

The most Northern tribes of the White Nile are the Dinkas, Shilooks, Nuehr, Kytch, Bohr, Aliab and Shir. . . Without any exception they are without a belief in a Supreme Being, neither have they any form of worship or idolatry; nor is the darkness of their minds enlightened by even a ray of superstition.

This was the blunt conclusion that Sir Samuel Baker, the Victorian explorer, announced to the Ethnological Society in London in July 1866. He had found people who had no religion. Not a trace of supernatural belief could be found in their culture. They had no gods.

But Samuel Baker was wrong—wildly and spectacularly wrong. All these tribes had their own religious systems, and some of them remarkably sophisticated; especially the Nuehr and the Dinka. It was just that their beliefs were so different to Baker's own that he failed to identify them. And so he lived among them in order to study them without ever noticing how religious they were.

Baker is one example of many people in history who have tried to find evidence of

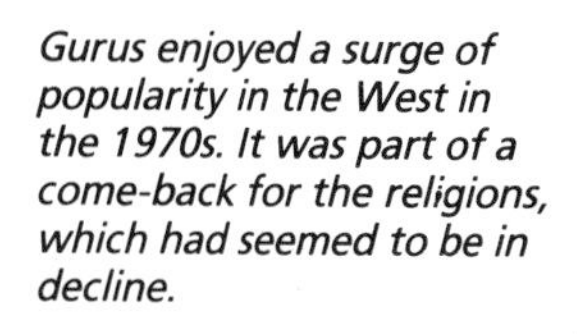

Gurus enjoyed a surge of popularity in the West in the 1970s. It was part of a come-back for the religions, which had seemed to be in decline.

human beings who are religion-free. And all have failed. There is not a single human culture where some form of religious worship has not been known. Even in civilizations that developed in complete isolation from one another—such as the South American cultures, and the great empires of Africa—we find exactly the same basic questions about human life being asked, the same sense of 'something else out there' being expressed, that we find in our own culture and those closest to it.

Human beings have always been religious animals. And there seems no sign, at the end of the twentieth century, that this is about to end. Even in the Soviet Union, after almost a century of atheist propaganda, there are calculated to be 97 million Christians—more than there were before the Revolution. In China, when the harsh repressions of the Cultural Revolution came to an end and churches reopened, far more people were found to be Christians than at the time when China turned communist.

Other religions are surging back as well. The growth of Buddhism in the West this century has been quite a success story. And fundamentalist Islam has added a whole new dimension to the political jigsaw of the Middle East. Clearly, what Muhammad started over 1,300 years ago is still potent enough for thousands of people to be willing to give their lives in its service.

And in the West, even those who do not see themselves as conventionally religious people often have guiding beliefs that shape their lives. The growth of astrology, mind-control therapies, yoga systems and Tarot reading has demonstrated clearly that people still have religious longings which need to be satisfied somehow. Successful actresses credit their success to the wise advice given by spirit beings who are 'channelled' by mediums in a trance. Businessmen take off their shoes and sit before an altar meditating, or chanting a phrase in Japanese, so as to attune themselves to the universe and change their lives for the better. And not long ago, all over the Western world, there was a wave of new religious movements—The Unification Church, the Children of God, Scientology, the Rajneeshis—all showing an alarming propensity to dominate the minds of young people and persuade them to make a violent break with their previous lifestyle. Just how far these new religions could go, in their power over adherents, was demonstrated when 900 people committed suicide one afternoon in a forest clearing in Guyana. Their group leader had told them to.

How did human beings first become religious animals? The question is important because, again, this is one of the things which marks us off from the rest of the animal creation. No monkey ever said a prayer, no beaver ever built a church. Yet wherever one looks throughout human civilization, the signs of religion are unmistakable—temples, mosques, ziggurats, shrines, altars, standing stones. How did it all begin?

How did religion begin?

The great psychologist Sigmund Freud believed that religion began when people lived in a tribe ruled by one male, the father of the group. This ruler would have had a large number of wives, and the younger men would have been forced out of the tribe to find mates for themselves. Finding this intolerable, they must have revolted, murdered the father—and then been so ashamed by what they had done that they had to find ways to ease their crippling feelings of guilt.

Freud conjectures that they took an animal to act as a symbol of the dead father, and honoured it throughout the year, giving it the kind of respect once paid to the murdered leader. And then, on the anniversary of the murder, they would kill the animal as a sort of recreation of their crime—thus assuaging their guilt, and also celebrating their new freedom.

In this way, says Freud, came about the basic ideas of religious ritual, sacrifice, symbols, guilt and forgiveness. It is a plausible theory. But is it correct?

Plainly no proof can be found for the truth of such a story, either for or against. But Freud's whole case depends on the idea that human primitive societies have a lot of similarities to ape societies, and we now know that this is just not true. What is more, enough data has been discovered about the origins of symbols and ceremonies to be fairly sure he was wrong about them. And did he really believe his own theory anyway? David Stafford Clark, a leading expert on Freud's thought, is not convinced.

Did Freud believe this to be a historical account? The answer to this is that he did and at the same time he didn't. He writes about the possibilities and probabilities, the unlikelihood and at the same time the certainty that this was part of the original mental inheritance of the human race. In a sense, he tends at this stage both to display ambivalence and to plead poetic licence. . . Freud the mythmaker has come a long way from Freud the scientist.

Freud's theory might just fit with religions which place a lot of emphasis on guilt and forgiveness—such as Judaism and Christianity. But it has little relevance to other faiths (Shinto, say, or Buddhism) which are concerned with very different things. It looks as though Freud was wrong. We have to look elsewhere for the origins of religion.

Another influential view is that human religion began with dreams. When we dream, people appear in our mind's eye in a peculiar, disembodied fashion; and that may have given primitive man the idea (said E.B. Tylor, whose theory this originally was) that souls can exist apart from bodies. From this, it was just a short step to ancestor worship (fearing and respecting those, souls which had broken free of their bodies); then to attributing to spirits the power to control rain, fire, fertility and other natural events; then to worshipping a whole variety of different gods; then finally to narrowing everything down to the worship of just one supreme God.

What about this theory? First, again there is no direct proof. Other researchers into primitive religions saw the chain of events a little differently. J.G. Frazer argued that it all started, not with dreams, but with magic; Herbert Spencer thought it began with ancestor worship, and goes back no further than that. Also, as Ninian Smart has observed, 'It makes primitive man very logical in his approach to religious belief.' The process of development from one step to another involves a fairly sophisticated use of reason and inference. We know that developments in human culture are not usually quite so neat. Were human beings really so remorselessly rational?

There is another possibility, advanced by anthropologist Wilhelm Schmidt. He reverses Tylor's sequence, by claiming that there is evidence, all over the world, that the original belief of humanity was in one High God; and that only later on did this primal conviction become distorted by polytheism and 'animism' (or spirit-worship). This idea would seem to fit well with the apostle Paul's account of how religion developed:

Since the creation of the world God's invisible qualities—his eternal power and divine nature—have been clearly seen, being understood from what has been made, so that men are without excuse.

For although they knew God, they neither glorified him as God nor gave thanks to him, but their thinking became futile and their foolish hearts were darkened. Although they claimed to be wise, they became fools and exchanged the glory of the immortal God for images made to look like mortal man and birds and animals and reptiles.

'In any event,' agrees Ninian Smart, 'it is a striking fact that many primitive cultures have a belief in some sort of High God, even though very often there is no specific ritual directed toward such a being.'

Inward and outward religion

We may not be sure where religion started from, but we can trace its major developments through history with some assurance. One period of three hundred years was most important. Just before 800BC, in most major civilizations, religious worship had become bureaucratized. It was the preserve of a body of officially-appointed priests, with elaborate rituals and centralized administration. And then over three centuries, quite suddenly in culture after culture, came challenges to the established power of the priesthood, which led to some of the most creative and brilliant developments in human religious history.

In India, for instance, where there were already some sacred scriptures connected to priestly worship, a new kind of writing arose—devoted to explaining the inner, personal meaning of faith. The older scriptures had stressed the existence of several gods and the

Statues of the Buddha carry the serene expression of one who both taught and practised renouncing earthly desires.

importance of sacrifice; they had taught that in a sacrifice a certain power is released, called Brahman, which can help the worshipper. Now these new scriptures were claiming much more: that Brahman was not just a kind of energy, but the very energy which lies behind the world itself, and holds it all together. The old belief in several gods was beginning to lose its grip. Perhaps there was just one vital force with which people had to do?

The Indian writings are called the Upanishads. In Hebrew culture too, this was the time when the prophets tried to understand God's feelings about his chosen people and their behaviour. The picture painted by the prophets of a God who was unique, unrivalled and endlessly caring for his creation, laid the basis for no less than three world faiths: Christianity, Islam and Judaism.

Another development in India at this time was the emergence of two unusual men with genuinely original ideas. Gautama Buddha, the 'Enlightened One', cut through all religious complication by announcing a direct and clear philosophy: Life is unhappy when we are in the grip of earthly desires; losing these desires is the way to true freedom, integration and wholeness. The Buddha's 'Eightfold Path' is the way to learn how to eradicate earthly desires. Vardhamana Mahavir, on the other hand, stressed the need to do good: that would destroy the evil of the human heart, harmonize with the inbuilt moral order of the universe, and win salvation for the individual. The recipes were different, but both teachers agreed about one thing. Priests and sacrifices were unnecessary; the response of the individual to the forces at work in the universe—that was what religion should be about.

Meanwhile in Persia a religious teacher called Zoroaster (or more correctly Zarathustra) was upsetting old ideas too. Unlike the other great teachers of this period, he actually was a priest. But he taught that before God all human beings stand on an equal basis; that

Buddhist young men often undergo a period of training as monks.

ARE RELIGIOUS EXPERIENCES FOR EVERYONE?

Over the last three centuries, scientific advances have completely transformed our world. It's not surprising that many people in Western society now see scientific facts as somehow more 'real' than others. If a claim cannot be tested in a laboratory—analyzed, photographed and documented—how do we know it is true? If something cannot be measured and explained in cause-and-effect terms—how do we know it is happening?

This has led, claims Lesslie Newbigin, to a split in the minds of many human beings between the 'public world' of hard, objective, scientific fact, and the 'private world' of values, opinions and prejudices. In the 'public world' you have to believe the same facts as everyone else—that two and two make four— but in the 'private world' you can believe whatever you like. There is no proof.

And so many people look sceptically at religious experience, and doubt those who claim to have had an encounter with God. Is it all a private fantasy? Or does it have any objective meaning in the 'public world'?

Religious experience seems to be just as common as ever it was. In many industrialized countries, churchgoing has slumped dramatically this century. This has been explained as the inevitable outworking of 'secularization', as industrial people lose their need for religious faith. But, as Harvie Conn points out, this is not universal; there are signs that 'religion seems alive and fresh in the secular city'. And even if there is a seeming lack of interest in religion, it may simply mean that the religious impulse is taking another direction: people still need answers to the basic questions of life and death, and still build their lives on religious assumptions, whether or not they go to church.

David Hay of Nottingham University conducted interviews with a random sample of adults, most of whom did not belong to an organized religious group. He found that a surprisingly large percentage spoke of sensing a power or presence in their lives which was greater than themselves. Many of them said that they had never told anyone else about their experience.

Hay became convinced that 'religious experience is something biologically natural to man'. He added: 'The common testimony of the religious traditions and of those who have spoken to us is that they normally lead in the direction of personal integration and just behaviour towards fellow human beings.'

This may show that religious experience is natural to human beings, but how do we know if it is true? Some religions simply state flatly that it is, but make no attempt to justify their assertion. Christians claim that it is possible to go beyond this instinctive awareness of a greater power, and establish a personal relationship with God himself, which provides the ultimate proof of his reality. The final chapter of this book describes the experience in more detail.

ARE ALL RELIGIONS SAYING THE SAME THING?

Human beings follow many different religious paths. And even within major religions, there can be bewildering numbers of competing denominations and sub-groups. Within Islam there is profound disagreement between Shi'ite and Sunni Muslims, and Sufis have sometimes been so unorthodox as to be suspected of not being Muslims at all. In Buddhism, the Hinayana and Mahayana schools have very different viewpoints, and fringe groups such as the influential Nichiren Shoshu actually believe very little that the Buddha would have approved of. Hindu personalists and impersonalists argue with one another; Christianity is estimated to have 21,780 denominations and sub-groups within it. It seems that human beings have an infinite capacity for falling out with one another over metaphysical questions. But is it possible that, for all the disagreement, everyone is saying the same thing?

Over the last century there have been many 'syncretistic' movements, which have tried to harmonize the claims of different religions. An important landmark was the World Parliament of Religions, held in Chicago in 1893, when leaders of a colourful assortment of faiths came together to share their perspectives. The academic discipline of Comparative Religion, which began at about the same period, provided a method of evaluating world religions without making any prior assumptions about which—if any—was true. It became much more attractive than ever before to believe 'All religions lead to God', or 'Every great faith boils down to the same essential truth'.

However, if one wants to believe this, there are some problems to be faced. For one thing, different syncretistic movements have very different ideas about what the essential core of all religions actually is. Theosophy locates it in the 'theosophia', a collection of arcane esoteric knowledge and wisdom. Transcendental Meditation claims (without any historical evidence whatsoever) that it is the meditation technique which TM promotes. The Baha'i Faith claims that it is the shared vision of a group of strategic prophets who taught a basically Islamic view of God. Others say that the core is a bundle of shared ethical viewpoints, such as 'Do as you would be done by' and 'Love your neighbour as yourself'. Which is right?

Another problem is: how do we define a 'religion'? The word covers all sorts of different practices—from the ethical idealism of Guru Nanak to the murderous insanity of Charles Manson and the debased magic of Aleister Crowley. Do all these paths lead in the same direction? Or do we exclude some? If so, which?

Again, syncretists often underestimate the real divergences in the world view of different faiths. Is God one or are there many gods? Is he a person, or is it a thing? Do men live once, or reincarnate? How do we achieve union with God? Where did evil come from? To all these questions, and many others, the great religions return radically different answers. It leads to one simple conclusion: if all religions lead to God, then none of them tells us very much about him. Their competing claims cancel one another out.

Finally, there are those religions which claim to be unique. Christianity claims to be a once-for-all revelation from God, which applies to human beings of every culture and background: 'God now commands all men everywhere to repent.' We can reject this claim, or accept it; but we cannot ignore it. Either Christianity is the unique faith it claims to be or it stands condemned as an over-ambitious mistake.

Hindus bathe in the waters of the holy river Ganges at Varanasi.

they have a personal moral duty to choose good and shun evil. Zoroastrianism was to become, by the time of Christ, the most powerful religion of the known world; then slowly to sink into the background, surviving today only as the religion of the Parsis in India, and a small group of about 17,000 believers in Iran.

In China too, these were important times for religious development. Just eight years or so after the birth of the Buddha, the great teacher Confucius was born. Confucius (or K'ung Fu'Tzu, to give him his proper name) argued that it was wrong to focus one's attention on the next life: here and now there are duties and responsibilities to be observed. It was not that Confucius did not believe in the gods; but he stressed (just like the Buddha, the Hebrew prophets and Zoroaster) that sacrifice on its own will not achieve much; that it is much more important to examine carefully one's own moral life, and check that one's conduct is all it should be. As we saw in chapter eight, Confucius' teaching about ethics and relationships in society became the foundation of Chinese society for 2,500 years.

But Confucius was not the only Chinese religious genius. There was also Lao-Tse, born at around the same time. Just like the

Upanishad writers and Mahavir, Lao-Tse conceived ideas about one energy source which holds the universe together. But where the Upanishad scholars talked of Brahman and Mahavir described the moral power of the universe, Lao-Tse spoke of the 'Tao', the Divine Principle which explains and comprehends all reality:

The Tao that can be expressed is not the eternal Tao; The name that can be defined is not the unchanging name. Non-existence is called the antecedent of heaven and earth; Existence is the mother of all things. From eternal non-existence, therefore, We serenely observe the mysterious beginning of the universe; From eternal existence we clearly see the apparent distinctions. These two are the same in source and become different when manifested.

This is not remarkably clear. But at least one thing is obvious from it: Lao-Tse saw reality as made up of two balancing forces, a harmony of opposites. Later Taoism developed the idea of the Yin and the Yang—two great forces which interact with one another. (It is interesting that a Christian fringe religion today, the Unification Church, uses the idea of Yin and Yang in its theology, and actually calls its sacred book *Divine Principle.* It owes more to the Taoist background of its Korean founders than many of its Western followers realize.)

Taoists never believed that the Tao could be talked of as a personal God: 'How can the Creator have a conscious mind?' And some Upanishads take a similar view. Equally, the Buddha declared himself unsure about whether the gods existed or not. Certainly we could expect no direct help from them; human beings needed the Eightfold Path because they had to struggle with the issues of life unaided. Clearly the trend in many of these major religious developments was towards a concept of God which saw him as a force, a remote essence, incapable of being communicated with in a personal relationship.

And so in many ways it was going against

Jews have a high reverence for the 'Torah', the Law of Moses. Readings form part of synagogue worship. Here the book of the law is raised to show its pre-eminence.

the grain of world religious development for the Hebrew prophets to insist stubbornly that God was personal, and can be known in a personal way:

When you pass through the waters, I will be with you; and when you pass through the rivers, they will not sweep over you. When you walk through the fire, you will not be burned... Since you are precious and honoured in my sight, and because I love you, I will give men in exchange for you, and people in exchange for your life.

But in the end it was their concept of God which was to have the biggest impact on the world. Indeed, the other religions started to show signs of needing the same kind of God. As Buddhism developed and spread, more and more of a need came to be felt for some supernatural figure to which the worshipper could relate; and (not surprisingly) the Buddha himself became an object of worship. Nowadays we have all seen statues of the Buddha; every antique shop has a few. But those statues did not generally exist before the first century BC. That was when *bhakti*, personal feelings of love and devotion to the Buddha, became popular. (This has led to a situation today in which there are two rival schools of Buddhism in the world: one stressing the element of personal devotion, the other largely ignoring it.)

In Hinduism, there was a similar change of direction. In the second century BC (or perhaps a little later) appeared the most famous Hindu scripture of all: the *Bhagavad Gita*, 'the Song of the Lord'. It takes the form of a poem in which Arjuna, a warrior prince facing a dangerous battle, receives a vision of the god Krishna himself, and begins to understand the vital importance of personal love and devotion to him. The *Gita* does not deny the earlier teaching about Brahman, but suggests that Brahman can take personal form in the shape of one of the gods, such as Krishna; and that devotion to a god might achieve forgiveness of sin and eventual salvation.

(Today the well-known Hare Krishna cult bases its entire faith on a literal reading of the *Gita*. Hare Krishna disciples devote themselves utterly to the person of Krishna, worship him with chants and meditation, and shave off all their hair except for a top-knot—which is retained, by tradition, so that Krishna can use it to haul the deserving disciple up to heaven.)

But from the heart of the truly personal faith—Judaism—sprang the most amazing surge of religious enterprise in world history. When Jesus Christ died on the cross in Jerusalem, he had only 120 followers, all of whom had fled and left him to die. Within a short space afterwards, they were travelling all over the ancient world boldly proclaiming their message, and founding churches as they went. What had happened? J.M. Roberts, a historian who is not a Christian, says of Jesus' teachings:

Though they were effective in his lifetime, they seemed to die with him. At his death his followers were only one tiny Jewish sect among many. But they believed that a unique thing had happened. They believed that Christ had risen from the dead...

Christians established themselves in Europe, North Africa and the Middle East, and indeed became so numerous that the Roman emperor Constantine finally decided to make Christianity the state religion of the empire.

This access to power and influence was not all good for Christianity. For less than three hundred years later, 'Christians' in the Arabian peninsula were leading such hypocritical lives that a young merchant was shocked. He came to believe that if God is all-high and all-holy, then Christians must have distorted the Scriptures to make life comfortable for themselves; for they did not show God any real respect. When one day the young trader, Muhammad, heard voices in his ears telling him to write, he obeyed; and so (in time) came about the Qur'an, the sacred book of the Islamic faith.

'Islam' simply means 'submission', 'Muslim' means 'one who submits'. The whole basis of Islam is that God has set rules for living, which when observed bring happiness and success, and when ignored bring chaos and disillusionment. Muslims do not talk of a God of 'love' as Christians do. God is the all-merciful; but nothing more than that. He is so highly exalted above humanity that it is blasphemous to speak of him in a familiar way.

Muhammad was a persuasive teacher, and the vision of brotherhood he offered to the Arabs made instant headway. Within fifty years Islam was the dominant faith of North Africa, much of Spain, parts of Central Asia, and almost the whole of the Middle East. Later it

Such figures as the Ayatollah Khomeini and Yasser Arafat are symbols of Islam's high political profile. Religious fundamentalism, of several different kinds, has a strong following today.

was to penetrate Africa further south, parts of Central Asia.

However, there were often violent clashes between Hindus and Muslims in India, and that was what provoked Guru Nanak (1469–1538) to begin a new religious grouping which would combine the best of Hinduism and Islam. The new religion has come to be called Sikhism.

Sikhs combine a Hindu view of life—such as a belief in rebirth after death—with the Muslim view of one highly exalted but personal God. Nanak was convinced that good insights could be had within each tradition; that the saints of Hinduism and Islam genuinely had, each in their own way, made contact with God. It was folly to stand apart and criticize the other belief.

Unfortunately, Sikhs found themselves cut off from both the Hindu and the Muslim communities. Rather than being a bridge between the two, they were forced to become a grouping on their own; and to defend themselves militarily, which involved doing some things which were against the strict code of *ahimsa* (non-violence) which they had been taught. Sikhs in India today feel themselves a beleaguered minority, threatened by the large groups around them.

Is there a god?

Many centuries before Christ, a Hebrew psalmist wrote, 'The fool has said in his heart that there is no God.' It has always been possible to be a complete unbeliever, at almost any stage of history; atheism is not an entirely new development. The ancient Greek philosopher Epicurus, for example, taught that the universe was simply a material object, that human beings were accidental, and the gods non-existent. But it is true that over the last two hundred years unbelief has become more popular in the West than it has ever been anywhere.

There are many causes for this. One is the movement of thought in the eighteenth century, called the Enlightenment (see chapter eight), when after a century of religious wars European thinkers despaired of ever making sense of religion and instead tried to reason their way to sensible principles of living. If God was still allowed to exist, he was thought of simply as the First Mover, the craftsman who had made everything and set it in motion; but impossibly remote from practical concerns on a day-to-day basis.

Then came the rapid industrialization of the following century. People were torn from their former community life and jammed together into city streets where the old certainties, the former symbols, did not seem to apply any more. Churchgoing dropped steadily, and the Western world started to see the beginnings of 'secularization'—the word sociologists use for the way in which modern styles of living are rendering religion peripheral to the lives of an increasing number of people.

Another pull against traditional beliefs was exerted by nineteenth-century scientific discoveries which seemed to call in question the claims of the Bible. When Charles Darwin finally published *Origin of Species* in 1859 (after sitting on it for over twenty years, scared of the reaction it would provoke), he appeared to be challenging the accuracy of the book of Genesis. Some defenders of the Bible were ill-informed, illogical and abusive, and many people started to assume that science was now undermining the foundations of Christian faith.

A major expression of unbelief gathering momentum at about this time was 'humanism',

WHEN DID ATHEISM BEGIN?

It is sometimes thought that in previous ages everyone was superstitious and credulous, and so believed in supernatural powers of all kinds. Only recently, on this view, in our more enlightened times, did humans dare to start believing, 'There is no God.' In fact this is not true.

■ We know that some of the great Greek philosophers were unbelievers: they cautioned their disciples to observe all the religious rites which society expected of them, so as not to scandalize the public and make trouble for themselves, but in fact thinkers such as Democritus of Abdera (c460-c370BC) were thoroughgoing materialists. Others such as Epicurus (341–270BC) did not deny the existence of the gods, but did deny that there is any divine providence or purpose, any supernatural intervention in this life or punishment hereafter, and any existence of the human soul after death. In fact, the gods had so little to do in his scheme of things that for all practical purposes they did not exist.

■ One of the founders of the great world religions was undecided about the gods. The Buddha was content to remain unsure whether or not they existed. Only one thing was certain about the gods, he taught: they were not going to help human beings. Buddhism is an applied philosophy to help human beings live their lives without supernatural assistance.

■ Atheism in the West started to become much more attractive after the rise of science, which showed that natural features of the physical world could be explained in terms of natural law, without any direct intervention from God or gods. Science had not disproved or undermined religious faith; but it had removed one 'proof' on which many people had naively built their faith 'There could not be a world like this unless God was constantly pulling strings to make things happen.' And so when Napoleon asked the astronomer Laplace what part God played in the *System of the World* Laplace had put together, he was told 'Sire, I have had no need to make use of that hypothesis.'

It needs to be remembered that many of the great scientists (such as Galileo and Newton) and the philosophers who struggled with the implications of their discoveries (such as Descartes and Kant) were convinced Christians. But their work opened the door to new possibilities for human minds, and atheism was one of them.

One influential figure was the eighteenth century philosopher Georg Hegel (1770–1831), who believed that God was the 'world-spirit' whom we encounter in the processes of the world—not an independent figure. 'Without the world God is not God.' Hegel influenced Ludwig Feuerbach (1804–72), who was more radical: for him, religion was just 'the dream of the human mind', and talking about God was simply a coded way of talking about what humanity wanted to be like. God did not exist at all.

The stage was set for the arrival of nineteenth- and twentieth-century atheism, which has taken too many different forms to describe. Three have been particularly influential. **Marxism** took its lead from Hegel and Feuerbach. They argued that the force which they saw running through history, was not to be identified with God; religion was simply 'opium for the people'. **Humanism**, which emerged from the thought of men such as Thomas Huxley and Leslie Stephen, who insisted that this is the only world there is, and human welfare within it must be our prime concern. **Atheistic existentialism**, which centred on French thinkers Jean-Paul Sartre and Albert Camus, claimed we must face the fact that we are living in an absurd universe, and bravely reckon with the contradictions and frustrations we cannot escape. 'Atheism is a cruel, long-term business,' Sartre wrote, 'I believe I have gone through it to the end.'

a school of thought which claimed that humanity could find true dignity in life only by facing up to the fact that we are alone in the universe, and must try to solve our problems for ourselves. Some of the humanists were brilliant people, such as the philosopher Bertrand Russell, who summed up the humanist viewpoint memorably in one famous statement:

That Man is the product of causes which had no prevision of the end they were achieving; that his origin, his growth, his hopes and fears, his loves and his beliefs, are but the outcome of accidental collocations of atoms; that no fire, no heroism, no intensity of thought and feeling, can preserve an individual life beyond the grave; that all the labour of the ages, all the devotion, all the inspiration, all the noonday brightness of human genius, are destined to extinction in the vast death of the solar system, and that the whole temple of Man's achievement must inevitably be buried beneath the debris of a universe in ruins—all these things, if not quite beyond dispute, are yet so nearly certain, that no philosophy which rejects them can hope to stand.

Interestingly, Russell's own daughter returned to religious belief; she became a Christian. Later she wrote:

I would have liked to convince my father that I had found what he had been looking for, the ineffable something he had longed for all his life. I would have liked to persuade him that the search for God does not have to be in vain. But it was hopeless. He had known too many blind Christians, bleak moralists who sucked the joy from life and persecuted their opponents; he would never have been able to see the truth they were hiding.

The other influential form of unbelief was Marxism, the faith which today controls the lives of millions of people worldwide. Karl Marx believed that religion was an instrument used by the ruling classes to keep the workers in their place; it had no objective reality, and must be fought as strenuously as possible.

Marx drew his ideas about religion from German philosopher Ludwig Feuerbach, who claimed that human beings create God in their own image—in other words, that the statements we make about God (God is good, God is loving, and so on) are really just declarations of our own ideals. The more we think about God, the less able we will be to progress. Said Marx, 'The more man puts into God, the less he retains himself.'

Can we accept this as a fair account of what religion is about? David Hay, a researcher into religious experience, thinks not. He remarks:

Convinced atheists like Freud and Marx certainly felt they had explained religion away, yet their criticisms. . . are purely functional: religion is false consciousness, or a neurosis, and leads to the diminishment of man.

. . .The evidence collected over the past two decades suggests that these attacks, partly determined by a nineteenth-century positivism which had already dismissed religion before examining it in details, were too sweeping. All recent studies of the 'experiential' dimension of religion show that it is typically associated with personal integration, a sense of meaningfulness in life, and concern for social justice.

THE FAITH THAT GREW AND GREW

Which religious teacher has had most impact on the human race? The answer has got to be: Jesus Christ. He started with no conventional advantages; he was not born in a prominent place geographically, nor was he a member of an important family, nor did he receive an extensive education. And he died at an early age compared with the founders of other religions. Yet Jesus has had a staggering impact on human history. He left behind no writings or even a visible organization; his committed followers, numbering about 120 when he died, are said to have lost their courage and deserted him at his death.

Yet today the Christian church exists in virtually every country in the world—including hostile societies such as Albania, where Christianity has officially been exterminated but secret fellowships are still known to meet. After seventy years of atheistic propaganda in the Soviet Union, the number of Christians there has actually increased. At the time of writing, the Soviet government is changing its policy, and seeking closer links with Christian churches instead of trying to undermine their activities.

Almost one-third of human beings today are associated with Christianity, at least to the extent of keeping the membership qualifications of a church. It has been estimated that 63 thousand people each week become Christians.

The amazing spread of Christianity is sometimes attributed to the fact that it is a religion of the West, and Western civilization has carried it throughout the world. But Christianity showed signs of unexpected vitality long before it became an accepted Western faith. In its earliest days, for example, Christians were severely penalized and persecuted by the Roman Empire, and there was every reason to expect that the faith would die out—or at least go underground as an esoteric minority belief. In fact Christianity had become so widespread within three centuries that the Roman emperor Constantine gave up trying to fight the inevitable, and established Christianity as the state religion of the empire. After many centuries of Roman state religion, this was a striking about-turn, and would not have happened unless Christianity's power to spread seemed quite invincible.

Christians attribute the impact of Christianity to the uniqueness of its founder. Jesus Christ made claims which are quite unprecedented in the history of religion. His followers said that he claimed to be the Son of God—a title which denoted an intimate special relationship with God which no other human being has ever had. He taught that through his death human beings could find forgiveness for their wrongdoing, and come to know God's presence in their lives as Father, guide and king.

His claims were not the only unusual thing about him. From the earliest times, Christians have asserted that Jesus was a worker of miracles, and that he rose from his grave after burial, since death could not defeat the Son of God. These ideas have often been derided as impossible, and yet there is a great deal of suggestive evidence which has often convinced sceptics. If Jesus did not do what Christians claim he did, there is a historical puzzle to be solved.

But all of this would not be sufficient to explain Jesus' impact. Early Christians believed that 'if anyone is in Christ, he is a new creation; the old has gone, the new has come!' And this experience of transformation, of 'new life', has been the clinching factor for many millions of people down through the centuries.

Christianity has spread further and faster than any other religion. One reason is the imagination and energy with which it has been made known. Here a street drama gives emotional impact to a Gospel story.

Can God be known?

Ultimately there are three positions we can take with regard to religious experience:

- We can simply say, 'Religious experience is not real or helpful.' This is Marx's position, and also the position of J.G. Frazer, whom we discussed earlier. Frazer believed that it was possible to trace the same symbols and myths—for example, of the dying and rising God—in a variety of different religious traditions, and therefore that we were not to think of *any* of the stories as literally true. At one stage of his life C.S. Lewis was an admirer of Frazer. Then he came to believe that there was a difference between Christian claims and the other myths:

Now the story of Christ is simply a true myth: a myth working on us in the same way as the others, but with this tremendous difference that it really happened.

- Or we can say, 'Religious experience is real, and it happens to just about everyone.' This is David Hay's position. He has studied for several years the claims made by ordinary people who feel that they have encountered God. He has found that these kinds of experiences happen over and over again:

Something woke me up. There was something or somebody by my bed; I wasn't frightened. Within ten minutes the torment I'd felt, for some strange reason left me. I think I had more peace then than I'd had for a very long time... I have enough knowledge to know that there's somebody there, to know that I need never be so alone again...

I began praying, not really sure that there was a God. At one particular time after a great deal of hought a relaxation came upon my mind and everything fitted together. It only lasted for a moment, perhaps four to five seconds... I really felt God was communicating with me.

This sounds like the sort of thing which the Bible predicts should happen:

From one nation God made every nation of men, that they should inhabit the whole earth; and he determined the times set for them and the exact places where they should live. God did this so that men would seek him and perhaps reach out for him and find him, though he is not far from each one of us.

■ Perhaps these fleeting experiences are all we can ever know of God. Or perhaps there is a third possibility? This would be to say, 'Religious experience is real, and can be a signpost towards God; but a *deeper* relationship with God is possible too.'

Jesus Christ is on record as saying, 'I am the way, truth and life; no one comes to the Father except through me.' One of the distinctive things about Jesus' teaching was the way he constantly referred to God as 'the Father'—an emphasis not much explored in Judaism, despite its strong belief in a personal, caring God. It was as if he was saying that it is possible for human beings to approach God more closely—to have an individual relationship with him which is as intimate as a father-child relationship. And that the only way to establish such a connection is 'through' Jesus.

We will examine this claim more closely in another chapter. But here we should note that what seems like the apparent staggering arrogance of his statement immediately sets Jesus Christ apart from other religious leaders. He was not content to be a prophet or a rabbi, a Guru Nanak or a Lao-Tse; he said he was the one direct route to God. And today, two thousand years later, almost a quarter of the human race claims to follow him and believe the claim.

Could he have been telling the truth? Let C.S. Lewis have the last word.

On the one side clear, definite moral teaching. On the other, claims which, if not true, are those of a megalomaniac, compared with whom Hitler was the most sane and humble of men. There is no half-way house and there is no parallel in other religions. . . The idea of a great moral teacher saying what Christ said is out of the question. In my opinion, the only person who can say that sort of thing is either God or a complete lunatic suffering from that form of delusion which undermines the whole mind of man.

THE HEART OF IT ALL

Human beings have a seemingly incurable habit of looking for patterns. You can test this by sprinkling ink blots at random on a piece of paper, and then showing it to some friends, asking them what they see. They may come up with different ideas, but most will be able to see some sort of picture there. The same is true of imagining faces in the clouds or melted snow, or guessing the next number in a sequence, or sensing a connection in the events that happen to you from day to day. (Which is why humans are often easily persuaded by the claims of astrologers and fortune tellers; and why we have to be careful with claims of answers to prayer.) The human mind does not like randomness; it always looks for meaning. Presented with a pile of bits of information, it instinctively sets about sorting them into an organized pattern.

And one thing we have discovered about patterns is that the whole can be more than the sum of the parts. You can describe a piece of wood in terms of its chemical composition, the pigment adhering to it, and the position of the molecules involved; but until you have also stated that it is a signpost bearing the message *Trespassers Will be Shot*, you have certainly not exhausted its meaning! Similarly, as we have seen, you can count up the chemical constituents of human life, and put them in a fairly accurate list, right down to the last traces of selenium and molybdenum. But you have not even started to assess the importance and meaning of human life.

In a famous book called *Holism and Evolution*, written in 1923, South African premier Jan Christian Smuts claimed that analyzing the elements of things would never give us the truth about the universe. He insisted that if we do not look at wholes, and appreciate the drive towards higher organization which is present in nature itself, we will never understand the significance of the isolated discoveries we make.

Examining the track is no way to discover what a railroad is for! We need to learn to see life whole.

More recently, a new approach known as General Systems Theory has taught that the component parts of any system are so intimately related in their interactions that it is dangerously misleading to consider them separately. A single variable can be both cause and effect within the system. We have to understand the whole, not just aspects of the parts. 'General Systems Theory is symptomatic of a change in our world view,' says Ludwig von Bertalanffy. 'No longer do we see the world in a blind play of atoms, but rather a great organization.'

The whole and the parts. . . This book about human beings has concerned itself with the 'parts'. We have explored the body, the brain, the personality, the successes and failures, the social life and sexual differences, of *Homo sapiens sapiens*. We have looked at fringe possibilities—extra-sensory powers, contact with alien races, fire-walking, vampirism, levitation. And even in our survey of the parts, we have left out a shamefully large amount. I am conscious, for example, that a Marxist would object that I have paid scant attention to the way in which economic forces shape society; and a mystic would look in vain for an adequate treatment of ecstatic experience, altered levels of consciousness, meditation and asceticism. I would personally like to have spent more time on hypnotism, yoga, the development of philosophical thought, sexual behaviour, the significance of clothes, body language, human ritual. But the list is endless. In no way can one book address all the aspects of the rich, variegated, paradoxical jumble of human life.

However, it has been on the 'parts' rather than the 'whole' that we have focused. Now I want to redress the balance a little, before the end of the book. And I need to do this for a very important reason: anyone who writes about the 'parts' will tend to do so in a way that reflects his view of the 'whole'. All writers make assumptions about the meaning and significance of their subject. I am no exception.

I have a suspicion that if this book had been written by, say, David Attenborough or Desmond Morris, it would have come out rather differently. This is because I am assuming a view of human life which is a little different from theirs, because I am a Christian. And although I have tried to be fair, and to present only facts which I can be sure are true, my starting point is inevitably going to colour the way I write.

And so it is time to tie all the loose ends together. What is the 'whole', where human life is concerned? What is the ultimate significance, the point and purpose, of this endlessly fascinating development in an otherwise lonely universe?

The point of life

As we have seen, some thinkers find no point in life. Our existence is merely absurd; we are a chance accident in space (admittedly a most improbable one), and there is no continuing meaning in what happens to us day by day. Death ends everything; there is no Creator in charge, and we could well end our own history by blowing ourselves up.

This does not mean that such thinkers merely opt out of life with nerveless resignation. Jean-Paul Sartre spoke of the need to achieve 'authentic existence', not just passively accepting whatever the universe happened to do to us. And some of the great humanists have been tireless workers for social justice and human liberties. But it does mean, that in the end, as humanist Kit Mouat put it, 'If it is necessary, humanists would rather state flatly that they have no final cut-and-dried reason why they believe that Man must live a good and constructive life.'

Other people teach that our present life is not the final truth about us. Indeed, this life is basically illusion: the real 'us' belongs somewhere else, as part of the great creative force which underlies everything and breathes through all life. And so the point of life is to realize that we do not belong here, that this world is not ultimately real, that only when we lose our individuality and stop being personally differentiated will we at last achieve integration and harmony.

This is the position of some of the great Eastern religions. But there are problems with this claim. C.E.M. Joad complained, in a famous passage, that it did not make much sense for 'me' to aspire towards a condition in which 'I' would cease to exist! I can believe, if I like, that this world is not real, and that my personality is basically illusory; but while I am on this planet, I have to live *as if* it is real and *as if* I am an individual. All the experiences of life supply me with evidence that this is actually true. If I want to believe it is not, I take a step of faith on the basis of no evidence whatsoever.

Christians like myself have a different view from either of these two. Looking at human beings, Christians see that one of the most significant things about us is that we are social animals: we exist in relationship to others, and it is through others that most of the important experiences of life come to us. Now there is nothing specifically Christian about this insight; Matthew Arnold, for instance, saw human relationships as the one source of meaning human beings can find:

Ah love, let us be true
To one another! for the world, which seems
To lie before us like a land of dreams,
So various, so beautiful, so new,
Hath really neither joy, nor love, nor light,
Nor certitude, nor peace, nor help for pain. . .

Paul Simon has expressed the same idea more starkly:

And so you see I have come to doubt
All that I once held was true
I stand alone without beliefs;
The only truth I know is you.

But to build our whole lives on the important relationships we have with other people is to risk disappointment, and in the end futility. The Western world is full of older people whose partners have died, and who consequently, although they are physically healthy enough to last for another twenty years, have no further reason for living. And since divorce rates have climbed so steeply in recent years,

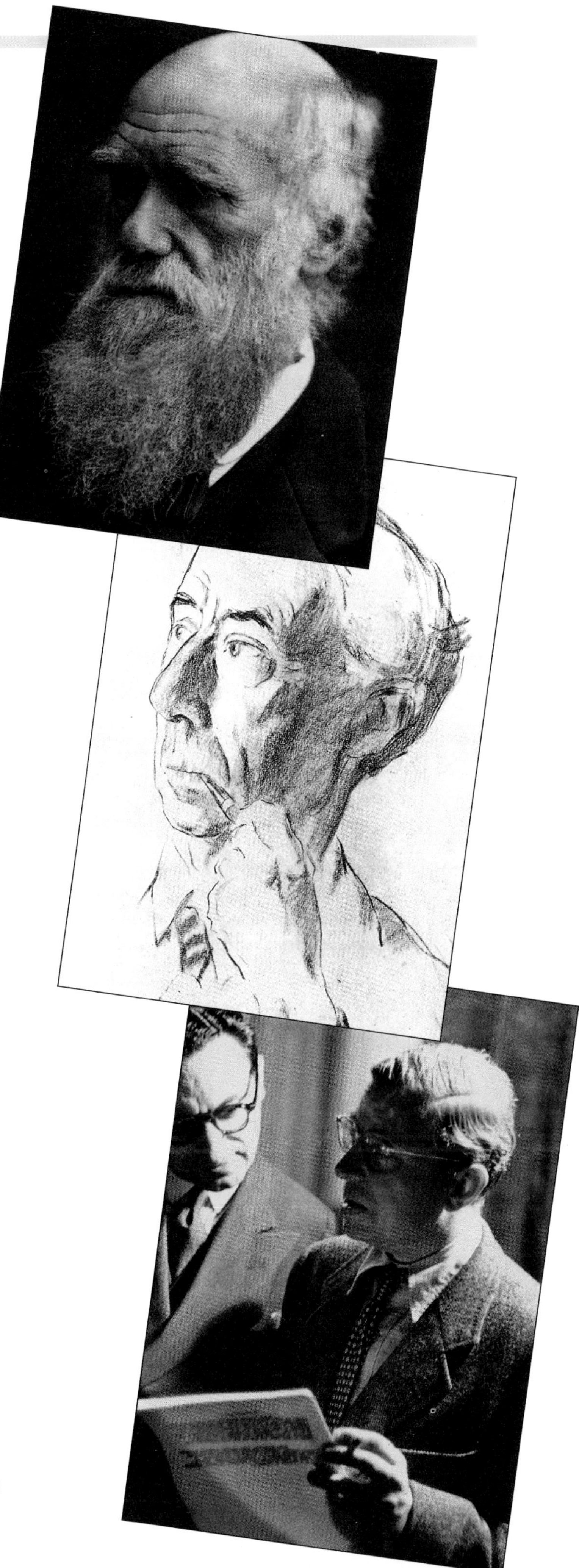

Darwin's theory of evolution made people rethink their belief in God's creation; the positivist philosophy of Bertrand Russell and the existentialism of Jean Paul Sartre were both avowedly atheistic. Christianity has taken some knocks in the last century, but it is still very much alive.

many sociologists have started to ask: is it because we look for too much from marriage nowadays? If we are looking to human relationships to supply the ultimate meaning of our lives, are we placing on them a strain they cannot bear? The words of a pop star's deserted wife—herself an intelligent, articulate actress—are instructive:

Ever since I was a little girl, I thought marriage was what comes at the end of the rainbow. Maybe I just put too much stress on it.

Christians claim that humans were created to be dependent on relationships, not just with other human beings—but also with God himself. And only in this permanent, unfailing relationship can true meaning and purpose be found. Paul the apostle wrote:

I am convinced that neither death nor life, neither angels nor demons, neither the present nor the future, nor any powers, neither height nor depth, not anything else in all creation, will be able to separate us from the love of God that is in Christ Jesus our Lord.

God is therefore not an impersonal force (as some religions believe) nor a remote lawgiver (as others see him). Neither is he a distant, mysterious figure who may have created us, but is now unknowable and beyond our grasp. God, if the Bible is correct, stands ready to establish a relationship of love and trust with any of his creatures who is willing to encounter him.

This is what the Bible means when it says that humanity was made 'in the image of God'. The resemblance is not physical; God is not a physical entity. Nor can we fix on one key quality of human beings (reason, or morality, or creativity) and say that is especially like something in God. Rather, says philosopher Arthur Holmes, it means:

A human being's relationship to God, seen both in dependency on God and in bearing God's image in the world, makes us all at heart religious beings. Our highest end, our all-inclusive supreme good, is to glorify God and enjoy him forever... As dependent, we must seek God in all we are and do. As responsible image-bearers, we represent the Creator in all of it, too.

Human relationships

'Representing the Creator' means that our relationship with God will affect all the other relationships we have in our lives.

- **It will affect our relationship to nature**. If we are creatures of the dust of the earth,

Alexander Solzhenitsyn is one of a galaxy of great men and women who have maintained Christian faith and values, often against great odds.

dependent on nature for our continuing existence, and yet responsible to God for the way we treat it, then there are certain things we cannot do. We cannot treat the world as if it does not matter. Christians take the human body seriously (and the rest of the natural creation as well), because they cannot accept the teaching that this world is basically evil or illusory. It is the real creation of a good God, and must be given its full value.

On the other hand, neither can Christians treat the world as if it is all-important. The kind of naturalistic, materialist viewpoint which reduces humanity to just one fortuitous component of nature—this cannot be a Christian attitude. Christians are always conscious that there is something beyond the physical; we are more than hapless machines. Our bodies and brains are subject to physical influences and conditioning, but there is still a real human freedom and responsibility which remains uneroded by the speculations of Pavlov, Skinner, Desmond Morris.

And so when it comes to ecology, Christians line themselves up with those who want to preserve the environment and protect our vital ecosystem. God's creation must be safeguarded, and we are responsible for that. On the other hand, there is a strain of nature mysticism running through the thinking of many campaigners for the environment—as if the world were some kind of deity in itself. Christians want no part of that. The world is God's creation; that makes it very important, but not somehow worshipped in itself.

- **Living in the image of God also affects our relationship to other people**. If all other humans are made in the image of God, as I am, then I cannot manipulate or abuse them; I cannot treat them as mere objects. Every human life matters, however useless or unproductive it may seem to be. I cannot 'write off' those I do not like, taking refuge in the thought that they are just accidents in the cosmos, or evanescent incarnations who will live again many times.

Of course, Christians have no monopoly on the idea that 'every life matters'. But if human beings are *not* the individual, personal creations of a loving God, such a belief becomes unexpectedly hard to justify. Humanists would unanimously condemn Hitler for the slaughter of six million Jews; but, as we have seen Kit Mouat admit, 'for no final cut-and-dried reason'. Mahatma Ghandi is a marvellous example of a Hindu who was motivated by infinite concern for other individual human beings; but there was no justification for his attitude within his philosophical system.

- **The image of God also leaves its mark on our relationship with ourselves**. On the one hand, we are created beings, operated on by an awesome variety of physical forces, which condition and shape us definitively. That should give us a proper humility, and an awareness of our own limitations.

This kind of humility has often been forgotten in Western culture. It happened during the Enlightenment of the eighteenth century, when reason seemed to be the key to all life's mysteries and the means by which the planet could be brought to perfection:

The shades of ignorance, of intellectual night Will fade and flee before the coming light.

It happened again in the mid-nineteenth century optimism of 'social Darwinism', when thinkers such as Herbert Spencer were proclaiming that 'progress is not an accident, but a necessity... It is the law of nature'. It happened again in the rise of humanistic psychology in the twentieth century, and the 'New Age' movement of the 1970s, with its belief that the human race was entering the 'Age of Aquarius', an era of staggering new potentials, cosmic powers and worldwide peace.

The history of the human being, and the way we are made, does not warrant any such optimism. Christianity focuses clearly on the smallness and dependence of human beings. As one of the Psalms puts is:

When I consider your heavens, the work of your fingers, the moon and the stars, which you have set in place, what is man that you are mindful of him, the son of man that you care for him?

It is a good question, and the answer is: 'You made him a little lower than the heavenly beings and crowned him with glory and honour'. The Christian view of human nature includes a realization that our lives have a real dignity and purpose. Human individuality matters, and I am responsible to shape my life by my own choices and calculations. I am not the plaything of fate; I am a free being.

Sometimes people have complained that the Bible's attitude is excessively gloomy. Christians have been criticized for talking too much about guilt and sin, for producing a cult of self-abasement which denies human beings the chance to stand on their own feet and take legitimate pride in their own achievements. Now certainly some Christianity has erred in this direction. There are some startlingly spineless hymns:

O to be nothing, nothing!
Simply to lie at his feet. . .

But this is not the Bible's picture of a free, responsible figure of dignity, 'crowned. . . with glory and honour'. Our relationship with ourselves need to be realistic, and humble; but not negative or dismissive.

In all of these ways, then—our relationship with nature, other people, and ourselves—it makes a tremendous difference to believe that we are made 'in the image of God'. But why *should* anyone believe it? Are there good grounds for believing that it is true?

Knowing for sure

Christians believe that much of the objective evidence about humankind points in the direction of a Creator God. For one thing, the chance of life emerging on earth at all was vanishingly small; it is hard to believe that something as complex and sophisticated as the human being should have emerged through mere accident. And if the highest form of life we know on earth is personal, it is reasonable to suppose that anything higher than ourselves might also be personal—and might attach as much importance to relationships as we do ourselves. Christians also look at the evidence about Jesus Christ, who claimed to be the ultimate revelation of God's nature, and find there things which cannot be explained unless Jesus was exactly who he claimed to be.

Considerations such as these are strong indications that God is real; they give good, but not conclusive, evidences. Is there a way we can know for sure? Only by putting God to the test: 'Find out for yourself how good the Lord is,' urges the Psalmist. The early Christians were confident that something had happened to them which had altered their experience of life permanently, and introduced them to the friendship of God.

But if this is so, why are we not experiencing it already? Because human beings are not automata, but have responsibility for their own actions. Arthur Holmes comments, 'To be responsible. . . implies that I can do something that will make the relationship different.' And the Bible asserts that this is exactly what has happened. The human race has misused its freedom and turned its back on God, preferring to live life independently. To quote the Psalms again:

There is no one who is righteous, no one who is wise or who worships God.

Writing in 1948, just after the discovery of the atomic bomb, Albert Einstein remarked, 'What terrifies us is not the explosive force of the atomic bomb, but the power of the wickedness

Who should we follow? There is a wide choice of blind guides. Are they a good bet?

HUMAN LIFE AS THE WRITERS DESCRIBE IT

But man, proud man,
Drest in a little brief authority,
Most ignorant of what he's most assur'd,
His glassy essence, like an angry ape,
Plays such fantastic tricks before high heaven
As make the angels weep.
Shakespeare, *Measure for Measure*

Glory to Man in the highest! for Man is the master of things.
Algernon Swinburne

The life of man, solitary, poor, nasty, brutish, and short.
Thomas Hobbes, *Leviathan*

But trailing clouds of glory do we come
From God, who is our home;
Heaven lies about us in our infancy!
William Wordsworth

Human life is everywhere a state in which much is to be endured, and little to be enjoyed.
Samuel Johnson

Created half to rise, and half to fall;
Great lord of all things, yet a prey to all;
Sole judge of truth, in endless error hurled;
The glory, jest, and riddle, of the world!
Alexander Pope

Man is only a reed, the weakest thing in nature; but he is a thinking reed.
Blaise Pascal

I am a man; I count nothing human alien from me.
Terence

Man is by nature a political animal.
Aristotle

If we may believe our logicians, man is distinguished from all other creatures by the faculty of laughter.
Joseph Addison

In a short while the tribes of living things are changed, and like runners hand on the torch of life.
Lucretius

If God does not exist. . . man is in consequence forlorn, for he cannot find anything to depend on, either within or outside himself.
Jean-Paul Sartre

What is man that you are mindful of him,
the son of man that you care for him?
You made him a little lower than the heavenly beings
and crowned him with glory and honour.
You made him ruler over the works of your hands;
you put everything under his feet. . .
Psalm 8

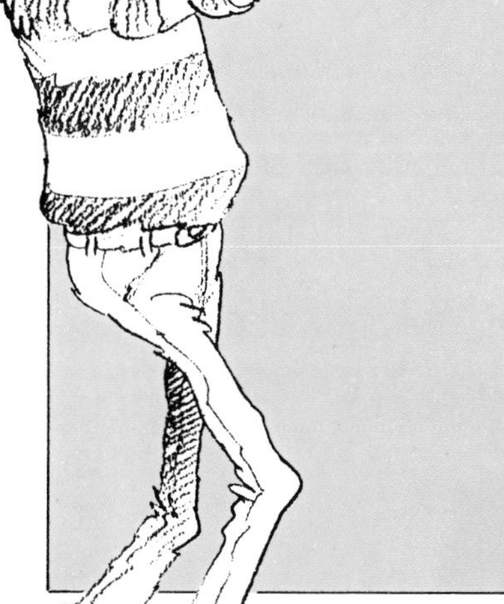

of the human heart, its explosive power for evil.' The greatest problem of humankind is the problem of our own moral failure—what the Bible calls sin. The history of our race demonstrates clearly just how fallible we are. And, as I have tried to argue in the chapter on the workings of our brains, we cannot blame our failures on our conditioning; we are free to choose for ourselves.

Sin affects all the relationships which human beings were created to enjoy. Our relationship with the world, for example; we are misusing the resources of our planet. Our relationship with other people is affected, too: racism, genocide, social and caste barriers are all evidence of the divisions that sin has brought between us. Our relationship with ourselves suffers: we feel guilty and annoyed with ourselves when we do now live as we feel we should, and we cannot make sense of our own existence. Rock singer Bruce Springsteen has been treated as a contemporary messiah by many young people today; yet he says, 'I don't have the answer to anyone's life, including my own. We're all just thumbing through the darkness looking for that bright spot.'

God's solution

All these broken relationships are serious. But the worst effect of sin on the human race is that it shuts us in to an existence without God, an empty universe in which contact has been broken with the infinite. Small wonder that existentialists such as conclude that God is just not there:

Up till now, man derived his coherence from his Creator. But from the moment that he consecrates his rupture with him, he finds himself delivered over to the fleeting moment, to the passing days, and to wasted sensibility.

Yet Christians insist that God has not left us, that the 'rupture' need not be final; that in fact God has taken the initiative and found a way of breaking through the barrier between human beings and himself. This way is, to use New Testament words, 'through the coming of our Saviour, Jesus Christ'. How did Jesus' coming make a difference?

When Jesus Christ died he took the brunt of the penalty we deserved—to pay for our sins and rebellion against God. He stood in our place and accepted our blame. As a result of his death, we can go free.

Because of Jesus' death for us, human beings are faced with another choice: to continue ignoring God, and live life in proud independence; or to accept forgiveness gladly and begin to experience the friendship of God. One man who chose the second option, while on the run from the American authorities, was Black Panther leader Eldridge Cleaver. He wrote of his experience:

That night I slept the most peaceful sleep I have ever known in my life. I woke up the next morning with a start, as though someone had touched me, and I could see in my mind the way, all the way back home, just as clear as I've ever seen anything. . . I had it within my power to get back home by taking that first step, by surrendering; and it was a certainty that everything was going to be all right. I just knew that—that was the solution, and I would be all right if I would take that step.

And so this is the 'whole' which Christians believe—I believe—makes sense of the fascinating 'parts' we have examined in this book. Human beings can 'get back home'. They can find, just as Eldridge Cleaver did, a relationship with God which unifies and integrates and intensifies and deepens all that it means to be truly human.

All the rest of this book remains true and valid, whether or not the reader accepts the truth of this closing personal statement of faith.

But it would be strange indeed to collect all kinds of data about the human experience, and yet not take time to weigh up the claims of Jesus which many people have found make sense of everything else. This is what it is all about. This is the ultimate meaning of humankind.

Today's young people look on into an uncertain future. What kind of life will they choose to live?

Books quoted in 'The Human Difference'

John Archer and Barbara Lloyd, *Sex and Gender*, Pelican 1982

Robert Ardrey, *The Social Contract*, Fontana 1970

Michael Argyle, *The Psychology of Interpersonal Behaviour*, Pelican 1972

Isaac Asimov, *The Universe: From Flat Earth to Quasar*, Pelican 1971

Peter Berger, *Facing Up to Modernity*, Basic Books 1977

Peter Berger, *The Social Reality of Religion*, Penguin 1973

P. Berger and T. Luckman, *The Social Construction of Reality*, Penguin 1971

P. Berger, B. Berger and H. Kellner, *The Homeless Mind*, Pelican 1974

H. J. Blackman and others, *Objections to Humanism*, Pelican 1965

M. Bolt and D. G. Myers, *The Human Connection: How People Change People*, Hodder 1984

Tal Brooke, *Riders of the Cosmic Circuit*, Lion 1986

J. A. C. Brown, *Techniques of Persuasion: from Propaganda to Brainwashing*, Pelican 1975

Carlos Castaneda, *A Separate Reality*, Penguin 1973

C. M. Cipolla, *The Economic History of World Population*, Pelican 1965

Eldridge Cleaver, *Soul on Fire*, Word 1978

Vernon Coleman, *Stress Control*, Pan 1980

C. W. Colson, *Born Again*, Hodder 1976

David Cook, *Blind Alley Beliefs*, Pickering and Inglis 1979

Francis Crick, *Life Itself: Its Origins and Nature*, Futura 1982

Richard Dawkins, *The Blind Watchmaker*, Penguin 1988

Richard Dawkins, *The Selfish Gene*, Oxford 1976

M. W. Dempsey, ed, *Everyman's Factfinder*, Galley 1988

Maya Deren, *The Voodoo Gods*, Paladin 1975

John Drane, *Jesus and the Four Gospels*, Lion 1979

Hoyt, Edge and others, *Foundations of Parapsychology*, Routledge and Kegan Paul 1986

Martin Esslin, *The Theatre of the Absurd*, Pelican 1968

Mary Evans, *Women in the Bible*, Paternoster 1983

C. Stephen Evans, *The Quest for Faith*, IVP 1986

H. J. Eysenck and D. K. B. Nias, *Astrology: Science and Superstition?*, Pelican 1982

Peter Farb, *Humankind*, Granada 1978

Marilyn Ferguson, *The Aquarian Conspiracy*, Routledge and Kegan Paul 1981

Antony Flew, *Darwinian Evolution*, Paladin 1984

George Frankl, *The Failure of the Sexual Revolution*, NEL 1975

Betty Friedan, *The Feminine Mystique*, Pelican 1986

Martin Gardner, *The Whys of a Philosophical Scrivener*, Oxford 1983

Martin Gardner, *Science: Good, Bad and Bogus*, Oxford 1983

Erving Goffman, *The Presentation of Self in Everyday Life*, Pelican 1987

Stephen Jay Gould, *Ever Since Darwin: Reflections in Natural History*, Pelican 1980

John Grant, *A Directory of Discarded Ideas*, Corgi 1983

J. A. Hadfield, *Childhood and Adolescence*, Pelican 1975

David Hay, *Exploring Inner Space*, Pelican 1982

Mary Hayter, *The New Eve in Christ*, SPCK 1987

Paul Hazard, *European Thought in the Eighteenth Century*, Pelican 1965

Paul Hazard, *The European Mind 1680–1715*, Pelican 1964

Arthur F. Holmes, *Contours of a World View*, IVP 1983

H. Stuart Hughes, *Consciousness and Society*, Paladin 1974

Morton Hunt, *The Universe Within*, Corgi 1984

Roger F. Hurding, *Roots and Shoots*, Hodder 1986

William Jones, *The Varieties of Religious Experience*, Fontana 1960

D. Gareth Jones, *Brave New People: Ethical Issues at the Commencement of Life*, IVP 1984

H. T. Kerr and J. M. Mulder, eds, *Conversions*, Hodder 1984

Leszek Kolakowski, *Religion*, Fontana 1982

Harold S. Kushner, *When All You've Ever Wanted Isn't Enough*, Pan 1987

Harold S. Kushner, *When Bad Things Happen to Good People*, Pan 1982

Christopher Lasch, *The Culture of Narcissism*, Abacus 1980

The Last Two Million Years, Reader's Digest Association/Hodder 1986

C. S. Lewis, *God in the Dock*, Fount 1979

C. S. Lewis, *Mere Christianity*, Fount 1979

C. S. Lewis, *Miracles*, Fount 1981

C. S. Lewis, *Surprised by Joy*, Fontana 1974

Gordon R. Lowe, *The Growth of Personality*, Pelican 1972

David Lyon, *The Steeple's Shadow*, SPCK 1985

Donald Mackay, *Human Science and Human Dignity*, Hodder 1979

Marshall McLuhan, *The Gutenberg Galaxy*, Routledge and Kegan Paul 1962

Marshall McLuhan, *Understanding Media*, Sphere 1969

I. Howard Marshall, *I Believe in the Historical Jesus*, Hodder 1977

Patrick Masterson, *Atheism and Alienation*, Gill and Macmillan 1971

Katinka Matson, *The Encyclopedia of Reality*, Paladin 1979

Margaret Mead, *Culture and Commitment*, Panther 1972

George Melly, *Revolt into Style: the Pop Arts in Britain*, Penguin 1970

John J. Mitchell, *Human Life: The Early Adolescent Years*, Holt, Rinehart and Winston (Toronto) 1974

Juliet Mitchell, *Psychoanalysis and Feminism*, Pelican 1975

Elizabeth Moberly, *Homosexuality: A New Christian Ethic*, James Clarke 1983

R. A. Moody, *Life After Life*, Corgi 1976

Stephen Neill, *Crises of Belief*, Hodder 1984

Lesslie Newbigin, *Foolishness to the Greeks*, SPCK 1986

Oliver O'Donovan, *Begotten or Made?*, Oxford 1984
Vance Packard, *The Hidden Persuaders*, Pelican 1974
M. Scott Peck, *People of the Lie*, Rider 1983
Clark H. Pinnock, *Reason Enough: A Case for the Christian Faith*, Paternoster 1980
J. M. Roberts, *The Pelican History of the World*, Pelican 1980
Steven Rose, *The Conscious Brain*, Pelican 1976
Sheila Rowbotham, *Women's Consciousness, Man's World*, Penguin 1973
C. I. Sandstrom, *Psychology of Childhood and Adolescence*, Pelican 1968
Donald Scott, *The Psychology of Work*, Duckworth 1970
W. J. H. Sprott, *Human Groups*, Pelican 1977
G. Rattray Taylor, *The Natural History of the Mind*, Secker & Warburg 1979
William Sargant, *Battle for the Mind*, Pan 1970
Ninian Smart, *The Religious Experience of Mankind*, Fount 1977
Anthony Smith, *The Body*, Pelican 1985
David Stafford-Clark, *What Freud Really Said*, Pelican 1983
Elaine Storkey, *What's Right with Feminism*, SPCK 1985
J. R. W. Scott, *Issues Facing Christians Today*, Marshalls 1984
John G. Strelan, *Search for Salvation*, Lutheran Publishing House (Adelaide) 1977
Gay Talese, *Thy Neighbour's Wife*, Pan 1981
Robert Thomson, *The Psychology of Thinking*, Pelican 1977
Alvin Toffler, *The Third Wave*, Pan 1981
Paul Tournier, *The Adventure of Living*, SCM 1966
Paul Tournier, *Learning to Grow Old*, Highland 1985
Peter Tyrer, *Stress*, Sheldon Press 1980
Peter Underwood, *Dictionary of the Supernatural*, Harrap 1978
Adrian Wilson, *Family*, Tavistock Publications 1985
Colin Wilson, *Poltergeist!*, NEL 1981
Robert Wrenn and Reed Mencke, *Being: A Psychology of Self*, Science Research Associates 1975

Index

Acknowledgments

B & C Alexander, page 50; All Sport Photographic Ltd, pages 37, 40 (top), 41, 46 (bottom); APA/Holger Holleman, page 48 (bottom); Associated Press, pages 10, 28, 67, 69 (right), 90/91, 111, 115 (bottom), 127, 144; Howard Barlow, pages 87, 153; Barnaby's Picture Library, pages 7, 25, 32, 39 (both), 58, 59, 82, 100/101, 108/109, 125, 131; Steve Benbow, page 104 (bottom); Bridgeman Art Library, page 107; Susanna Burton, pages 4 (top right), 36; Camera Press, pages 26, 27, 61, 74, 85, 103, 104 (top), 130 (bottom), 132, 152; Church Missionary Society, page 34 (left); Richard Dean, pages 4 (bottom right), 14, 15 (centre), 17, 23, 57, 97 (top), 98/99, 135; Mary Evans Picture Library, pages 75, 76 (both), 77 (both), 84, 88 (both), 151 (top and centre); Format Photographers, pages 40 (bottom), 89, 97 (bottom); Hulton Picture Company, pages 24/25, 64 (both), 151 (bottom); Hutchison Photographic Library, pages 42 (both), 43, 56, 78, 106 (top), 115 (top), 129, 130 (top), 142; Lion Publishing: David Alexander, page 55 (bottom)/Fritz Frankhauser, page 54/David Townsend, pages 5, 55 (centre); London City Mission/Peter Trainer, pages 146/47; Richard Opei, page 104 (centre); Photo Co-op/Vicky White, page 30; Picture Point, page 140; Popperfoto, pages 68, 69 (left); Rex Features, pages 4 (centre left), 48 (top); Gerald Rogers, page 12; Nick Rous, page 33; Science Photo Library, pages 80/81; David Simson, page 15 (top); Tony Stone Worldwide Photolibrary, pages 3, 9; David Townsend Photography, pages 34 (right), 35, 55 (top), 94, 95; Janine Wiedel, page 19; Zefa (UK) Ltd, pages 16, 45, 46 (top), 51, 86, 106 (bottom), 109, 110, 121, 136, 139, 141